THE RURAL TRADITION IN THE ENGLISH NOVEL, 1900-1939

By the same author

John Cowper Powys: Novelist
The Ancient People (poems)
Paradise Stairway (poems)

THE RURAL TRADITION IN THE ENGLISH NOVEL
1900—1939

Glen Cavaliero

ROWMAN AND LITTLEFIELD
TOTOWA, NEW JERSEY

BROOKLINE PUBLIC LIBRARY

4/86

STACK 814
C29r
copy 1

© Glen Cavaliero 1977

All rights reserved. No part of this publication may be
reproduced or transmitted, in any form or by any means,
without permission

First published in the United States 1977
by Rowman and Littlefield, Totowa, N.J.

Library of Congress Cataloging in Publication Data
Cavaliero, Glen, 1927–
    The rural tradition in the English novel, 1900–1939.
    Bibliography : p.
    Includes index.
    1. English fiction—20th century—History and criticism. 2.
Country life in literature. I. Title.
PR888.C67C3   823'.03   76–30536
ISBN 0–87471–952–6

Printed in Great Britain

For John Skidmore

The business of art is to reveal the relation between man and his circumambient universe, at the living moment. As mankind is always struggling in the toils of old relationships, art is always ahead of the 'times', which themselves are always far in the rear of the living moment.

D. H. Lawrence,
'Morality and the Novel'

Contents

Preface

The writers whose novels about country life succeeded those of Hardy have, with the exception of T. F. Powys, been neglected by academic criticism. That neglect, however understandable in view of the predominating urban character of our civilisation and culture (and thus of our assumptions and preoccupations) does disservice to a body of work which has been as widely read in its own day by an intelligent reading public as those books now held to be most representative of their time. The reason for this is not so much the contrast between 'rural' and 'urban' novelists, but rather a matter of limitation. Those novelists who are generally accepted as being of major significance extend their area of concern both geographically and psychologically beyond that of the writers considered here: in this respect the rural novelists have been neglected because their achievement seems, in a derogatory sense, provincial. But it is none the less an achievement – one that, in addition to its intrinsic merits, sheds a valuable light on the condition of life and literature in the four decades preceding the outbreak of the Second World War. The writers discussed below all possess a certain individuality, are gifted in various degrees, and are representative of their time: they are thus even more valuable to historians than are greater artists, who are usually ahead of it. In the history of literature, best-selling novelists like Hugh Walpole, Francis Brett Young and Mary Webb may not be of great importance; but in the history of reading they are. They reflect the taste and outlook of their time so well precisely because they lacked the major writer's capacity to transcend it.

The rural fiction of this period shows a traceable development. The essentially literary and artificial concept of an isolated 'peasantry', found, in the early years of the century, in the work of Eden Phillpotts, changed to a more integrated picture of a whole rural society in the novels of Sheila Kaye-Smith and Constance Holme, writers whose best work appeared in the second decade. The 1920s were years of rural fantasy and romance, of the sudden posthumous success of Mary Webb and of the discovery of T. F. Powys. With the 1930s the revived literary concern with social realities was reflected in the popularity of a number of farmer novelists and of the early fiction of H. E. Bates. There was a general movement away from imaginative abstraction towards documentation, as can be seen in the virtual demise of any significant rural fiction after the end of the Second World War. What work has been produced has continued earlier traditions, and of the writers discussed here only Henry Williamson and H. E. Bates have added substantially to their achievement.

My emphasis in the present study, however, does not lie on chronology but on the novelists' approach to their material, and on an examination of what they single out for treatment in the rural theme. I am concerned with methodology, with the way in which their work reflects the fluctuations of creativity in a context which was particularly unfavourable to its intelligent expression. After a preliminary discussion of popular romantic attitudes towards the country, attention is focused on a number of writers who wrote of it in the naturalistic mode, proceeding later to the more subjective novelists for whom the record of country life is a medium for personal and philosophical explorations. The study begins and closes with two novelists, E. C. Booth and H. E. Bates, who serve to illustrate with especial clarity the literary issues confronting the rural novelist at the beginning of the period, and their solution at the end of it. I have hoped to demonstrate what the factors were that went to the making of successful art in rural fiction; for although the creative impulse remains mysterious, some study of the ground in which it flourishes is both possible and useful. It is with this in mind that greater attention has been paid to some novelists than to others.

Two writers who are obviously relevant to the matter in hand have been omitted from any detailed consideration. D. H. Lawrence has already been discussed extensively by other critics, and I have been content here to use his achievement as a touchstone. The other writer is John Cowper Powys, about whom I have already written at length elsewhere. Rooted though his work is in the rural tradition, it goes so far beyond it that I have limited myself to a substantial footnote indicating his significance.

In allotting space to the various writers I have been governed by a sense of their literary worth, and by a desire in the case of several of them to draw attention to interesting, enjoyable and rewarding novelists belonging to a neglected literary tradition. My interest in all of them has been two fold: a historical interest, in which they are studied as representative of trends and tastes of their time; and a literary interest, in which the presiding factor is the novelist's handling of his material. The interrelation of these two approaches seemed necessary in view of the peculiar position of the rural school in twentieth-century English fiction. It may also prove rewarding in its own right.

My thanks are due to Mr Nigel Hancock and the staff of the Cambridge University Library Reading Room; to Mr Donald Hopewell and the Oxford University Press for access to letters and manuscripts by Constance Holme; to Mr and Mrs Basil Saunders for allowing me to inspect certain of the manuscripts of E. H. Young and to Mr Kenneth Hopkins for his help with the proofs. For valuable criticism I am especially grateful to Mrs Gillian Beer and Professor Raymond Williams; and also to Mrs Irene Cavenaugh, Dr Paris Leary and Mr John Toft for discussing so helpfully with me the novelists described below. Finally I would like to thank the Master and Fellows of St Catharine's College, Cambridge, whose kindness made it possible for me to write this book.

Acknowledgements

The author and publishers wish to thank the following who have kindly given permission for the use of copyright material:

The Bodley Head for the extracts from *The Tree of the Garden* by E. C. Booth, published by Putnam & Company.

Curtis Brown Limited, on behalf of the Estate of Winifred Holtby, for the extracts from *South Riding*.

Jonathan Cape Limited, on behalf of the Executors of the Mary Webb Estate, for the extracts from 'The Vagrant' in *Poems* and *The Spring of Joy* by Mary Webb.

Faber & Faber Limited for the extracts from *The Beautiful Years, Dandelion Days, The Dream of Fair Women* and *The Pathway* by Henry Williamson.

Oxford University Press for the extract from *Beautiful End* by Constance Holme (The World's Classics, 1935), reprinted by permission.

The publishers have made every effort to trace the copyright holders but if they have inadvertently overlooked any, they will be pleased to make the necessary arrangement at the first opportunity.

1 The Land and the City

I

Thomas Hardy's account of Egdon Heath is famous. His portrayal of the Heath's indifference to human beliefs and aspirations, though orchestrated in verbal rhythms that to some extent belie its theme, was to prove a formative influence on later novelists of rural life. It is not hard to see why: Hardy made of it an unforgettable image of that alienation from past traditions, and, more significantly, from past relationships with the world of nature, that afflicted so many late nineteenth-century writers.

> Haggard Egdon appealed to a subtler and scarcer instinct, to a more recently learned emotion than that which responds to the sort of beauty called charming and fair.[1]

The Heath is not a metaphor for human drama, but a commentary upon it. It is the means of evaluating the various characters and of assessing their tendencies towards self-destruction or survival.

For example: in Eustacia Vye, Hardy draws a forceful picture of a woman whose emotional life is at odds with her social circumstances, and who as a result imposes her own feelings upon the world around her. She has some affinity with Emma Bovary, but Hardy gives her situation a wider application than is attempted by Flaubert. Eustacia is destroyed not simply by her own passions and the pressures of society, but also by her estrangement from the natural world in which she finds herself. She rebels against the Heath – understandably but none the less fatally. Preparing to elope with Damon Wildeve (the name is significant – was Hardy thinking of Marvell's Damon the Mower?) she finds in the storm a reflection of her inner self.

> Skirting the pool she followed the path towards Rainbarrow, occasionally stumbling over twisted furze-roots, tufts of rushes, or

oozing lumps of fleshy fungi, which at this season lay scattered about the heath like the rotten liver and lungs of some colossal
animal. The moon and stars were closed up by cloud and rain to the
degree of extinction. . . . Never was harmony more perfect than that
between the chaos of her mind and the chaos of the world without.[2]

Alienated from impersonal nature, Eustacia is destroyed by its embodiment in her own emotions.

Thomasin Yeobright, on the other hand, a native of the Heath and
destined to be the wife of a farmer, is at one with her surroundings.

To her there were not, as to Eustacia, demons in the air, and malice
in every bush and bough. The drops which lashed her face were not
scorpions, but prosy rain; Egdon in the mass was no monster whatever, but impersonal open ground. Her fears of the place were
rational, her dislike of its worst moods reasonable. At this time it
was in her view a windy, wet place, in which a person might experience much discomfort, lose the path without care, and possibly
catch cold.[3]

The two responses towards the natural world embodied here had been
expressed in fiction nearly seventy years before. ' "It is not everyone,"
said Elinor, "who has your passion for dead leaves." '[4] The contrasts
in outlook which Jane Austen presented in her first published novel
were to be known in uncomfortable separation in a good deal of
early twentieth-century fiction.

On the one hand the scientific method of working upon the
structures and energies of the non-human world, by analysing and
directing them, had been accompanied by a growing self-consciousness.
That world could either be used as an illustration of human moods and
feelings, or have human moods and feelings imposed upon it. In both
cases the sense of belonging to it was secondary to a sense (painful in
Hardy's novels) of being unrelated to it at the most distinctively human
level; or else of being related to it simply in perceptual terms. Man and
what may be called 'the earth' merely reflected each other; or if they
were related, it was only to the degree in which the human imagination
could make the relation real. This is perhaps the inevitable outlook of a
predominantly mechanistic and urban civilisation.

That civilisation was also aware of a still greater alienation. Geology,
the Darwinian revolution, and the discoveries made by astronomers
were rendering time and space both vaster and yet more trivial than
had been supposed. Hardy was acutely conscious of these changed

perspectives; but he complemented his assertion of man's alienation from the natural world with a portrayal of the rural way of life as being suggestive, if only at the moment of its departure, of a more organic relationship, one known both physically and socially in terms of manual work and of inherited traditions. It is this retrospective view of rural life as an escape from loneliness, fragmentation, uniformity, artificiality and all the outcomes of the social developments of the industrial age that was to appeal to the popular imagination: the idea of 'the land', the earth as tilled and cultivated by man, was a predominant symbol of harmony in these years. And it was Hardy's abandonment of this view of the land in *Jude the Obscure* (1895) which was at the root of that novel's unpopularity with a hitherto admiring public.

Hardy was indeed prophetic in this, as in so much else, for certain implications of the Industrial Revolution were making themselves inescapably felt in a world that was still only partially willing to accept them. Wordsworth might declare in 1800 that 'Poetry is the breath and finer spirit of all knowledge; it is the impassioned expression which is in the countenance of all science';[5] but by the end of the nineteenth century the polarisation of scientific and of poetic and religious thought was virtually complete – with results that D. H. Lawrence, for example, although rejecting the orthodox Christianity of his time, saw as being potentially fatal to civilisation. Nor was he alone in this. In *The Place of the Lion*, a novel published in 1931, the year following Lawrence's death, Charles Williams, the most imaginative Christian writer of his generation, envisaged a world laid open to destruction by archetypal energies, those spiritual powers in which it no longer believed. The sterility of modern attitudes is here embodied in the person of Damaris Tighe, a young woman at work on a doctoral thesis about Pythagorean influences on Abelard. To her horrified amazement she encounters one of the very archetypal principles of creation about which Abelard wrote; but she sees it, not as it truly is, but only as her dessicated intellect is capable of seeing it. To her the Eagle of Divine Wisdom has become a stinking pterodactyl. Her collapse is the result of her refusal to take the beliefs of the past with proper seriousness. She is an example of the type of scientific mind that ignores any living relationship with the material on which it works: hers is the reverse of the poetic vision defined by Blake:

I question not my Corporeal or Vegetative Eye any more than I would question a window concerning a Sight. I look through it and not with it.[6]

Damaris, Williams observes,

> In general . . . associated peace with her study, her books and her manuscripts rather than with the sky, the hills and the country roads; and not unjustly, since only a few devout followers of Wordsworth can in fact find more than mere quiet in the country.[7]

That Williams should fasten upon this point is the more significant in that he himself was a townsman and preferred the urban way of life, endorsing in his poems, novels and theological writings the Christian image of heaven as life in the redeemed City.[8] Nonetheless, like most of his contemporaries he could see in country life an image of that unity of inward and outward experience which had been lost in the course of the Industrial Revolution. The sense of that loss can be seen in both a mental and a social context.

Williams's reference to 'devout followers of Wordsworth', although serious, has an element of playfulness. The insights of Wordsworth and the other romantics as to the creative power of the imagination and the significance of human perceptive faculties have not, outside the world of academic scholarship, been taken very seriously; and the later nineteenth-century trivialisation of the romantic tradition has led to a false and limiting notion of the poetic which has in turn engendered a reaction, one that ignores the romantic insights altogether. There is more dividing Wordsworth from Hardy than the Age of Tennyson. It is the difference between the reciprocal relationship between man and nature celebrated in Wordsworth's 'Tintern Abbey' lines, and Hardy's description of Egdon Heath as itself a symbol of man's own alienation from the natural world.

This alienation is, of course, in terms of philosophy: it is man's emotional life that is alien, his ideals and imaginative gifts. Of his physical union with the natural order there are constant examples in Hardy's novels; moreover, it is notable that these are most vivid in *The Woodlanders* (1887) and *Tess of the D'Urbervilles* (1891), the last two works to precede his definitive picture of alienation in *Jude*. And the austerity of his outlook could, on occasion, be tempered. The much-quoted lines 'The Oxen' are a clue to one aspect of his enduring popularity among people to whom his outlook is otherwise uncongenial.

> If someone said on Christmas Eve,
> 'Come; see the oxen kneel,

> 'In the lonely barton by yonder coomb
> Our childhood used to know,'
> I should go with him in the gloom,
> Hoping it might be so.

This poem was written in 1915; and the note of wistfulness is a characteristic of much literature of that period. Its natural focus was the life of rural England. There, if anywhere, might be found not only a valid image of the good life, but also a sense of the numinous which could ease the passage from religious dependence to spiritual autonomy. The apparent simplicity of country life appealed to the frustrated religious feelings of the age; but attitudes towards it were indicative not only of changes in religious belief but of social change as well.

II

The widespread hostility aroused among both reviewers and the reading public on the appearance of *Jude the Obscure* in 1895 was the result not only of outrage but also of disappointment. By moving into the present day from the rural world of his boyhood and earlier, Hardy was turning a source of pleasant if melancholy contemplation into an occasion for disquiet. The tragedy of Jude and Sue was not, like that of Tess, to be attributed to a conveniently remote President of the Immortals: it was planted explicitly as the door of contemporary society. And as he was to observe,

> Artistic effort always pays heavily for finding its tragedies in the forced adaptation of human instincts to rusty and irksome moulds that do not fit them.[9]

And again, commenting on the reviews,

> Tragedy may be created by an opposing environment either of things inherent in the Universe, or of human institutions. If the former be the means exhibited and deplored, the writer is regarded as impious; if the latter as subversive and dangerous. . . .[10]

In drawing attention to the decaying rural life of England, Hardy was drawing attention to something that, amid the rising prosperity of suburban England, tended to be forgotten; moreover, he was putting the rural novel to a use that was fundamentally at variance with what it had stood for hitherto. In spite of the accounts of rural squalor in such novels as Disraeli's *Sybil* (1845)[11] and Charles Kingsley's *Yeast* (1851) the country was, by the 1890s (and this partly as a result of the popularity of Hardy's earlier books), associated with all that was desirable in the England that was being changed. The industrial towns, on which the nation's prosperity was largely based, were decried as ugly, and deadly to the human spirit – in terms of architecture and the working class slums, a fair assessment. But Victorian fiction had not for the most part been concerned with the actual living conditions of the contemporary rural population, except as an appendage to the charitable or sporting activities of the rich : the novels of Charlotte M. Yonge and of Surtees and Whyte-Melville come to mind in this connection. Trollope, it is true, dealt peripherally in *The Last Chronicle of Barset* (1868) with the sufferings of the labouring poor; but more often he uses the countryside as a backcloth against which his nobles and squires and country gentry carry out their love affairs, their hunting and political intrigues. George Eliot in *Adam Bede* (1859) made a young artisan, with his family and friends, the central figure of a novel; but the picture is set back in the times of her girlhood and softened in the haze of memory. The novel to that extent celebrates an England that was already an object of nostalgia. It is noteworthy, however, that George Eliot was herself aware of this tendency, and in the opening of *Felix Holt* (1868) described it with characteristically balanced irony.

That George Eliot was governed by more serious motives the novels themselves make clear; but the tendency to turn back to a suppositious pastoral world of peace and plenty in times of insecurity and change is perennial. It is evident in the Elizabethan age and is evident in our own – the greater rapidity of change being reflected in the current turning still further back to mythological fantasy. (The enormous popularity of J. R. R. Tolkien's *The Lord of the Rings* (1954–5) with its homely Shire and diverse landscapes is a case in point.) In the nineteenth century this emotional predisposition was linked with nostalgia for natural religion, a nostalgia that the revived ecclesiastical interests of the Oxford Movement did little to assuage; and with the actual waning of agricultural prosperity it produced an increasingly sentimental and self-conscious attitude to country life. So Wordsworth was reduced in the popular mind to the status of a 'nature poet', and (despite the evidence of the 'Westminster Bridge' sonnet and of the seventh book of *The Prelude*) as the champion of a purely rural sensibility. In fiction there is evidence of the contrasted views of town and country as early as 1841 in *The Old Curiosity Shop* – a novel, however, in which both rural peace and industrial squalor are presented in sentimentalising rhetoric. The directly emotional approach here is far less effective than the biting satire of Dickens's later novels – one thinks of *Little Dorrit* (1857), with its account of Bleeding House Yard and Mrs Plornish's wall painting, where the human imagination is seen as both a defiance of the greed of the exploiters and a comment on it. Still more effective is the description in *Hard Times* (1852) of how the town and country overlap. An analytical approach replaces the simple contrasts in the earlier novel. The undermined countryside round Coketown is a powerful image of the dangers attendant on the exploitation of the earth; while Dickens's particular style of humour enabled him to emphasise the contradictions inherent in the separation between a town and the people who inhabit it.

These attributes of Coketown were in the main inseparable from the work by which it was sustained; against them were to be set off comforts of life which found their way all over the world, and elegancies of life which made, we will not ask how much of the fine lady, who could scarcely bear to hear the place mentioned.[12]

Dickens, however, is concerned specifically with industrialism; in an earlier economy the urban and rural ways of life were not so out of touch with each other as they were to become. Both George Eliot's account of Middlemarch and Hardy's of Casterbridge make one keenly aware of the country world surrounding those towns and of their interaction with it. The nature of the new industrial cities contrasted markedly with what 'George Bourne' was to observe about the old ones.

For the old towns . . . were not in their origins places where rural life ceased; they were the places where it grew tense and vital. . . . If you are a native of one of them, and know it well, the steadfast houses and the turnings of the streets seem to add to your personal memory recollections from times long before your own, and every memory of them all smacks not of town but of country.[13]

Perhaps the most satisfactory treatment of the town-and-country theme in nineteenth-century fiction comes in Elizabeth Gaskell's *North and South* (1855), where the worlds of Milton-Northern and of Helstone are not only contrasted but also dynamically related, most notably in the book's deliberate qualifying of the popular view of the rural south as being the cradle of the human virtues.[14] In this the author is making a distinction between nature and what man makes of nature; even in the more idyllic pastoral stories, like *Cousin Phillis* (1865), she is more concerned with country people than with landscape as such, although in *The Life of Charlotte Brontë* (1857) she writes of the Haworth moors with an intensity unmatched in Victorian fiction outside the work of George Meredith and of Henry Kingsley in *Ravenshoe* (1861) and *Austin Elliot* (1863).

To mention Meredith is to mention one Victorian who, in his poetry and prose alike, proclaimed the need for the society of his day to accept and not resist the creative energy of natural forces; but it is disputable whether *Rhoda Fleming* (1864), his one sustained excursion into contemporary rural life, reveals his genius in its most appropriate sphere: the style is pitched above the material upon which it works – though 'above' may be a misleading term here. But for any would-be novelist the contrast between an idealistic appreciation of landscape and the actual conditions of life among the rural poor was an uncomfortable one. Certainly, as the century proceeded, the greater sophistication of fictional method and presentation made it increasingly difficult for novelists to write about the working class, whether agricultural or urban, with naturalness, let alone with knowledge. (E. M. Forster's comment on this is notorious: 'We are not concerned with the very poor. They are unthinkable, and only to be approached by the statistician or the poet.'[15] The irony is self-defeating in its sophistication.)

With the exception of Richard Jefferies and of Hardy, late nineteenth-century novelists tended to use the rural scene in historical rather than contemporary settings. The novels of R. D. Blackmore are a case in point, as are those of the Scottish novelist S. R. Crockett (1860–1914), whose *The Raiders* (1893) makes effective use of the Galloway landscape in an adventure story of a Stevensonian kind, but whose tales of contemporary life, such as *The Lilac Sunbonnet* (1896) are whimsical and over-sweet.[16] Even Jefferies, in *The Dewy Morn* (1884) and *Amaryllis at the Fair* (1886), depicted rural life idealistically, though the novels are saved from sentimentality (and this is especially true of *Amaryllis*) by the author's reasoned belief in the inherent superiority of that life when properly ordered. His most forceful condemnation of industrialism comes in *After London* (1885), with its superb account of the overgrowth of industrial England by the returning forces of vegetation. The paradox here is a painful one: the increase in population made urban development inevitable; and yet in the national literary consciousness this meant exchanging a natural and healthy way of life for a mechanical and inferior one. The fact that the country in its turn was interpreted through the eyes of the town only made the situation more confused. And at the back of all was a social situation of genuine tragedy.

III

A classic account of the human implications of that tragedy can be found in the writings of George Sturt (1863–1927), who used the pen-name 'George Bourne'.[17] Sturt was almost alone among his contemporaries in seeing the state of rural communities as it really was. Of the agricultural labourer he wrote that 'He is between two civilisations, one of which has lapsed, while the other has not yet come his way.'[18] The lapsed civilisation Sturt defined as that of the peasant tradition which 'permitted a man to hope for well-being without seeking to escape from his own class into some other'.[9] But the increasing mobility of modern society, both physical and social, and the influx of cheap food from abroad, meant that life had become competitive, and based on money in ways that left the agricultural labourer at a signal disadvantage.

> Under the new system a far larger population is able to live in the parish than could possibly have been supported here under the old; for now in place of the scanty products of the little valley and the heaths, the stores of the whole world may be drawn upon by the inhabitants in return for the wages they earn. Only there is the awkward condition that they must earn wages. Those limitless stores cannot be approached by the labourer until he is invited – until there is 'a demand' for his labour. Property owners, or capitalists, standing between him and the world's capital, are able to pick and choose between him and his neighbours as the common never did, and to decide which of them shall work and have some of the supplies.[20]

It is a limitation of Sturt's account, however, that he does not stress sufficiently that the old system had been based on landownership: it was essentially feudal in spirit. The landowner was responsible for the provision, maintenance and improvement of all the fixed capital on his estate, so that 'In practice this meant that the well-being of one of the nation's greatest industries was in the hands of a minute proportion

of its people.'[21] But with an increasing economic pressure on landowners, and the necessary diminution of rents,[22] they were often unwilling or unable to keep up their extensive properties; and the small
tenant farmer and the agricultural labourer alike were victims of the
decline of one form of paternalist system and the delay in its replace-
ment by another.

Low wages, bad housing, tied cottages, long and irregular hours,
poor schools and few provisions for leisure all made country life un-
attractive for the working man, and the move to the towns was continuous. Only those who worked their own farms remained constant;
luckily the break-up of the great estates meant an increase in owner-
occupancy. But agriculture remained a neglected source of national
revenue, and the transformation of England into a primarily indus-
trialised society was, by the outbreak of the Second World War,
complete. The tragedy was that, while rural England lost its pre-emin-
ence, it did not gain fast enough from the material benefits of the
age. In 1939 there were still over 5000 parishes in Britain without a
sewage system. The anonymous essays published in 1925 under the
title *England's Green and Pleasant Land* were rightly disenchanted.[23]

By the 1940s the elegaic message of Sturt had taken on a more
urgent note in the writings of H. J. Massingham and of F. R. Leavis
and Denys Thompson. The last two, although their tone is sharper
than Sturt's, were traditionalists in seeing rural England as the source
of a genuine and vital culture that was rapidly being lost; their emphasis
was on quality of life rather than on any economic roots that life might
have had.[24] H. J. Massingham (1888–1952), on the other hand, was
aghast not only at the philistinism and ugliness of the industrial age,
but also at what he regarded as the crass folly of modern farming
methods. A son of the journalist and editor H. W. Massingham, he
became one of the most consistently outspoken opponents of twentieth-
century commercialism and its effects on people, places and the Western
world as a whole. Through a long line of books – essays, topography,
studies of craftsmen and village life – he argued persuasively and pro-
phetically for a halt to be called to a process that for him spelled moral
and economic ruin. He is a writer in the line of Cobbett and Sturt,
and his message is the same as theirs.[25]

In the process of change something infinitely precious was being
destroyed. As Sturt wrote,

I know now that the landscape is not peopled by a comfortable folk,
whose dear and intimate love of it gave a human interest to every

feature of its beauty; I know that those who live there have in fact lost touch with its venerable meanings, while all their existence has turned sordid and anxious and worried; and knowing this, I feel a forlornness in country places, as if all their best significance were gone.[26]

The tragedy lies in the fact that, while the destruction of the old world is inevitable, the awareness of what is lost rebounds damagingly upon those who necessarily lament it. The kind of organic community rooted in the seasonal round and responding creatively to a stable tradition of humane and liberal values is, even if it did once have an existence,[27] something unattainable in an overpopulated island. And yet the beauty and craftsmanship that are the products of the rural life of the past remain as a rebuke to the standards of the age that has succeeded them.

IV

Nostalgia for the England of the 'open' villages of independent yeomen and cottage industries was not new; it had cultural antecedents in the work of Ruskin and William Morris. In the ethical field the pioneer writings of Edward Carpenter (1884–1929) influenced both Lawrence and Forster.[28] Carpenter, like them, was acutely aware of the dessicating, not to say destructive, effect of contemporary middle-class manners and moral priorities; and this awareness was painfully sharpened by the fact that, again like Forster, he was homosexual. 'Natural' was indeed a key term for him, and his poetry and political writings alike were pleas for a renewed recognition of man's physical nature. Much is summed up by the clothes of the period, the constricting garments of the Edwardian age giving way in due course to the more flowing wear of the 1920s and 1930s; and this sartorial change is matched by a quest for a simpler way of life. The latter, indeed, became a necessity for the middle classes as servants became hard to find. The purchase of weekend cottages, with all the implications of a divided work-and-play, town-and-country outlook, grew with the spread of the motor-car; and Forster has some tart comments on this in *Howards End* (1910), a seminal novel for understanding the issues of the period, both in its positive criticisms and in its limitations of response. But in general the cult of the simple life was to be matter for comedy in the fiction of the time – for example, in *The Caravaners* (1910) by 'Elizabeth', and in Radclyffe Hall's *The Forge* (1924).

Carpenter himself, however, devotedly lived out his ideal of the 'natural' as he ran his Derbyshire market garden with working-class companions (he was a follower of Whitman and Thoreau); and similar ideals can be found in Lawrence's letters and novels, though in them, perhaps because of his working-class background, we find little sentimentality where the simple-life ideal is concerned. His enthusiasm was for the idea of community; but he shared Carpenter's belief that

> familiarity with the wind and waves, clean and pure food, the companionship of the animals, the very wrestling with the Great Mother for his food – all these things will tend to restore the relationship which man has so long disowned.[29]

The gamekeepers who appear in Lawrence's first and last novels embody a belief in the virtues of natural man; and Forster's *Maurice* (written in 1913–14, after a visit to Carpenter) provides a further example. Alec Scudder, however, is a less romanticised character than are Annable or Mellors. But Forster is more sentimental than is Lawrence about the lure of what he calls 'the greenwood': to see the difference between them one has only to compare the scene in Chapter 8 of *Women in Love*, where Birkin strips naked in the fields, with the altogether more frolicsome tone of Forster's account in *A Room with a View* of how George, Freddie and Mr Beebe dance around the woodland pool. Lawrence clearly believes in man's affinity with the non-human in a way that is beyond Forster's capacity; while the latter's rather arch and dated treatment of Pan in such stories as 'The Curate's Friend' and 'Other Kingdom' – they appear in *The Celestial Omnibus* (1911) – has an Edwardian playfulness which detracts from the seriousness of what they have to say.

But Forster can be more intelligent about human sexuality than this: there is the genuinely forceful and challenging 'Story of a Panic', written as early as 1902. And both *The Longest Journey* and *Howards End* contain formal laments for the passing of rural England which are tinged by savage anger at the exploitation of people and places that accompanied it. This negative feeling is in fact more persuasive than are the positive touches. The accounts of Wiltshire in *The Longest Journey* and of Dorset and Shropshire in *Howards End* have the wrong kind of eloquence to counterbalance the negative stresses: charming though they are, there is something overstudied about them. Forster was still in his twenties when he wrote these novels, and was too imprisoned in the Edwardian world to make that kind of protest effectively.

The house Howards End is far less impressive a symbol of the continuity of rural England than is, say, Groby in Ford Madox Ford's *Last Post* (1930). Forster's most trenchant writing in this kind was not to come until the Second World War and after.

Indeed, only Lawrence among his contemporaries succeeded in making a positive protest against the trivialisation of rural life and sensibility, and in *The White Peacock* (1910) and *The Rainbow* (1915) and many shorter tales he provided touchstones by which one can assess the work of numerous lesser writers who concerned themselves primarily with rural themes. For the greatness of Lawrence's achievement in this field lies in the way in which he was able to dismiss the corruption and degradation of industrialism without resorting to mendacious nostalgia for a rural past that never was. His concern with nature was without illusions as to what men would do when in a state of nature. Civilisation was for him something more than either an urban or a rustic ideal. It was a matter of integrating a man's bodily and imaginative awareness of life around him, of accepting his part in the on-going process that is 'nature': sensitivity and responsiveness are key terms for Lawrence in his attack on that spirit of exploitation which governs a technological civilisation.[30] But he did not fall into the trap of seeing in rural life simply an alternative to the age of the machine. He would have sympathised with these words of Adrian Bell, a writer whose first book was published in the year of Lawrence's death:

> No one decries civilization who has not experienced it *ad nauseam*. Modernity offers dim but infinite possibilities to the young country-man if only he can rid his boots of this impending clay. Pylons, petrol pumps and other 'defacements' are to him symbols of a noble power.[31]

It was the living power of natural forces driving all aspects of life which interested Lawrence. But the more exclusively rural novelists were concerned with the individual and particular responses to the process of change, with the predicament of Bell's young agricultural labourer:

> The old men had their defence. They knew what they knew. But he can't stay where they are. The contentment of it is gone.[32]

2 Problems of the Rural Novelist: E. C. Booth

A mordant parable of the divorce between town and country can be found in John Christopher's novel *The Guardians*, a book for children published in 1970. Set in the future, it portrays an England divided rigidly into urban and rural ways of life: the Conurbs, conformist, mechanised, gregarious and imaginatively stifling; and the County, gracious, conservative, quiet and apparently free. The County embodies the longing for beauty and order, spontaneity and freedom of spirit, that the country has come to mean in the experience of city dwellers. But this peace is had at a price. The two worlds must never meet; and the County is preserved from contact with the Conurb by the Guardians, a ruling élite who maintain its idyllic tranquillity by operating on the brains of all those restless and imaginative enough to seek to break the barrier between the two worlds: peace and order are secured by a process of spiritual gelding. The fable is apt.[1] Arcadia is a dangerous province to evoke, for to do so always involves leaving something out.

But such fragmentation has for a long time been apparent in literature. By the beginning of the twentieth century the compendious all-purpose three-volume family novels of the great Victorian writers had had their day. The reading public demanded shorter works of more specialised appeal: 'Society' novels, such as those of Ada Leverson and E. F. Benson, or historical novels like those of Stanley Weyman. There were urban novels and there were rural novels.

Of these it was the urban novel which proved most lasting in appeal and productive of the most important work. Dickens's *Our Mutual Friend* (1865) may be seen as the precursor of such deliberate treatments of city life as James's *The Princess Casamassima* (1886), Gissing's *The*

Nether World (1889) and Maugham's *Liza of Lambeth* (1897), while in the Edwardian period the tradition was enriched by the very different achievements of Arnold Bennett's tales of the Five Towns and Conrad's *The Secret Agent* (1907). Though varying in treatment and profundity, they were all concerned with the life of cities as such; their impact was in part the result of timeliness, and their relevance has by no means ceased. But, Hardy's novels alone excepted, the exclusive handling of rural themes did not lend itself to effects of equal power. The country was too readily regarded either as an Arcadia or as a static, not to say stagnant, society to be naturally conducive to the more serious kind of treatment. It was difficult to relate it to the changes in social conditions and mental horizons that were quickening the vision of the better novelists of the period. The country and what it stood for were beginning to have an emotional and literary significance at odds with historic fact.

The early twentieth-century rural novel itself came in a number of different types. There was, for example, the rural novel proper, confined to a particular locality and, for the most part, to that locality's native inhabitants; it was concerned with the exhibition of rustic idiosyncrasy, and made great use of dialect for ornamental or anthropological purposes. The novels of Eden Phillpotts are examples of this, as are, for all their very different intention and achievement, those of T. F. Powys. More strictly naturalistic was the type of novel, written for the most part from the countryman's point of view but with a townsman's sophistication of outlook, which was first seriously essayed by Sheila Kaye-Smith, and brought to its most effective expression by H. E. Bates; while the farmer novelists of the 1930s used a documentary rather than a novelistic approach. Again there was the romantic rural novel, which presented country life as something more intense and personally fulfilling than life in the towns: Mary Webb and, in a more hard-headed manner, Henry Williamson were the most notable practitioners in this mode. Other writers, such as Constance Holme and Francis Brett Young, explored the life of a particular region, attempting with varying success a fusion of naturalism with romance. And there were writers of fantasy, such as Kenneth Grahame, who wrote of rural life as an embodiment of dreams and personal impulses; one finds a variant on this treatment (though inspired by the same kind of awareness) in the work of a more formally urban writer like E. H. Young. Nor should one forget the telling use of country backgrounds and folklore in ghost-story writers, such as M. R. James and Walter de la Mare. The variety of modes makes it difficult to be dogmatic about questions of genre; and even within any one mode the novelists are apt to use methodology appropriate to another. More interesting than the mode as such is the variety of attitudes to be found among these writers, attitudes which involved a good deal more than the difference, say, between symbolism and naturalism. What matters most is their understanding of what may be called the rural experience and its potentiality for fiction.

II

To speak of 'the rural experience' is of course to imply its opposite, and leads to the question of what, in contrast with life in the town, that experience really is. It can be understood in a number of ways, both from the point of view of the townsman and from that of the countryman. In the country, people who live in villages and hamlets tend to have a stronger sense of community than, working-class areas apart, is to be found in the town. There also tends to be a close relationship between classes, who, however much they may be separated by economic disparity and social custom, are, by sheer geographical proximity, more aware of each other's needs and habits. To the townsman this can seem idyllic or constricting as the case may be. But country life has another side to it, making for an unthinking conformity and a concern with one's neighbours that can be obsessive. The rural novelists present both aspects, at their best refusing to stress one at the expense of the other.

But this quality of life is the *result* of living in the country: it is not country life as such. The rural experience in this sense involves not only freedom from the tensions and pressures of town life, but also a far closer acquaintance with the realities of weather and of seasonal change; it means hard work and it can mean isolation. And since the latter condition is more distinctively rural even than the social life of the village, it is not surprising that the farmer, the isolated human unit, is the character most often chosen by the rural novelists for their protagonist.

The rural experience of the townsman, whether as a visitor or as a settler in the country, tends on the other hand to be essentially aesthetic. It is he who is inclined to romanticise country people, to patronise them, to exploit them. For to the townsman the appreciation of scenery, human or otherwise, has become a mode of consciousness fed by literature and art. For him the country is a mental as much as a physical world; and the solitary visitor leaning over a gate and admiring the pattern of the fields is inclined to feel awkward in the presence of the man who rides the tractor.

In view of their variety of standpoint, and the distinction most of them made between the world about which they wrote and the world that was their audience, to produce good novels the rural novelists needed tact and sensibility as much as narrative power or the ability to draw living characters. Their subject matter called for exceptional skill in handling, involving as it did the portrayal of people whose social life and sensibility were alien to the largely urban readership. For by the rural population one means those whose lives were confined to the country through economic necessity: it was they and not the potentially mobile middle-class inhabitants who underwent the rural experience in its fullest sense. There is in this respect considerable diversity in the way in which the various novelists approach their subject. Eden Phillpotts, for instance, usually centres his tales on the native inhabitants of Dartmoor, who were often freeholders, so that we have a closed community in which individual quirks of humanity can flourish unencumbered by external factors. John Trevena, on the other hand, is more concerned with the outsider's point of view, and with those peasants who are economically dependent on and exploited by their richer neighbours. Sheila Kaye-Smith's main interest is in farmers, clergy and shopkeepers, Mary Webb's in local craftsmen and followers of old-world trades: her work is thus more 'picturesque' than that of Sheila Kaye-Smith. The landed gentry figure conspicuously in the novels of Constance Holme and Winifred Holtby; in those of Henry Williamson the social element is minimal. T. F. Powys describes all types and walks of life, but these social differences are subordinate to the overriding literary style and parabolic theme.

The rural novelist's task also involved something that urban fiction generally omits: a response to a way of life more directly conscious of living from, and of being in touch with, non-human forces – what may be called a more elemental way of life; and this aspect in particular called for intelligent treatment if absurdity or pretentiousness were to be avoided. (That it often was not avoided the success of Stella Gibbons's parody, *Cold Comfort Farm*, makes clear.) Most especially were these novelists faced with a problem of relatedness. To the degree in which he is genuinely of the people and way of life which he describes, to that degree will the rural novelist seem eccentric to the majority of his readers; while the degree in which he approximates to the expectations of that public will also be the measure of his unreliability as a chronicler of the rural scene. As Jefferies wrote,

> The shepherd has never surprised an Immortal reclining on the thyme under the shade of a hawthorne bush at sunny noontide; nor has the ploughman seen the shadowy outline of a divine huntress through the mist that clings to the wood across the field.[2]

Only the genuine artist can bridge the gap between the dictates of his material and the expectations of his readers; and he can do so only by transcending both. The success and failure of the various rural novelists, like the success and failure of all novelists, is a question of their art.

A further quotation from George Sturt is apposite here.

> Those people from whom the enclosure of the common . . . made room in the valley – I mean the well-to-do residents – employ local labour, not for profit at all, but to minister to their own pleasure, in their gardens and stables, and the majority of them would be genuinely glad to be helpful to their poorer neighbours. The presence of poverty reproaches them; their consciences are uneasy; or, better still, some kind of regard, some kind of respect, goes out from them towards the toilsome men and over-burdened women whom, in fact, they have displaced. Yet compassion is not the same thing as understanding, and the cottagers know very well that even their best friends of this kind have neither the knowledge nor the taste to appreciate them in their own way. Sympathy for their troubles – yes, there is that; but sympathy with their enjoyments hardly any property-owner dreams of cultivating; and this is the more true the more the property-owner has been polished by his own civilization.[3]

This social division is an aspect of the more fundamental one between man and his environment: with 'civilization' pursuits become more sophisticated, become more self-conscious, more unrelated to natural processes. And just as the physical world is regarded as material for dissection and free exploitation, so, in second-rate fiction, the alienated and underprivileged and even unfashionable elements in society are used mechanically as stereotypes. They are not considered and respected for their own sakes. And what is true of fictional characters is true of fictional themes. The theme of rural change is doubly significant in this respect. In the first place, it provided a sensitive context for the exploration and questioning of evolving social and economic values; and secondly, by virtue of association, it provided a fruitful field in which traditional values could grow and in which significance for human life could be found. To this extent the Wordsworthian legacy had not been squandered.

III

For an example of the kind of problems and pitfalls that confront the rural novelist one can turn to certain of the novels of Edward C. Booth (1873–1954),[4] a characteristic regional writer whose fiction is centred on the Holderness district of the East Riding of Yorkshire. He was well-to-do, and wrote to please himself, appearing to be without literary ambition. His novels are celebratory rather than critical, with a strong interest in primitive types of character. At his best he had a vigorous command of words and phrases; and *Fondie* (1916) and still more *The Tree of the Garden* (1922) retain their interest, the latter being an exercise in the Lawrentian manner by one whose literary habits had been unaffected by the Lawrentian stylistic revolution. Booth is a writer who rebelled ineffectively against a bad tradition.

As a regional novelist he relies mainly on an elaborate and rather exhausting use of dialect. He can catch not only local idiom, but also the essential quality of the abrasive North Country humour; and this humour can be telling, as when the eager Farmer Suddaby escorts his over-refined landlady, Mrs Openshaw, around the farm from which she draws the rents but which she has never visited. The situation typifies the theme that runs through the whole novel – the divorce of the artificial life of town respectability from the spontaneous and healthy freedom of the country.

'Why, it's bad land, marm,' Suddaby told her, absorbed in his task like a terrier at a rat-hole, so that the plainest signs of fatigue would have been lost on him, '. . . and takes ower much work by half to keep i' fettle. It grows nought but wicks and rubbish nobbut it's left tiv itself. Land's been robbed fro' the start. Soil was very nigh hungered to death when first I cam'. Punds and punds I'se put intiv it. Loads o' good stable muck, wi' slag an' guano an' such-like. Why, marm! there was acres an' acres wi'out a drain-pipe under 'em, and the outfall i' yon seeds-close was set as much as half a foot higher than

B

main-course. You've nobbut to ask aud Bobbie Chambers 'i yon second thatched cottage at Beachington – poor aud man; he's helped me to drain many a chain, me bottoming and him laying oot pots. He'll tell you same, his-sen.'[5]

The strength of Booth's humour is the strength of his best work – an intimate knowledge of the people and landscape which he describes: the first third of *Fondie*, for instance, is mediated largely through the gossip and sayings of a small town. At times the humour becomes too knowing and complacent (regional novelists can be self-indulgent in this respect) but it is capable of a more astringent turn. *Fondie* contains a good example of this. The vicar's tomboy daughter Blanche (a sympathetic study of an unruly hoyden) has been seduced by the son of the neighbouring squire. When the vicar complains to the rector of the squire's parish, he meets with scant sympathy: the rector is a more belligerent Mr Collins. He readily believes the young man's denial of the charge.

> 'Besides . . . he's still a minor. Even if he had the misguided chivalrous impulse to some suicidal act – and you know what a generous-hearted fellow like that might do – it would be his father's duty not less than mine to dissuade him. Fellows like Leonard D'Alroy have not only themselves to think of: they haven't the freedom of these discontented working men, that don't know how to appreciate it. They have their country and their social duty to consider.'[6]

The possession of a great estate is presented as sufficient reason for ignoring all humanitarian claims: Booth's criticism of the existing social ethos is here explicit. The choice of a suitable wife has become for the squirearchy as much a matter of social obligation as it is for royalty. As the rector points out, 'What would happen to us all if such a place as Marsham came to ruin, I daren't really contemplate.' The operative words here are 'all' and 'daren't' – the use of the one lends inevitably to the other.

Fondie is a tale of small-town life, centring on the character of a simple wheelwright's son; the contrast between the strenuous humour of the portrait of the father and George Sturt's factual restraint in *The Wheelwright's Shop* (1923) is instructive. Booth's novel seems to belong to another age: indeed, it is like a more pungent version of a novel by George MacDonald. The rich, almost clotted verbal texture disguises the thinness of the actual imaginative conception; and there is a curious uncertainty of tone. We can never be altogether sure whether the author is laughing with his characters or at them.

This is true at times of *The Tree of the Garden*. Here a potentially interesting theme is spoiled by kid-glove treatment. The suffocating of a son's emotional life by his mother is linked to the especial kind of ethical upbringing he has received: Guy Openshaw 'had been trained in sentiment as other boys are taught their drill; brought up to know only so much of life as might be loved'.[7] Mrs Openshaw is an odiously sentimental, self-deluded woman, emotional and pretentious; but Booth lacks the nerve to follow his insights through. Mrs Openshaw, having almost manœuvred her son into a fatal marriage and indirectly caused the fall of his rural lover into prostitution, is allowed a last-minute repentance, and remains firmly in possession. If we were sure that this was intended to be a cynical ending the book would retain a healthy tartness: as it is, its earlier points are blunted.

It remains, however, a vivid and singularly interesting novel, and a useful measure by which to compare the far-greater achievement of D. H. Lawrence. The pastoral theme is here related to dawning sexuality. Mrs Openshaw takes her son to live on the Suddaby's farm for the sake of his health: the account of the country on the journey down prepares us for what is to follow.

It was an afternoon in mid-June, warm and humid. The corn was in milk, and all the air seemed softened with balmy fragrance of fattening grain. Everywhere one felt the sense of flowing sap that freshens and subdues the face of nature like the blood behind a girl's cheek. Now and again the flesh-warm fragrance that floated from ripening pith and juicy stalk rose up in a sudden access of sweetness to the ravishing breath of honeyed clover, that supreme ineffable sweetness as though perfume were on the poignant border-line of the sense allotted to her, and must next moment burst through every limitation into the empire of the other senses and become sweet sound and swooning sight, tremulous music and a passionate white body.[8]

Fortunately the book is not all pitched in this key. The life on the farm is described with simple zest. The account of the animals at feeding time is quite Chaucerian.

At the first rattle of the bucket a porcine scream arose, spreading with flame-like rapidity from sty to sty as if it had been a conflagration, until the whole foldyard was afire and ringed with lurid screams, and the two sows at grass raced furiously up the whinfield, with their noses in the air, swinging their double row of dugs like bells, and squealing over the whole gamut of a bassoon; and the poultry – always quick to misinterpret commotion into a meal – would come running too : agile hens with the most unladylike abandonment of leg, and red-cheeked cockerels, casting dignity and chivalry to the winds, and chickens swept along by the current like autumn leaves in a storm; and aimless cackling ducks, that seemed to run without knowing why, and that look foolish everywhere but at table and in the water; and great, harsh-voiced, greedy geese, too fat to squeeze under the foldyard gate, and too stupid to go round, that would push their necks through all the bars as far as the gizzard, one after another, with an absurd patience, and flop down on the grass with the despair and helplessness of lost children in the wake of a school treat.[9]

As to the farmer himself, one might compare Booth's description of him with Jefferies's account of Iden in *Amaryllis at the Fair*. Jefferies's technique is to provide a gradual building up of a picture by a series of momentary vignettes – Iden in the garden, Iden at table, Iden dozing after his meal – each one of which is an implicit comment on an entire way of life. Booth, less of an artist, confronts his subject head-on :

Suddaby seemed the incarnation of all wisdom; his local history huge; his grasp of facts enormous. The name of every bird was known to him, from the great brown 'muck-bird' coasting overhead, to the busy white-cheeked Billy-biter, or the voluble Peggy-white-throat (own cousin to the nightingale), chattering in the hawthorn hedge; the name of every grass and weed and hedge-side flower, from cockfoot and timothy to fat-hen and crake-needles and the yellow runch. Suddaby it was who showed Master Openshaw the old-time fashion of playing fiddle with the figwort, and gave him his first lessons in hedge-lore and the mysteries of banking, dyking and draining. Not all the farmer's familiarity with the facts of life had blunted his zest for it, or weakened his interest in the things that were his daily portion.[10]

The mass of detail serves to restrict rather than to expand the significance of what is being implied : a sense of fussiness is induced by the local bird names – the whole passage savours of the self-consciously 'quaint'. Booth has one mark of the amateur – he always seems to be trying too hard.

When it comes to the love affair, the earnestness of his approach almost undoes him. The character of Thursday Hardripp, the country girl to whom Guy is too inhibited to make love, is sensitively drawn, her speech natural, her simplicity without mawkishness; she can be compared not unfavourably with Hardy's Marty South. So long as Thursday is *talking*, the novel rings true; but the language in which the love-making is described is more in tune with Mrs Openshaw.

At that overwhelming contact with realities so firmamental high above experience, it seemed to Guy Openshaw as if his soul held breath, prostrate before an altar, in expectation of some tremendous epiphany. Think! This sex he had been taught from boyhood to worship from afar; whose ostensory of flesh and wonder had been elevated with such portentous reverence by his mother's hands for the eyes of chivalry to rest on; that had inhabited heretofore the extreme and outward region of his mind – could it be incarnate close beside him at last? Was the deity already half-divulged to the vision of the devotee?[11]

The paragraph from which this comes is extremely long, and continues on the same note. One can the more appreciate the need for the particular kind of plain speaking that Lawrence called for: Mrs Openshaw is own cousin to his version of Irene Forsyte.[12]

Somewhere in the gesturing of Booth's novels a notable talent was lost. How notable can be illustrated by Thursday's account of her drift into prostitution. This is speech perfectly heard, speech sounding off the page.

'Yes, it's true. Does it sound very awful? I suppose it must, to you. It did to me, once. It does now – nobbut I get started to think what might a' been. But once folks loses hope and hasn't anything to live for, it's easy to be anything. One doesn't notice it so much then. Nothing seems to matter. Nothing's mattered to me for a long while. Maybe I should never a' been what I is now if you'd wanted me sooner. I'se not one o' the worst. I never ask people. And I won't take anybody. . . . And I'se never grown to like it, like some girls. That's the worst of all. I've allus wished it had been different, and done it because I didn't care. I've made up my mind what to do as soon as things got too bad. I was allus hoping . . . why, I was

allus hoping I might see you again. If you hadn't come across road
last night when you did, an' stopped him, an' spoke to me . . . I don't
know: I think sight o' you would a' finished it.'[13]

The trouble with Booth's fiction is that his world is not in fact primitive or provincial enough: despite the fidelity of his descriptions,
it never quite rises out of the world of popular fiction, so that however
felicitous in parts, the novels as a whole seem artificial. 'Surgery or a
bomb' – one sees Lawrence's point that the novel has 'got to have the
courage to tackle new propositions without using abstractions; it's got
to present us with new, really new feelings, a whole line of new
emotion, which will get us out of the emotional rut'.[14]
    The interesting thing about Booth is that he is such a signal case of
how much surgery was needed: truth and falsehood are so closely
intertwined in his writing. It is hard to tell whether he was aware of
this. One passage, coming from the very start of *The Tree of the
Garden*, by its abrupt switch of language seems to suggest that he was;
but the implied comment is never followed through. The 'placing' of
Mrs. Openshaw, if placing it be, is allowed to pass.

> 'O! how could you! How could you!' [Mrs Openshaw] ex-
> claimed. Out of the first weakness of imploration the fire of indignant
> passion burst like a red flame blazing unexpectedly through grey
> ash. 'To steal my husband's love and loyalty from me! To poison his
> allegiance to wife and child, and corrupt all that was good and noble
> in him for your sinful, selfish ends; O, how could you! How could
> you! Was there no other sphere of wickedness left open to you but
> you must invade the very home? Are you utterly lost to the sanctity
> of love? It was shameful of you. It was shameful.'
> 'That'll do!' the woman said, with defensive indignation. 'That'll
> do. If that's all you've come to say to me, I won't listen to you. I
> suspected what had brought you, from the first. I won't submit to be
> trampled on, for all you're his widow. If you'd 'a had any respect
> for yourself you'd 'a thought twice before coming to my house to
> make a scene. I've never troubled you in yours.'[15]

In the undeveloped contrast between those two voices one sees a failure
to recognise the changing times and thus to produce work of any lasting significance. The divorce between town and country, social and
economic, was to have its parallel in literature. What other, more
serious artists were to make of the rural theme was indicative therefore

of something more than a literary convention trying to establish itself: it showed the need to reconcile economic and social change with individual liberty and emotional fulfilment; and to find a strong enough creative outlet for the human spirit to replace effectively the waning of more formal religious sanctions. Underlying the purely literary problems facing the various rural novelists lay the issues facing a nation's way of life, whether they were consciously concerned with them or not.

3 Rural Fantasies: Kenneth Grahame, T. H. White and others

I

Stilehouse Farm lay back from the road on the rising ground between Durham and Tarring Neville. The house, mellowed by age and sun, stood foursquare to the salt winds blowing inland from the Channel.

These are the opening sentences of *Barren Leaves* by Nora Kent, which was published in 1926. Two years later appeared *Endless Furrows*, which begins as follows:

Mopbeggars Farm lay in a fold of the hills between two rises, and from where young Adam Harmer toiled in the oat-field on the other side of the brow he could see no more of the house than a single spiral of blue smoke from a chimney, flattened and twisted by the wind sweeping up the valley from the Channel.

Three years after this Naomi Jacob confirmed her already established popularity with *Roots*. Its opening is according to the by now recognisable rural novel pattern:

The Whitelaws of Fellow's Top, in the West Riding of Yorkshire, were a family which could only have been bred in that land of broad acres and narrow prejudices.

The conclusion is written with an equal confidence:

Sarah Ann Whitelaw, at seventy-six, mistress of Fellow's Top, Fellow's End and Basset in the West Riding of Yorkshire, had paid her debt and finished her work.

The End

Sermione, Lago di Garda

The place of composition indicates the profitability of this kind of fiction.

Certainly the publication in 1932 of *Cold Comfort Farm*, Stella Gibbons's famous satire on the contemporary rural novel, was well timed. The rural novel as a specialist branch of fiction had been exploited by too many writers in a hackneyed way, and the conventions of plot, characterisation and atmospheric description laid themselves open to parody. But this particular satire indulged in more than parody: by causing her heroine to reorganise the lives of that collective embodiment of literary mannerisms, the Starkadder family, the author exercised a criticism of a more serious kind. Flora Post was a character with whom the reader was invited to identify; and her attitudes had been anticipated by critics and reviewers for many years, Katherine Mansfield, for instance, writing that she had

> grown very shy of dialect which is half prophecy, half potatoes, and more than a trifle impatient of over-wise old men, hot-blooded young ones, beauties in faded calico, and scenes of passion in the kitchen while the dinner is hotting up or getting cold.[1]

However amusing this may be, the tone of it refers not only to the style of this kind of novel but to its subject matter also. It patronises the rural theme as such, and country life is in the very dismissal being depicted as something outside the ordinary course of human affairs. It is a townsman's approach.

Cold Comfort Farm remains a very funny book; but as a weapon it only damages the more violent rural novels of the day, a species of fiction that stemmed in part from an oversimplified appreciation of *Wuthering Heights* ('elemental' being a stock adjective for a stock response to that book). Nevertheless, *Cold Comfort Farm* must hover like a warning presence in any consideration of the rural novelists of its time, as a touchstone for cliché though not as the dismissal of a mode. And it certainly has outlived most of the books that were its occasion.

But the unreality it pilloried was not the only one that infected the treatment of rural themes in fiction. There was a more insidious kind. One source for it was Mary Russell Mitford's *Our Village* (1824–32). These essays are charming, observant and seriously intended; but, however inadvertently, they have the effect of putting the village and its people on display. What Mary Mitford and Elizabeth Gaskell, in *Cranford* (1853), did with intelligence and tact, their imitators in the twentieth century did with a heavy hand. One has only to compare the average 'country book' of the 1930s with the sober dignity of Flora Thompson's account of country life in *Lark Rise* (1939) and its successors to see the difference between an approach that sees the country primarily as something to be enjoyed and one that knows it as a means of livelihood. For Flora Thompson (1877–1947), unlike most rural writers, came from a labouring family. She worked for some time as a post-office clerk, and in her own life made the transition from country to town. Her four books were written after she was sixty: the trilogy *Lark Rise to Candleford* is probably the best account of late nineteenth-century village life that we have, outside of the work of George Sturt.[2]

At the turn of the century, however, there was a market in old-world charm, embodied, for instance, in the kind of illustrations to popular classics associated with the names of Hugh Thomson and C. E. and H. M. Brock; and it was the more picturesque areas which tended to be chosen by novelists for their backgrounds. In the more prosaic 1930s, Suffolk became the favoured county with several writers; but earlier in the century Devonshire was a frequent subject of novelists – among them Gwendoline Keats, who used the pen name 'Zack', and the more popular 'Beatrice Chase' (Olive Katherine Parr) who was a well-known Dartmoor personality. Her tone was rather proprietorial:

> I know our fields love me, just as the moor loves me, and the tors . . .
> I know that something in the land answers silently to my call, thrills
> to the mighty forces of the love I pour out on it.[3]

This is like Wordsworth through the looking glass. Beatrice Chase was the subject of a novel by the best-selling 'John Oxenham' (William Arthur Dunkerley), *My Lady of the Moor* (1916). It is dedicated to 'Beatrice', and an advertisement for her own works appears on the fly-leaf. She repaid this in 1944 with *My Chief Knight, John Oxenham: A Memoir and an Appeal*. The appeal, surprisingly, is not financial: it is a summons to the men of England to dedicate themselves to sexual purity. The book also contains an account of the author's excursions into the drama. One play, adopted from her novel *Lady Avis Trewithen* (1922) is described by her as 'a comedy full of new milk, new-mown hay, old world wit and a perfect love story'. Another, *The Little Cardinal*, is more far-ranging, 'a sort of suggestion of *Under the Red Robe, The Sign of the Cross,* and *Little Lord Fauntleroy.*'

In these 'Devonshire years' nostalgia was unaccompanied by any precise anxiety as to where the forces of change might be tending: there was no alarm, merely regret for the 'quaint old ways' which were being lost. But to call something quaint is, in popular understanding, to belittle it; and it is a fault of self-consciously 'rustic' fiction that it dehumanises its characters. There were, however, two minor writers who avoided this tendency, Walter Raymond (a Somerset man who retired from business in order to devote himself to writing) and Mary J. H. Skrine. The latter, a clergyman's wife, had, like Mrs Gaskell before her, a sensitive appreciation of the human aspects and human mitigation of economic hardship:

> The two dim thoughts, old and young, groped after the love that wasn't anywhere. The big world around meant to protect. My Lady was good. In everyday reality, neither fact meant anything practical. In the last and final resort the poor depend on one another.[4]

Novels like *A Stepson of the Soil* (1910) and *Shepherd Easton's Daughter* (1925) appear to have been written as much *for* the country people as about them.

The same can be said of the work of Walter Raymond (1853–1930), though it has a greater veneer of sophistication; it attained a memorial edition after his death.[5] Most of his novels were published before the turn of the century, though *Verity Thurston*, the tale of a farmer's daughter who marries a smuggler, appeared as late as 1925. Raymond's principal concern is to describe faithfully a bygone way of life which he cherished and remembered; but he realised that this was itself a symptom of alienation.

> Rural folk live very little in the past. The present absorbs their cares, and they are shy of talking to a stranger of bygone people and conditions. If you enquire of the aged, they cannot 'call to mind', or they have heard 'a summat', but really couldn't 'tell the rights o' it.' If you ask of the young it was before their time. You cannot

gather anecdotes in an ale-house as you can pick nuts in an October wood.[6]

Here the use of the word 'folk' and the quoted dialect presuppose an urban readership wishing to be informed about a way of life different from and better than its own. But Raymond is never trivial or patronising: he tells only of what he knows for himself. His virtues and liimitations can be assessed in the light of the following account of rural migration when compared with a similar passage in *Tess of the D'Urbervilles.*

Such waggons are to be met with on every road now all the changing folk are ridding house. I suspect a reluctance concealed beneath the greater number of these heterogeneous piles of household sticks. Some are going to finer dwellings, and yet for a moment there is a sadness at leaving the old home. The greater number, perhaps, are moving because they have not been able 'to make a do of it.' But whether the change be to a better place or to a worse, a true democratic spirit pervades the journey there. Utensils, buckets, dairy tubs and vats associate awhile with parlour tables and chairs. A highly respectable old horsehair sofa, decorated with brass-headed nails, back to back with a very common kitchen dresser, nurses a lapful of pots, pans, jugs, basins and bedroom ware of no distinction whatever. The grandfather clock must needs chum with a baby's cradle. The occasion is destructive not only of class distinction, but of all true modesty. Decent tables, habitually draped, get on their backs, like ewes heavy in wool before shearing, and lie with legs pointing up to the sky. Even a thoroughbred mahogany Chippendale will expose its elegant calves and feet to a staring world without a blush. All things became equal at house-ridding as at the greater passing which men call Death.[7]

The emphasis here is pictorial, and the narrator's voice – playful, sympathetic but detached, a shade portentous – controls the tone. It is like a peepshow; everything is at once clearly seen and very distant.

Compared with Raymond, Hardy is sparing of detail; but his analytic approach involves his readers far more effectively.

[The house-ridding] proceeded with some cheerfulness, a friendly neighbour or two assisting. When the large articles of furniture had been packed in position a circular nest was made of the beds and bedding, in which Joan Durbeyfield and the younger children were to sit through the journey. After loading there was a long delay before the horses were brought, these having been unharnessed during the ridding; but at length, about two o'clock, the whole was under way, the cooking pot swinging from the axle of the waggon, Mrs Durbeyfield and family at the top, the matron having in her lap, to prevent injury to its works the head of the clock, which, at any exceptional lurch of the waggon, struck one, or one-and-a-half, in hurt tones. . . .

The day being the sixth of April, the Durbeyfield waggon met many other waggons with families on the summit of the load, which was built on a wellnigh unvarying principle, as peculiar, probably, to the rural labourer as the hexagon to the bee. The groundwork of the arrangement was the family dresser, which, with its shining handles, and finger-marks, and domestic evidences thick upon it, stood importantly in front, over the tails of the shaft-horses, in its erect and natural position, like some Ark of the Covenant that they were bound to carry reverently.[8]

Here the emphasis is on people rather than on objects: in place of Raymond's serio-comic catalogue we have a careful choice of material, designed to reveal the essence of the family life that is being uprooted. Moreover, the ridding is seen as part of a wider social process, something which extends beyond the boundaries of the immediate occasion. Instead of being invited to contemplate a static society, we are involved in a changing one. This is exactly what does not happen in the old-fashioned pastoral tradition, which for all its virtues of modesty of aim faithfully fulfilled does not measure up to the actualities of the rural world as Hardy's informed astringency can do. It suffers from a certain fatal softness.

II

This softness is still more evident in the various novels about gardens, which are a feature of the earlier twentieth-century literary scene. The garden, a valid image of Paradise when nature remained untamed and faith was strong, diminishes, like all the greater religious images, in an age of industrialism and doubt; and from a vision of lost Eden it becomes an embodiment of a social Eden threatened by democracy. The shading of one view into the other can be seen in Forster's *Howards End* (1910);[9] and the central critical problem arising from that novel is to decide whether it succeeds in resolving the contradictions inherent in the situation. One such was the association of the garden, in the public mind, with a private retreat, a view which the best-selling *Elizabeth and Her German Garden* (1898) had already made popular.

'Elizabeth' was the pen name of Mary Annette Beauchamp (1886–1941). A cousin of Katherine Mansfield, she married a German count and went to live in Prussia – engaging for a while E. M. Forster, and later Hugh Walpole, as a tutor to her children. Her dislike of the Prussians evinced itself in a number of sweetly savage novels, and her two 'garden' books, in which she celebrated the charms of withdrawal from an uncongenial world. The garden becomes a token of its owner's sensibility and a retreat from the alien life around her. And it is *hers*: the garden is one aspect of nature (and thus of life itself) which can to a degree be controlled. It is Eden without Jehovah. Elizabeth subsequently married Bertrand Russell's elder brother, with results disastrous to her happiness, but beneficial to her art: the later novels are far more mature and interesting than the earlier ones, uneven though most of them are. She rarely treats of the English country scene, but *In the Mountains* (1920) and *The Enchanted April* (1922) demonstrate with characteristic wit the effects of sunlight and natural beauty when thawing out frigid northern temperaments. But it was the Elizabeth of the early German period who was to be influential: she possessed a tone of voice that was unmistakable, and one which allured imitators – the voice of the humorous, whimsical, commonsensical, occasionally sharp but always feminine Englishwoman who was aristocratically connected, kind to (but amusing about) her servants, and always elegant, even in an old mackintosh and gardening gloves.

Her progeny were many. Perhaps the most attractive were three books by Flora Klickmann, editor of *The Girl's Own Paper*. The accounts of her cottage and garden in the Wye Valley in *The Flower Patch Among the Hills* (1916) and its successors are written in an agreeably confiding manner and are less sentimental than their titles might suggest. They were marketed in lavender-coloured bindings, as were the enormously popular novels of Florence L. Barclay (1862–1921), of which *The Rosary* (1909) is the most famous. Though not exclusively rural in setting, these books inculcated the gentler rural virtues as well as more strident patriotic ones. A clergyman's wife, Mrs Barclay believed roundly in all she wrote.

Mrs Herriot was enjoying an afternoon drive. Her barouche, so well known in the park, drawn by a high-stepping pair of dapple greys, bowled in stately fashion through the Surrey lanes, and along the wide roads on the common above Dinglevale. . . . Here was no trotting dog-cart, or rushing motor. No startling hoot preceded her; she left no bewildering cloud of dust behind. The old village women dropped long forgotten curtseys, and went smiling on their way; the labourers touched their caps, as the carriage swept by; then wondered, in surly fashion, why they had done so.[10]

Indeed Florence Barclay and her imitators would seem to have valued country society all the more because of its innate conservatism. The above passage continues:

With the passing of a great queen and of a great century, there seems also to have passed the spirit of courtesy and gracious manners; the consideration of the rich for the poor; the respectful deference of the poor towards the rich. In this age of push and hurry, of attempts to level all class distinctions by those to whom the levelling means a step up, at the expense of others who stand higher, England is invaded by the spirit of Liberty, Equality, Fraternity – which practically means: I am at liberty to grab the things which belong to my brother – and the term 'early Victorian' carries with it somewhat of a sneer. But a reaction must come before long, for Englishmen are staunchly conservative at heart, faithful to traditions of Church and State, loyal to the great names, which in the past have made Britain great. And supreme among these, standing for all which is purest, noblest, and most truly British, will ever be the name Victoria.

It can have been given to few authors to state so exactly what they mean: one can almost hear the satisfaction with which that page must have been turned.

In the Florence Barclay world, rural scenes are usually productive of spiritual healing: thus in *The Broken Halo* (1913) Mrs Herriot, the 'Little White Lady' converts the young scapegrace 'Doctor Dick' during his country locum. A similar function is performed by another small coloured woman, the 'Little Blue Lady', in Mildred Garner's *Harmony*. This lush product of the Barclay school was published in 1916, and the advertisement for it cunningly capitalises on the fact.

The scent of old-fashioned flowers, the drowsy hum of bees, and the quiet spell of the countryside is realised in every page of 'Harmony'.

Peacewold is a harbour of refuge where gather those in need of the sympathy which the Little Blue Lady unfailingly has for her friends when they are distressed in spirit or body. To her comes Star worn out with months of settlement work in Bethnal Green, and Harmony whose sight is restored after years of blindness . . . Willow, whose story the book is, also has reason to love the Little Blue Lady who has been as a mother to her.

The novel, though not quite as funny as it sounds, is a good deal more exciting: it also includes a runaway nun, a small boy known as the Little Tin Trumpeter, and an abduction by brigands in Algeria. It is a real goose of a book, and clearly designed as an antidote to wartime anxieties: the nineteenth-century paternalistic ideals are still operative. Willow inherits an enormous fortune, Star is a daughter of the aristocracy – it is a story for the well-to-do. The virtues inculcated are all on the side of restraint and sweetness, even though 'the Little Blue Lady does not love a tidy garden. She cares too much for the ideas of the Greatest Gardener of all.'[11]

Genteel and sentimental, *Harmony* was the product of a decadent tradition, self-indulgent and insidiously silly. For one result of all writing of the kind is a quality of smugness: emotion is automatic and second-hand, the result of a pseudo-gnosis of the initiated. The rural scene becomes the preserve of an élite.

III

But there is a genuine and healthy nostalgia (the nostalgia described in Wordsworth's 'Immortality' ode), one related to the experiences of childhood when they are seen as correctives to the limitation of adult perceptions. In early twentieth-century literature there have been many evocations of country life as experienced by the child, works of which Jefferies's *Wood Magic* (1881) and *Bevis* (1882) are the forerunners, and Alison Uttley's *The Country Child* (1931) and Eiluned Lewis's *Dew on the Grass* (1934) among the more attractive and original examples. In these books an affectionate regret for the past is for the most part untroubled by uncertainty about the future. The English rural scene takes on the character of an Arcadia. And just as memory covers a rural childhood with a fine haze of happiness, so a would-be mystical strangeness becomes an element in the rural novel, making of the countryside not merely an idyllic world, but also a gateway into worlds greater than itself. Instead of being an object of fantasy (as in some of the works discussed above) it becomes an occasion for it.

The most widely read fantasy of this kind has probably been *The Wind in the Willows* (1908) by Kenneth Grahame (1859–1932), a book whose influence upon the popular imagination springs from a blending of an idyllic Thames Valley landscape with a reflection of deep-rooted psychological attitudes, of a wistful romanticism with the workaday and cosy. Mole, Rat, Badger and Toad are elements within the self as well as portraits of social types: as Peter Green points out,

> There is the idealized river-landscape with its peaceful Epicurean inhabitants; the menace, finally destroyed, of the Wild Wood; the conflict between a paternalist society and the hubristic, Bohemian individual, as exemplified by Toad; and the stabilization of the traditional *status quo* by the realization of a completely self-contained and self-sufficient myth.[12]

But the book's continuing vitality obviously springs from more than this. Grahame's peculiarly tender attitude to his animals (in noteworthy contrast to the more salty works of Beatrix Potter) allows for a large measure of self-identification on the part of his readers; and Rat messing about in boats, and Mole pining for his home, and Toad poop-pooping in his motor car along the country roads are emblematic of the various ways in which the Englishman enjoys his native country. But it is perhaps too narrowly masculine in sensibility: the society of the river bank is an exclusively bachelor one.

In one chapter, 'The Piper at the Gates of Dawn', we find a better exposition of Edwardian nature mysticism than in the early work of Forster: it is picturesque and optimistic, pagan and yet tinged with Christianity. Mole looks 'in the very eyes of the Friend and Helper'.

> 'Rat,' he found breath to whisper, shaking. 'Are you afraid?'
> 'Afraid?' murmured the Rat, his eyes shining with unutterable love. 'Afraid? Of *Him*? O, never, never! And yet – and yet – O, Mole, I am afraid!'[13]

The ambivalent attitude to religious mystery is beautifully expressed. But for the most part *The Wind in the Willows* keeps to the realm of the known. ' "Beyond the Wild Wood comes the Wide World," said the Rat. "And that's something that doesn't matter, either to you or me." '[14] The book's lasting appeal, below all it's charm and fun and sheer inventiveness, is to the Mole in one, the Mole who

> saw clearly that he was an animal of tilled field and hedgerow, linked to the ploughed furrow, the frequented pasture, the lane of evening lingerings, the cultivated garden-plot. For others the asperities, the stubborn endurance, or the clash of actual conflict that went with Nature in the rough; he must be wise, must keep to the pleasant places in which his lines were laid and which held adventure enough, in their way, to last for a lifetime.[15]

On the other hand, the book contains a chapter in which the alternative to this cosy resignation is romantically displayed. 'Wayfarers All' disturbs the prevailing mood far more than does the Wild Wood chapter: the latter enhances the river bank's charms by very contrast, but the lure of the wanderer is something more dangerous than the ferrets or the stoats. The transformation of Toad with his caravan to Toad with his motor car is representative of the increase and scope of travel that is still altering our imaginative assumptions. The call of the road is to be found in much popular fiction: Jeffrey Farnol's *The Broad Highway* (1910), where it is combined with Regency romance; H. G. Wells's *The History of Mr Polly* (1911), where it represents escape for 'the little man' besieged by conventions and the economic laws that support them; and as late as 1940 in Francis Brett Young's *Mr Lucton's Freedom*, the escaping hero now being a business man of a more prosperous kind than Mr Polly. The great popularity of *The Roadmender* (1901) by 'Michael Fairless' is another case in point, though this book was more serious and thoughtful than most of its kind. It is not a novel, but a fictionalised autobiography in the form of discursive meditations, rather in the manner of Gissing's *The Private Papers of Henry Ryecroft* (1903), which was, significantly, the only one of its author's books to have any real popularity in this period. But the half-bitter resignation of *Ryecroft* is nowhere present in *The Roadmender*. The author's real name was Margaret Fairless Barber: her book, which she dictated on her death bed, is shot through with mysticism. She herself, like many mystics, was tough, working for several years as a nurse in the London slums. When forced by ill health to retire to the country, she devoted herself to the care of a mentally retarded child, and ministered to tramps.[16] Her vision was hard-earned. But most books of the open-air type were full of cheer, and treated the industrial and commercial changes with rueful scorn: for all its bonhomie (of which the essays of Hilaire Belloc provide notable examples[17]), this literary traveller's world was narrow in outlook.

A more adventurous writer of fantasy than Kenneth Grahame was T. H. White (1906–64), whose *The Sword in the Stone* (1939) is probably the most popular book of its kind since *The Wind in the Willows*. White, a sometime schoolmaster, did not begin by writing fantasies (though *Darkness at Pemberley* (1930), a thriller which is part parody and part pastiche of contemporary models, comes near to being one). His first serious novel, *Farewell Victoria* (1933), chronicles through the eyes of a gamekeeper the changes overtaking England at the century's turn. The method is panoramic, the mood elegaic and opposed to a world that thrusts aside

the agriculturalists who are the true blood of England and have for a hundred years been cheated even of their small security; so that coal miners and factory hands, and the brood whose bloody vehicle is the motor bicycle, possess the rights of citizens, while their brothers are allowed to starve.[18]

But the tone here is too shrill: White's personal prejudices, while making him the extraordinarily individual writer that he is, also made him an ill-balanced assessor of social change. And yet for all his waywardness and frequent triviality, he again and again evinces a directness of perception and an awareness of the actual that makes his fantasies acceptable. The latter develop out of the rural experience explored in *Farewell Victoria* and the autobiographical *England Have My Bones* (1936). He can be a trenchant commentator, as when writing of the gamekeeper Mundy's reaction to his wife's elopement with a fellow keeper:

Perhaps a romantic character would have ridden after her and brought her back. But Mundy had gone out as Sir William's second horseman, as he had been trained to do.[19]

And his innate conservatism is balanced by his delight in learning things, in finding out how things work. This helps to offset the hostility he shows towards the world of the machine.

The cavalry was bucketing along the hedge and the toad was hopping towards it, transversely. It progressed in tedious, flurried hops. It landed on the grass with the whole of its undercarriage. It was exquisitely mottled. It was a toady toad and Mr Marx adored it in his soul.[20]

So the Professor (White's self-portrait in a number of books[21]) after catching a mermaid in a trout stream is at a loss what to do with her:

Apart from the question of close seasons and kelts and whether eighty pounds might not turn out to be quite an insignificant weight for a mermaid after all, apart from all this there were her brains. One can't beat people's brains out. One can't take the thick end of a gaff to something which is a lady from the waist up at any rate.[22]

Fantasy in White's work is always rooted in the actual – it is an extension of the natural world, not a corrective to it, or a substitute. Merlin in *The Sword in the Stone* turns the young Arthur into a perch, a hawk, a snake, and a badger: only with a close knowledge of the animal world and of the true workings of nature can he be the deliverer of England. The parable is obvious. The success of the book (for its rather facetious humour is not to everyone's taste) lies in the careful and delighted accounts of woodland life and its understanding of what may best be called the mechanics of nature. White's command of English reflects the clear, matter-of-fact quality of his understanding; for him, the country is man's true environment, not simply the ministrant to his needs or the vehicle for his emotions.

Night does not sleep, it wakes; not so much with the wakefulness of all the woodland creatures whose carnival is man's absence in the dark, but with the wakefulness of man the solitary, pattering home with his ears pricked to his own footsteps, or the insomniac, listening to the fizzings of the walls.[23]

Like Kenneth Grahame, T. H. White is a writer whose actual influence upon the English imagination may well be greater than that of academically more established writers. He succeeded perhaps better than any of his contemporaries in voicing the pleasure, the boyish pleasure, to be found in field sports and in mastering one's environment. The vulnerability and sensitivity to pain that so nearly makes his Arthurian tetralogy a masterpiece never turns to sickliness or rant: the compensatory turning to fantasy and farce give, surprisingly, a note of health and sanity.

The seriousness of his attitudes and achievements can be recognized when one turns to his friend David Garnett's *Lady into Fox* (1922). This book was much admired on its appearance, and its virtues – restraint, a clear style, an unswerving development of its theme – can still commend it. But its reticence and very clarity are also its undoing. As a parable of loss, of estrangement, of the engulfing of one partner in an experience impossible for the other, the novel is genuinely moving – and disturbing: the uneasy relationship between the civilised and half-wild is finely developed. But the book lacks a dimension. 'Wonderful or supernatural events are not so uncommon, rather they are irregular in their incidence.' The non-committal ambiguity of that opening, and the abruptness of Mrs Tebrick's change into a vixen, convey a sense of scorn for the medium employed: the literary effect is solipsistic. Though T. H. White no more believes in supernatural happenings than Garnett does, his less inhibited approach makes fantasy a statement about the world of nature, and not the other way round. His novels, even the weakest of them, because of their essentially reverential attitude to that world remain imaginative growing points, while Garnett's, economical and shapely as they are, do not. The rural novel does not lend itself to overmuch sophistication, which may account for Lawrence's comment, 'That lady into fox stuff is pretty piffle – just playboy stuff.'[24]

IV

Not all urban incursions into the country have, in fiction, been productive of peace and healing. A different pace of life and different perspectives cause their own disturbance. In *Bachelor's Knap* (1935), by the Dorset novelist Eric Benfield, the painter who visits the village of Buttery Corner is told that

> By now you must know that all this land is crossed and recrossed by lanes and cuttings underground, and so you'll understand that a man often breaks through into old workings that have been shut down for years.[25]

This novel, with its Purbeck quarry backgrounds and the oblique obscenity of its occult elements, is characteristic of another kind of rural fantasy, the exploitation of folk-lore and a feeling for the 'picturesque'. It is a sophisticated reworking of unsophisticated material. Its amoral approach to evil and its interpretation of witchcraft as a lust for power that can prove artistically fruitful (the painter leaves the village knowing that his liaison with the witch and exploration of the quarries are going to make him a famous artist) suggest the 1890s rather than the post-Lawrentian era. (Indeed, this kind of supernatural novel had already been written definitively in Arthur Machen's *The Hill of Dreams* (1907), where the whole attitude to 'evil' is far more subtle, being related to the psychological experiences of the protagonist.) Benfield's picture of the quarrymen in this novel and in *Saul's Sons* (1938) is more interesting than his treatment of the occult. The traditions, the family pride, the hardships, the rivalries seem part of a civilisation in miniature. In this use of a secluded community to give perspective to life at large, Benfield is reminiscent of T. F. Powys, a writer whom he admired and to whom he seems to be indebted for the more self-consciously bucolic element in his books. (He was to make some interesting comments on the Powys brothers as Dorset writers in his book on Dorset published in 1950). And T. F. Powys's influence is also to be seen in David Garnett's *The Sailor's Return* (1925) and *Go She Must* (1927). The former, named after the inn at Powys's home village of East Chaldon, depicts the countryman in fashionably lurid terms as full of intolerance and smallmindedness.

Novels about rural witchcraft are frequent in this period, though Benfield's is more torrid than most. Frances Carmichael's *The Witch of Brent* (1934) makes restrained use of landscape as an influence on belief: weather conditions and scenery as much as creeds and customs affect the tragedy. Charlotte M. Peake, on the other hand, in *Pagan Corner* (1923) focused on the psychology of witchcraft, revealing, however, a talent put to happier use in *Eli of the Downs* (1920), a portrayal of a shepherd that is innocent of any sense of merely exhibiting its subject, the vice of novels that explore the darker sides of rural life.

Easily the most interesting novel of this kind – indeed it is a corrective to the kind – is Sylvia Townsend Warner's *Lolly Willowes* (1926) The author (b. 1893), although not strictly a rural novelist (for her novels and stories cover a wide variety of backgrounds and themes) writes of country life with freshness and authenticity, above all with a remarkable feeling for the tangible that expresses itself most vividly in *The True Heart* (1929), the touching story of an orphan servant-girl in Victorian England. Here the Essex landscape gives strength and dimension to a tale that in hands less sure and able might have declined into whimsy. As it is Sylvia Townsend Warner achieves, by instinctive tact and an understanding of the use of words, a complete integration between urban and rural points of view. And the same is true of *Lolly*

Willowes. Its plot is simple. Laura Willowes, after a country girlhood, goes to live as a conventional spinster aunt with her brother and his family in London: at last, bored with her role to the point of rebellion, she retires to Buckinghamshire and becomes a witch. The novel is free from whimsy and sensationalism. Laura's progress is inevitable: by temperament she is solitary and adventurous, and society can offer her no outlet.

> 'That's why we become witches: to show our scorn of pretending life's a safe business, to satisfy our passion for adventure . . . It's . . . to have a life of one's own, not an existence doled out to you by others. . . .'[26]

The Devil is the natural guardian of all such rebels.

> Hid fast in that strong memory no wild thing could be shaken, no secret covert destroyed, no haunt of shadow and silence laid open.[27]

The irony is two-edged: our sympathies are with Laura, and yet the Satanic associations make one question, faintly, her own standards. So it is with Great Mop, the Chiltern village, which is at once sinister and harmless.[28] The 'Satan' who appears at the Sabbath is a fraud, and the real Satan is not so much a hunter as a guardian. All the supernatural phenomena (there are very few of them) can have a rational explanation. The book is a delicate readjustment of the conventional novel of witchcraft. Laura's commitment to Satan takes place when, without quite knowing why, she throws her guide-book down a well.

Slight though it is, the novel makes its impact. The writing, close, crisp and rich in imagery, maintains an even, watchful pace. The account of Laura's girlhood prepares us both for her passivity in London and for her final rebellion in Great Mop.

> She did not want to leave her father, nor did she want to leave Lady Place. Her life perfectly contented her. She had no wish for ways other than those she had grown up in. With an easy diligence she played her part as mistress of the house, abetted at every turn by country servants of long tenure, as enamoured of the comfortable amble of day by day as she was.[29]

A whole civilised way of life is suggested in that passage: it is the steady assured life, threatened by change, that so much rural fiction reflects and, in doing so, asks to be perpetuated. But that very life con-tains more of mystery than its routine suggests; and the passage con-tinues,

> At certain seasons a faint resinous smell would haunt the house like some rustic spirit. It was Mrs. Bonnet making the traditional bees-wax polish that alone could be trusted to give the proper lustre to the elegantly bulging fronts of tallboys and cabinets. The grey days of early February were tinged with tropical odours by great-great-aunt Salome's recipe for marmalade; and on the afternoon of Good Friday, if it were fine, the stuffed foxes and otters were taken out of their glass cases, brushed, and set to sweeten on the lawn.[30]

The charm has just a whiff of menace: and Laura's final destiny can be seen to be prefigured.

Lolly Willowes uses the rustic myth, with its body of ideas and as-sociations, as a parable of the human craving for individual liberty of choice; and it 'places' the darker aspects of that myth with a sophisti-cation that is far from superficial. Both mordant and good humoured, it is one of the body of 'side-line' novels – those which, while standing outside the mainstream of English fiction, isolate one particular ex-perience and put it in a fresh perspective. As a fable it is surpassed only by the best work of the author's friend and neighbour, T. F. Powys;[31] and even more successfully than his fiction it uses fantasy as a means of placing the rural experience for an urban consciousness.

Lolly Willowes does this by a blend of physical sensitivity and mental sophistication: it presents a literary solution. More profound, however, because more far-ranging in its application, is the comprehensive vision embodied in Edward Thomas's one novel (if novel it can be called), The Happy-Go-Lucky Morgans (1913). Here the author, among the most critically perceptive poets of his time, draws an affectionate portrait of a Welsh family living in a large and comfortable house on the edge of London, in Balham as it then was. This siting of his story enables him to depict forays made from it both into the country (the 'Our Country' of the boys Arthur and Philip) and into a suburban hinterland. Plot in the ordinary sense there is none; but we are made aware inferen-tially, through the recollections of the narrator, of how the family have come to move from Wales by way of Wiltshire – from Celtic romance, as it were, through the landscape of Jefferies (a writer whom Thomas intensely admired) to the present day. Family jokes are mixed up with poetic legends, facetiousness with personal tragedy, dry social comment with beautifully realised accounts of weather and landscape. Jefferies, James Stephens and E. Nesbit all seem to rub shoulders here, but the controlling sensibility is Thomas's own – the balance found in the servant Ann, who comes from Wales and who stays on in London after the family have returned to their original home, adapting to change when the generous, romantic, extravagant Morgans, of necessity it would seem, have withdrawn to the world of their origins.

The several worlds or dimensions of the novel are all subtly related, so that, while we are told of how the boys 'treated the streets like woods, and never complained of the substitute', or that 'no wonder Our Country was supernaturally beautiful. It had London for a foil', we are told on another occasion of how the boys see in a group of chimney stacks 'a sublimer St Michael's Mount' And against the obvious 'romance' of David Morgan's quest for the Absolute in his lonely tower in the Welsh mountains, we have a more immediate note struck by the Wiltshire village woman's recollections of the Morgan family, when she shows Arthur, the narrator, round their deserted house. The family of the London present are now felt to be almost eerie beings in the landscape they have vacated. The whole book, though inclined in places to an over-easy chattiness, is a remarkable picture of how memory and imagination can bind together disparate experiences and make them one. Thus on the one hand we have a moving restraint in the account of David's mystical quest among the hills :

In the rain and wind I have sat against one of the rocks in the autumn bracken until the sheep have surrounded me, shaggy and but half-visible through the mist, peering at me fearlessly, as if they had not seen a man since that one was put to rest under the cairn above; I sat on and on in the mystery, part of it but not divining, so that I went disappointed away. The crags stared at me on the hilltop where the dark spirits of the earth had crept out of their abysses into the day, and still clad in darkness, looked grimly at the sky, the light, and at me. . . .[32]

This is disturbing and compelling; yet Thomas has already provided a perspective on the experience.

But gradually [David] formed the opinion that he did not understand town life, that he never could understand the men and women whom he saw living a town life pure and simple. Before he came amongst them he had been thinking grandly about men without realising that these were of a different species. His own interference seemed to him impudent. They disgusted him, he wanted to make them more or less in his own image to save his feelings, which, said he, was absurd. He was trying to alter the conditions of other men's lives because he could not have himself endured them, because it would have been unpleasant to him to be like them in their hideous pleasure, hideous suffering, hideous indifference. In this attitude, which altogether neglected the consolations and even beauty and glory possible or incident to such a life, he saw a modern Pharisaism, whose followers did not merely desire to be unlike others, but to make others like themselves. It was, he thought, due to lack of the imagination and sympathy to see their lives from a higher or a more intimate point of view, in connection with implicit ideals, not as a spectacle for which he had an expensive seat.[33]

That association of 'higher' with 'more intimate' refers us to Thomas's particular quality as a poet; and the whole passage probes deep into many of the attitudes underlying the town–country literary confrontation. Thomas had the greatness to give each side its due, both to see the place of the country in the imagination of his time and to be aware of the physical realities of the situation as well. His novel shows the same awareness as we find in his poetry, that complex interplay between intimations of experience beyond our normal consciousness and a keen response to the tangible world, a response that was accompanied by a startling honesty as to his own feelings with regard to what he knew to be the truth. His work provides a balance that only the finest of the other rural writers were to emulate.

V

The wide variety of types of rural fantasy have this in common, that they all bear witness to the increasing hold of the English landscape over the English imagination. In all of them (with the notable exception of *The Happy-Go-Lucky Morgans*) the town is the enemy and the country the place where life is to be experienced at its fullest and richest. The nature of the fantasy to which the rural scene gives rise is itself indicative of the outlook and stature of the author. In the minor sentimental writer its quality is narrow, and self-protective; in the truly original artists, such as White and Sylvia Townsend Warner, the idea of a rural Arcadia becomes a springboard for psychological and philosophical speculation. It is an escape *into* reality, not an escape from it.

For the most part these writers are more interested in the aesthetic response to landscape as mediated through recollections of art and literature and folklore than in the people who actually live in and work the landscape. In Hardy's best novels we do find the fusion of place with people, but the fantasy writers are less balanced. Their central characters tend to be outsiders, recording instruments, and it is their experience which is treated as being the rural experience – the experience in rural surroundings of feelings of peace or resignation or spiritual enlargement. The appeal to the reader is one of familiarity, and the aim diversion. Not for nothing is it that the most enduringly successful rural fantasies have been books for children : *The Wind in the Willows*, Kipling's *Puck of Pook's Hill* (1906), John Masefield's *The Midnight Folk* (1927), and the tales of Beatrix Potter (most of which were written between 1900 and 1913). And it is in children's fiction that the tradition has continued to flourish, as in the play upon the mythological associations of specific English landscapes in the work of William Mayne and Alan Garner, and in Richard Adams's *Watership Down* (1972), where the beast fable receives a sustained and essentially adult treatment in a readily recognisable locality.

But these rural fantasies are not in the fullest sense 'the rural novel' : their authors, by ignoring the disparity between the subjective experience of the country and the social and economic experience of its hardships, are peripheral to the rural writer's most urgent concerns; though they do voice with particular clarity what the country meant in the average townsman's imaginative experience. For the more deliberate treatment of rural life we must look elsewhere. There are no real English equivalents of Zola's *La Terre*; but at the start of the twentieth century it began to look as though there might be. As against the idealisation of rural life found in much popular fiction of the first two decades of the century, readers could point to the more overtly realistic novels of John Trevena and Eden Phillpotts. Here if anywhere before 1914 was the English novel of the soil.

4 The Cult of the Primitive: Eden Phillpotts, John Trevena

I

Edward Thomas's account of the withdrawal of David Morgan from London to the Welsh hills reflects one aspect of the sensibility of his age. The growth of towns and cities, which had advanced at an unprecedented rate in this period, had modified the popular view of what constituted country life. As town life in its threefold aspect of smart society, bourgeois conventionalism and slum brutality and squalor could be considered 'artificial', so the identification of country life with the 'natural' and 'unspoiled' followed. But a growth in population had also meant a further swallowing up of common land and the spread outward of industrial cities,[1] so that villages were seen as being 'threatened' by the town. The hostility to industrialism and a desire to call a halt to it therefore led to a glorification of country which man could not change. However, nothing could in fact be more unnatural from the human point of view than a cult of the 'natural' in this sense, for country life was understood less in terms of living in a working community than as a means for undergoing various uplifting spiritual experiences. With this muddled thinking we find a turning towards the figures of the farmer and the agricultural labourer as types of primitive simplicity from which the urban consciousness could learn. The ideals of Carpenter and the Fabians were reduced to an aesthetic. The particular appeal of Hardy's novels in this respect has been well summed up by Lawrence:

> Upon the vast, incomprehensible pattern of some primal morality greater than ever the human mind can grasp, is drawn the little pathetic pattern of man's moral life and struggle, pathetic, almost ridiculous. The little fold of law and order, the little walled city

within which man has to defend himself from the waste enormity of nature, becomes almost too small, and the pioneers venturing out with the code of the walled city upon them, die in the bonds of that code, free and yet unfree, preaching the walled city and looking to the waste.[2]

Those writers who attempted to portray the primeval had inevitably to stress the difference between rural and city dwellers. Hardy's Wessex, as *Jude the Obscure* conclusively showed, was part of a larger world and a wider society (one reason for that novel's contemporary unpopularity); yet the novelists writing about specifically primitive people stressed, necessarily, the isolation of their world. But since the audience for these novels thus became outsiders, a degree of self-consciousness inevitably resulted.

A case in point is that of Eden Phillpotts (1862–1959), eighteen of whose novels were published in a collected edition of Dartmoor novels, selected from a large and varied body of work that included novels and stories, detective fiction, plays, verse, essays, topography and books on gardening. Phillpotts had worked as an actor and in an insurance office before taking to journalism, but when he began to make money by writing he retired to Devonshire and thereafter rarely left it, living to the age of ninety-seven. His first novel (inappropriately called *The End of a Life*) was published in 1891; the last, *There Was an Old Man*, in 1959. Between them are well over 120 more. His popular reputation rests mainly on his plays – notably *The Farmer's Wife* (1916) and *Yellow Sands* (1926) – and on his books about boyhood, *The Human Boy* (1899) and its successors. But it is in the Dartmoor novels that he expressed himself most seriously.

These novels are something of a problem for criticism. They belong to a kind of literary tradition of which the general run of academic study takes no account at all. Phillpotts's novels are as much commodities as serious works of literature, but as such they are representative of the problems facing any writer about rural life in the twentieth century. Introducing the Widecombe Edition in 1927, Arnold Bennett wrote of Dartmoor:

> What a district for a novelist – compact, complete, withdrawn, exceptional, traditional, impressive, and racy! Eden Phillpotts found it and annexed it.[3]

The characteristically business-like comment is illuminating: there is something mechanical and overdeliberate about these books. Phillpotts set out to write a novel about each area of the moor – and succeeded. In every case topography is important, especially the contrast between the wild and the cultivated districts: but in few of the novels – *Brunel's Tower* (1915) with its portrayal of the moorland earthenware industry is one exception – does the geological nature of Dartmoor play a part. In *The Secret Woman* (1905), for instance, the tragic story of Ann Redvers is integrated aesthetically into its background in a persuasive and effective manner; but the story could just as well have taken place on Exmoor or in Bowland Forest. The scenery and local colour, diligently though they are described, are significant in their general rather than their particular aspect, so that the stress on 'Dartmoor' as the novels' subject is in fact a spurious one. Hardy may well have been aware of this false significance attached to specific place-names when he generalised his Wessex backgrounds by inventing pseudonyms.[4]

Bennett deplored the comparison of Phillpotts's work with Hardy's but, despite the former's claim that he had already written a number of the Dartmoor novels before he had read a line by Hardy,[5] it is unavoidable, for the motifs and setting are often similar to those in such novels as *The Return of the Native* or *Far from the Madding Crowd*. A typical Phillpotts novel will open with a lone figure outlined against a moorland sky or trudging along a moorland road; or else with two lovers deep in converse beside a wooded stream. A triangular love story may soon develop, usually with a smallholder pitted against a dissolute squire, or a labourer against a farmer. The women are frequently capricious – Honor Endicott in *Sons of the Morning* (1900) bears a strong likeness to Bathsheba Everdene – and the plot takes many twists and turns before reaching what is frequently a bleak, astringent resolution. The author's respect for his characters is notable, *Demeter's Daughter* (1911), for instance, containing a finely balanced study of a heroic wife and mother, battling with poverty, unsatisfactory children and a feckless husband. Here the primitive ideal is effectively actualised. And Phillpotts's humanism informs all the books:

' 'Twill cure a lot of sickly thinking when you start to serve man instead of God. Maybe our whole duty to the one is our whole duty to the other, if we could see it.'[6]

One signal merit of these novels is their freedom from any rustic sentimentality: the nearest they get to it is in some of the rather pawky humour of the peasants – always a trap for novelists, and one which even Hardy did not escape.

At his best Phillpotts can write convincingly of rural character, with a nice blend of humour and irony. One example can serve for many. In *The River* (1902) a tragic turning point is Nicholas Edgecombe's desertion by his bride, who elopes with the dissolute farmer Timothy Oldreve on her wedding day, before the ceremony takes place. The incident is recorded indirectly:

> Farmer Snow and his wife drove up from Cross Ways at this moment. They were clad in full splendour for the ceremony; and Mrs. Snow had insisted on providing Hannah's bouquet – a noble, if solid mass of white roses and candid lilies. These had their anthers plucked out, that the gold pollen should not sully the purity of the petals.
>
> 'Good mornin', all!' shouted the farmer as he drew rein. 'A brave day for a brave deed, my dears. But wheer's the triumphant arch to? And wheer's the man hisself?'
>
> 'The arch be throwed down for winter firing,' said Scobhull; 'an' the man have just turned his back an' be walking home again very slow.'
>
> 'An' so can the rest of us,' concluded Mart Trout, not without satisfaction; 'for there's no wedding vittles for any belly to-day. An' I be the only one that won't suffer, 'cause I wasn't axed.'[7]

There is considerable literary tact here: Edgecombe has been consistently in the centre of the picture hitherto, a man of simple faith, a solitary; and the distanced picture of his lonely figure is the more eloquent by comparison. The wry conclusion of the passage is typical of Phillpotts, who had no illusions as to the tough selfishness of the average man. A similar note is struck earlier in the novel:

> Very slowly, and with appreciative chuckles, Edgecombe repeated the Commandments, with his eyes on the poacher.
>
> 'A wonnerful various lot,' he concluded, 'an' such as they be you've scat 'em all, 'tis said. Honour your God you don't, else you wouldn't kill fish 'pon Lord's Day; an' honour your parents you don't, else you wouldn't let Cherrybrook Farm go to rack and ruin; an' there's eighth commandment gone to the tune o' six rabbits. You've lied against your neighbour, an' will again when you tell this story down to the Ring o' Bells; and you've coveted your neighbour's wife, as all Dartymoor knows, including the woman herself. That leaves murder for 'e – well, you'm young yet.'[8]

There is a satisfying vigour in this: Phillpotts's use of dialogue is often fresh and lively, and at times can rise to heights of finely sustained intensity. He can catch the genuine note of exasperation in a daughter-in-law's voice:

> 'Cruel, hateful, blundering old idiot! No common sense, not a shred! To see her here – even a man would pity me, – any man but my man! She must be touching! Can't even let a blasted chair bide where I put it. Now she's watering the plants in the window; now she's up messing over Samuel's clothes; now I see her out of the corner of my eye looking at my darning, till often and often 'tis in me to scream at her and to tell her for Christ's sake to get home. Then the questions she asks – sly questions she thinks I won't understand; but they all mean Samuel. Good God A'mighty! can I help the man coughing?'[9]

This has an authentic ring; so, for all its 'poetic' qualities, has this speech of a mother to the girl who is to bear her dead son's child:

> '. . . Hold your head high an' pray when none's lookin', pray through every wakin' hour an watch yourself as you'd watch the case of a golden jewel. What odds if a babe's got ringless under the stars or in a lawful four-post bed? Who married Adam an' Eve? You was the wife of yun 'cordin' to the first plan of the livin' God; an' if He changed His lofty mind when 'twas too late, blame don't fall on you or the dead. Think of a baby – his baby under your breast! Better face the people an' let the bairn come to fullness of life than fly them an' cut your days short an' go into the next world empty-handed. . . .'[10]

Unfortunately Phillpotts was not content to let his rendering of rural life and manners speak for itself, but sought to impart to his essentially novelistic plots a cosmic significance that they are incapable of sustaining. His characters are not inherently interesting enough to bear the load.

> As for her own existence now, Ann moved through it like an embodied grief, and stood for a state of sustained but passive suffering. So from the twilight of pagan drama those Titan figures of tragedy gaze upon us, each with the face and voice of different agony. The genius that drew their immortal desolation, and left them more en-

during than the kingdom of earth, had been needed to paint this woman aright.[11]

This genius Phillpotts did not possess: Ann Redvers's tragedy is presented with an insistent rhetoric that estranges sympathy. The rural scene is here being exploited as a means to dramatic sensation, and the characters are not flattered by the process.

But Eden Phillpotts can at times write movingly about the moor and make of it a satisfying symbol. His actual descriptions are usually too meticulous to do their work, but more indirectly, through the consciousness of his characters, he can bring it vividly to life.

She turned to the Moor, as one who began to feel something of its secrets. She mused whether these terrific transitions of steepness and slough, these alterations of blazing heat and light, darkness and bitter cold, would find their image in her own brief days. She felt dumbly, as all feel, that here the very soul and spirit of truth encompassed her. Sometimes she was caught up by it, sometimes depressed and saddened. Yet here was greatness, if she might but see it. The Moor rang men like metal; proclaimed the strong and true; revealed the weak and false; challenged humanity; tolerated no middle courses; played the loadstone to drag elemental best and worst from human hearts. For a moment she pitied those men whose work daily called them to its high places. Because in the lowlands was escape from one's own heart, and many hiding-places opened on the road of life, where her kind tramped it together and practised those arts of simulation vital to gregarious living among men. But here it seemed that there was no evasion.[12]

The sincerity of this passage seems evident, though the rhythms are dangerously insistent.

How inflated Phillpotts's language can be is well seen in the opening of *The Forest on the Hill* (1912).

Where certain high-climbing hills take leave of the lowlands, there spread, beneath the eastern frontiers of Dartmoor, extended ranges of forest; and amid these far-flung groves, lifted mightily upon the bosom of her proper mount, crested with the ragged wilderness and bound on north and south by little valleys, where streamlets draw a silver thread through the fringes of her robe, lies Yarner – a fair kingdom, peopled by many myriads of the unconscious.

C

Page after page continues in this strain: Yarner Forest is described out of existence. The book ends on a fine flourish with a sweeping invocation of Reality.

> She harbours not with darkness but light; a frozen soul is no habitation for her; she wings with the dayspring and the rainbow; she shares the substance of human dreams and inspirations; she is one with the ideas and beacons and golden hopes that reign for ever in mankind's unconquerable heart.

The rather trivial story that lies between hardly warrants such grandiloquence.

But at his best Phillpotts can write with economy and penetration; and when his philosophical reflections are mediated through dialogue they are far more effective than when embodied in his rather turgid prose. *The Whirlwind* (1907) has a good example of this. One of his more effective melodramas, it contains, like *The Thief of Virtue* (1910) and *Children of Men* (1923), a study of religious fanaticism. Daniel Brendon, the gigantic labourer who 'gets religion' is in love with Sarah Jane, a delightful pagan who is gallant enough at the novel's end to commit suicide in order to spare Daniel the guilt of murdering her. The difference in outlook between them (and Phillpotts endorses the views of Sarah Jane) is amusingly illustrated in the following piece of dialogue.

> 'Why couldn't Jesus Christ have hastened into the world quicker,' she asked. ' 'Twould have saved a deal of sad doubt about all them poor souls.'
> 'You ought not to think such questions. I lay Woodrow said that.'
> 'No, he didn't. 'Tis my very own thought. Suppose, Dan, that He'd been the earliest born of a woman, and comed into the world Eve's first li'l one? How would that plan have worked?'
> He stared at her.
> 'Who would have crucified Him?' he asked.
> She sighed.
> 'I forgot that.'[18]

This illuminates not only the theological issues but also the characters involved. Phillpotts's own agnosticism, and his optimistic belief in evolution, with man as its crowning product, is typical of his time in the defensive–aggresive mode of its expression; and too often he stood in need of Lawrence's advice to 'trust the tale'. When he does trust it, as for example in *The Virgin in Judgement* (1908) or *Demeter's Daughter*, he can write with admirable simplicity and humanity.

He is perhaps best remembered for his comedy, the kind of genial undemanding comedy that made a success of his play *The Farmer's Wife*. The novel on which it was based, *Widecombe Fair* (1913), is a rambling portrait of a village, the humour being of the sort that gets the adjective 'mellow' attached to it. At times it attains a kind of sharpness that goes beyond the mere surface observation of manners and quiet country ways. The scene where the rather pompous Gabriel Shilling-ford goes to tea with the Smerdon family to discuss the marriage of his daughter to their son is a good example.

[Gabriel] flushed.

'I object to my private affairs being discussed, Mr. Smerdon. It is not seemly.'

'God forgive me, then,' answered Peter, 'for 'tis the last thing I meant. I was only going on for to say that our Whitelock be a proper nipper over money, and can make sixpence do the work of a shilling. I thought perhaps 'twould cheer you to know that. For, by all accounts, you'm one o' they open-handed heroes that forget you've spent your cash, till you look round for it and find it gone. Now, I can say in all sober honesty that us don't know the meaning of money out here at Bone Hill. It comes into my right hand and goes out of my left. . . . With two maids and Blackslade all your own, I should have thought as you could have put by a pinch for a rainy day or a daughter's wedding,' continued Peter, 'but that's your business of course. And as you say, she'll have the farm when you be gathered in. And if you make a clean breast of it to White-lock about what be owing, you'll never repent it. For he'll set to work to straighten the figures – and beg, borrow or steal you out of your fix.'

'I'm *not* in a – good gracious, man – how can you say these in-decent things?' gasped Gabriel.

The nakedness of the Smerdon mind was only equalled by its absolute sincerity. But Mr. Shillingford resented such artlessness with all his might. No air-drawn dreams made atmosphere for them; no visions, no comely if nebulous imaginings ever softened the stark reality of their lives. The master of Blackslade felt as one fallen among naked aborigines, who were stripping him of his clothes also. Their simple, innocent eyes went through him.[14]

It is not often that Phillpotts makes so overt a moral criticism: his novels for the most part merely relate and underline their points. And it is here that we come to the real critical problem attached to Phillpotts's work. He is a novelist who still commands readers, and who can write well, with a keen sensitivity to the natural order and a genuine interest in, and sympathy with, the varieties of human character: indeed characters like Primose in *The Portreeve* (1906) and Rhoda in *The Virgin in Judgement* suggest a deeper understanding of psychology than he usually chose to display. In view of all this why must he be reckoned a minor figure? Here, as in so much twentieth-century literature, Lawrence is our touchstone. What we simply do not find in Phillpotts is what we do find in Lawrence – a deep, personally involved awareness of the changing world in which he lived. When he does refer to change it is defensively.

> Education progressed, but its evidences were often painful, and along with it, things worthy of preservation departed for ever. Ambition at Brent was only understood in terms of cash; among many of the young men and women cleverness became only another name for cunning. Then dawned class consciousness and class prejudice; and the fresh point of view took shape in creation of new values. The timid admired the bold, who had courage to scant his service, yet drew his wages. The worker who robbed his employer, confident that trade unionism would support him in any open conflict, became the hero of the shop; while the employer retaliated without patience or perspicuity. Thus unsocial ideals were created.[15]

The stilted prose betrays a negative outlook.

Of Phillpotts's seriousness of purpose there can be no doubt; but the essentially standardised character of these books, the absence of any vital feeling of personal engagement on the author's part, or of development in style or treatment, preclude their being read today with the kind of pleasure with which one continues to read Hardy. One book is very like another; carefully composed, earnest in intention, sure of their direction, they remain in the last analysis mechanical in conception. And Phillpotts's Dartmoor is sealed off from the rest of the world, and thus cannot be invoked persuasively to correct it. That it was geographically sealed off at the time of which he wrote is not really relevant: one has only to think of what T. F. Powys made of a similarly isolated Dorset world. For all their faithfully recorded speech and landscapes, the Dartmoor novels are essentially bookish creations born of the English rustic myth, ultimately means of escape rather than of illumination.

Their failure to achieve greatness is the more disappointing in that Phillpotts was alive to the challenge facing the rural novelist of his day. Although only in *The Beacon* (1911) is there any effective confrontation between new ideas and old, in the sense that the heroine, Lizzie Denster, comes from the town (for many of the other novels are set back some fifty years in time), his eye was on the future development of fiction. In a preface to the first edition of *Widecombe Fair* he justified his concern for landscape against those who protested that it was excessive.

> To me . . . the phenomena of man's environment are as interesting as man himself; I can conceive possible fiction enriched with a far closer understanding of unconscious life than we have yet attained; when our intellect shall gauge the brain of the tiger and penetrate the bark of the tree, so that the artist may look out of the brute's eyes and from the tree's leaves, not with human values – a thing done in books for children – but with measures animal or arboreal.

This looks forward to the work of Henry Williamson and John Cowper Powys. Phillpotts continues,

> Comparative biology, while enlarging human compassion for all things called to the task of living, will also lift man to a juster estimate of self-conscious life in its greatness and littleness, and make a wider loyalty to his own race, seen struggling against the immeasurable background of the universe and its multitudinous interests, from the welfare of blade and bud to the fate of suns and systems.[16]

The waste lands of Dartmoor are an image of a greater barrenness. In the austerity of his best work Phillpotts faced the fact with courage; and, if he lacked the genius to transcend the knowledge, he was at least aware of where the opening for genius lay. A later generation may rate him more highly than our own can do.

II

In the fiction of this period, moorland is a recurrent symbol of the un-tamable human passions. As one character declares,

> 'Sometimes I think that we're nothing but the moor turned into persons. It gets into you when you're a child. Father's its rage and storms and its dominance. Maxwell's its instability; Hilda's its seeking, its terrible, unending seeking.'[17]

While Eden Phillpotts's account of his 'primitive' people is relatively restrained, there were abundant tales of passion from lesser writers, to the increasing irritation of reviewers. 'Mrs. Dawson-Scott has laid another psychologically implausible tale at the door of the long-suffering Cornish folk', complained one of them of *They Green Stones*, published as late as 1925. Even Phillpotts's *The Mother* had come in for similar criticism.

> Coming to it only a few days after laying down *Furze the Cruel* by Mr Trevena, we are constrained to fear that something drastic will have to be done soon either by the railway companies or by the associated hotel and lodging-house keepers of Devonshire, lest the British father, overfed on the sombre fiction of this country, shrinks from trusting himself or his family again in holiday time among so dark, revengeful and unmanageable a populace.[18]

As a comment on the marketing of rural fiction, the tone of this is singularly apt; but it is not altogether fair to the author of *Furze the Cruel*.

'John Trevena' was the pen name of a Canadian poet and novelist (Ernest G. Henham, 1870–1946) who settled in Devonshire for reasons of health. He caused great local offence with his trilogy *Furze the Cruel* (1907), *Heather* (1908) and *Granite* (1909) in which his portrayal of the residents of Dartmoor spared nothing of their brutality and limitations:

> the last dregs of the folk, still ignorant and primitive, who are being killed like the Red Indians by the civilization which has for a long time surrounded and is now breaking over them, driving out the old, bringing in the new, ringing out the age of mettle, of muscle,

sinew and simplicity, and heralding the age of skill, brains and trickery.[19]

These novels have at their best a harshness that has outlasted the sentimentality that infects them. That sentimentality in Trevena's case showed iself as whimsy: it is one of his besetting sins as a novelist, as it is of so many rural writers. The title of his early novel, *A Pixy in Petticoats* (1905), is a case in point: the eroticism in his work is apt to be flurried. But equally often the novels reveal a raw brutality. *Heather* contains a horrible picture of a couple brawling their days away in drink; but, whereas T. F. Powys, for instance, would make this an example of the brutality of life in general, John Trevena particularises: social conditions are responsible for drunkenness, and human wickedness trades upon it.

[Mr Odyorne's] sharp eyes saw the bottles scattered about the place. His knowledge of country folk told him how weary they were of the long, unlighted evenings and how ardently they desired the town when they were tied to the land. He had the public house in his mind and could get them in; and they would not know, until it was much too late, that the license had only a few more months to run and would not be renewed.[20]

Moreover, Trevena can portray directly what most contemporary novelists were only prepared to intimate:

'I be a young woman,' she shouted, her slo-black eyes running over with maudlin water. 'And I ha' nought but work. . . . What did I marry a mucky old stinking lot o' pig's dung like yew vor?'
'I wur vule enough to court yew, that's why,' John shouted.
'Aw, dirty toad. Get's an innocent woman into his home and makes a rag o' she, and a slave o' she, and uses she vor his own trade. If I'd ha' knowed what yew wur I'd a took father's razor and cut me throat avore going into church.'
'Aw, aw,' cackled John, rolling about by the huge sooty fireplace. 'Why didn't ye du it, woman?'[21]

The social criticism in these novels is complex, for the author's attitude to town and country alike is an ambiguous one. On the one hand the town can offer nothing to the country people:

The folk of the moor had been socialists for centuries, content and
fairly prosperous. . . . There was no competition, and property was
distributed equally. Each man had an acre or two; when a building
was required there were stone quarries held in common; for fuel
the peat bogs, for gravel and sand the rivers; horses, cattle, and sheep
fed upon the commons, which provided their masters with sticks
for the fire, reed for thatching, fern for bedding, materials for hedge-
making. And yet, when these people left their homes, and became
swallowed up by the towns, they very quickly departed from the
traditions of their ancestors, allowed themselves to become dependent
upon others, and would cry aloud that Socialism was the only remedy
of the evils which they suffered from; when it was in fact that very
state from which they had wilfully divorced themselves because life
was lonely and had no evenings.[22]

But Trevena's Devonshire is itself an unfriendly place. The starkness
of the country and the harshness of the life have a debasing effect upon
the inhabitants. Patience, the farmer's daughter in *Granite*, is no simple
cottage lass out of the pages of Walter Raymond : she goes to Plymouth
and becomes a harlot.

Her eyes were small, rather a light blue normally; but if a boy put
his arm round her waist and squeezed her they became instantly
dark and unpleasant. Even a glance would bring that wild darkening
of her eyes. Still, Patience was pretty from the cottager's point of
view; and an artist also would have found her pretty, but he would
have added to her face the beauty which was not there, the light
of reason, the glow of intelligence; he would have suggested some
moral reflections in the sleepy darkness of those eyes.[23]

This correction of the conventional notion of the peasantry is a constant
feature of Trevena's work. Just as he attacks rural novelists for their
depiction of romantic scenery 'which has been described in somewhat
inflated language, six-syllable adjectives, and mixed metaphors, as something absolute and unassailable' (was he thinking of Phillpotts?), so
he brusquely corrects the common notion of pastoral idylls :

Thomasine's ideas of love were simple enough; just to meet a man,
and walk with him in quiet places, and sit about with him, and be
mauled by him. That was the beginning and end of love according
to Thomasine, for after marriage it was all hard work.[24]

How hard the work was is seen in Trevena's account of the wife of a Dartmoor farmer. Old Barseba has no time to worry about either poverty or riches:

> if her husband grumbled about the one, she at least was making for the other, always at work, seven days a week and no holidays, half the work of the farm and all the work of the house – Hercules himself would have tottered to see her – and she did the mending for the hind and preached a little gospel to him sometimes, and she cut the faggot-wood and did all the dairy work. She was famous for her butter, which she made in the slow old-fashioned way, churning the cream with her hands, turning it out in great amorphous masses which were sent out to market, cut up by the trader, mixed with ninety percent of cheap foreign butter and sold to the public as best Devonshire after the manner of business. Barseba was a hyperphysical bee. She bred turkeys, geese, fowls and ducks; she brought up the calves and orphaned lambs; she made the cider without much assist-ance, turned out for the threshing, and in some miraculous way cooked a good dinner at the same time; she attended to the vegetable garden; she divided her physical self into a corps of personalities, appearing to toss hay in Stockey Furzen with one hand while with the other she made the beds in Love Lane. On the whole it was a wonderful life, and there was no reward, for she was only a woman getting very white about the head. She was not a worker like a man, she only messed about the place; and one day she would take to her bed and the next she would die, because she had no time to be idle, and then perhaps Caleb would remember that she had been 'wonderful handy', and would remind the undertaker that it must be a very cheap funeral.[25]

This passage is typical of Trevena's style and method. The rich use of detail, the caustic tone, the cynical awareness of the world outside the one he describes, the fury and despair underlying it, are all indicative of the imagination and energy that inform his best work: there is an urgency about it that suggests that he might have been another Lawrence had not other literary influences been at work. For Trevena unhappily lacked the courage of his own naturalism. Some of his novels are very strange indeed. He was interested in the paranormal and the occult, an interest which finds its most powerful expression in *The Feast of Bacchus: A Study in Dramatic Atmosphere*. This was published under his real name of Ernest G. Henham in 1907. As an

account of an ancient haunted mansion it bears comparison with the
work of Sheridan Le Fanu; but its opening is suggestive of a very
different writer.

> The silence upon the river was broken by a vivacious voice, –
> 'My lady, out of the depths of your wisdom define for me the word
> asymptote.'
> 'Spell it,' murmured beauty in laziness, from a heap of pink
> cushions.

Ronald Firbank did indeed write his own rural novel with *Valmouth*
(1919): its blend of burlesque rusticity and sly erotica develops out
of the kind of awareness we find more solemnly present in much of Trevena's work. It is there in *Bracken* (1910) and *Sleeping Waters* (1913),
which deal respectively with hypnotism and amnesia; and also in *No
Place Like Home* (1913) which contains an embarrassing religious
element. *Off the Beaten Track* (1925) declines into a self-parody that is
curiously enjoyable.

For Trevena is rarely dull: an immense forcefulness lumbers
through his work, and he is, for his time, singularly outspoken. He
had little use for the clergy or landowners or the well-to-do.

> Mrs Allen was a woman who would have profited by being
> abandoned on a desert island for two years with a few sacks of dog-
> biscuit, as she might have learned to do something during that
> period.[26]

His sympathies lie mainly with the old and exploited – silly country
girls like Thomasine, helpless old men like Brightly in *Furze the Cruel*.
Indeed, the latter novel, with its miserly farmer Pendoggatt who
tramples on the simpletons and harmless, strikingly anticipates the
early work of T. F. Powys; but Trevena lacks Powys's poise and objectivity. He constantly overwrites, and strains his effects. His descriptions of landscape, though more vigorous and precise than those of
Phillpotts, frequently run off into triviality and whimsy:

> The heavy fragrance of gorse was in the hot air. It was a well-hidden
> spot, and somewhat weird, a tainted kind of place. The ruins of a
> miner's cot were close by, and what had been its floor was then a
> mass of bracken. The stones were covered with flowering saxifrage.
> There was a scrubby brake here and there, composed of a few

dwarf trees, rowan and oaks, only a few feet high, ancient enough but small, because their roots obtained little nutrient from the rock-bedded peat. Their branches twisted in a fantastic manner, reaching across the sky like human limbs contorted with strange agony. They were the sort of trees which force themselves into dreams. Some of them were half dead, green on one side and black upon the other; while the dwarf trunks were covered with ivy and masses of poly-podies; overgrown so thickly with these parasites that the bark was nowhere visible. . . . Beneath the river tumbled; a rough and wild Tavy; the river of rocks, the open sun-parched region of the high moor; the water clear and cold from Cranmere; and there was a long way to go yet before it reached cover, the hanging trees, and the mossy bogs pink with red-rattles, and the woods white with wind-flowers, and the stretch of bluebell-land, the ferns, bracken, asphodel, and the pleasant winding pathways where fairy-tales and decent love abide, and the little folk laugh at moonlight.[27]

The quality of the writing goes downhill with the river; only one sentence is omitted between the two portions of the passage. The fertility of Trevena's invention is unaccompanied by discrimination; one of his heroines is called Boodles.

All these novels are long and slow-moving, with confused plots; their interest today centres on their powerful feeling for the primitive and inarticulate in country people. The outsiders who are the ostensible centres of the action – the artists and writers (such as so often frequent rural fiction of this period), and the patients in the sanatorium in *Heather* – are colourless, and described in that affected literary jargon which was the contemporary backwash of the Meredithian tide. But the more primitive the type, the more surely does Trevena depict it. The portrayal of the old woman Mary and her brother Peter in *Furze the Cruel* is among the most remarkable things in Trevena's work: their simple, cunning, canny minds, their shiftiness and naïveté seem representative of something aboriginal that will outlast all civilisations. The comedy of Peter and Mary's first ride on a train borders upon patronising farce; but their vitality is a condemnation of a way of life that cannot contain them. The fight between Peter and Pendoggatt illustrates this point, besides being in its terse vigour an example of Trevena's writing at its best.

Peter was a stumpy little creature with no idea of running; and he was captured at the end of the wall, and received a blow upon the

head which nearly stunned him. Pendoggatt stood over him, half mad
with fury, striking at him again and again; while Peter made quaint
noises, half passion and half pain. . . . Neither of them had spoken
a word. Pendoggatt had growled and spluttered; Peter had choked and
mumbled; the river far beneath roared because it was full of rain.
These were all incoherent noises. Pendoggatt began to slink away, as
if he had received the beating, shivering and looking back, but seeing
nothing except a dull little heap beside the wall, which seemed to
have many hands, all of them scrabbling in the dirt. Peter panted
hard, as if he had been hunted across the moor by the whist hounds,
and had come there to take shelter; but all the time he went on scrap-
ing up the clay, gathering it into a ball, spitting on it, moulding it,
and muttering madly from time to time, 'You'm him! You'm him!'[28]

Here the practice of witchcraft is made both explicable and dramatically
convincing: it is integrated into the outlook and character of the life
portrayed.

The humour in Trevena's novels springs from the same source as the
drama, and has a harsh edge to it; Trevena both laughs at his characters
and savages his readers for requiring him to do so. This anger, half
turned upon itself, is responsible both for the books' uncertainty of
tone and for their extraordinarily strong flavour. In the following passage
it is hard to determine where sympathy ends and contempt begins.

[Thomasine] was plump and full of blood; it seemed ready to burst
through her skin. She was somewhat grossly built; too wide at the
thighs, big-handed and large-footed, with not much waist, and a
clumsy stoop from the shoulders. She waddled in her walk like most
Devonshire farm-maids. . . . She was part of the exaggeration of
Dartmoor, which exaggerates everything; adding fierceness to fierceness, colour to colour, strength to strength; just as its rain is fiercer
than that of the valleys, and its wind mightier. Thomasine . . . was
of the Ger Tor family, the strong mountain branch which knows
nothing and cannot think for itself, and only feels the river wearing
it away, and the frost rotting it, and the wind beating it. The pity
was that Thomasine did not know she had a mind, which was already
fading for want of use. She only knew how to peel potatoes and make
herself wanton underwear.[29]

The assimilation of character to landscape is integral to the novels:
indeed Trevena, in the preface to *Furze*, emphasises this in explaining

the projected titles of his trilogy. For him the furze of Dartmoor suggested its cruelty, heather its endurance, granite its strength. 'The Furze is destroyed by fire [as is Pendoggatt in the novel] but grows again; the Heather is torn by winds, but blossoms again; the Granite is worn away imperceptibly by the rain.' Elsewhere he writes that 'it is place rather than time which makes people what they are'.[30] Like Phillpotts, Trevena writes in the shadow of the withdrawal of Christian faith, and the landscape of the moor is for him too an emblem of the fate of man.

> Men never know when they are beaten, they are the hardiest things alive; that is why they are splendid. If they could see right into those years, which seem to stretch beyond in a glittering row of stars, but are probably nothing more than a lot of dry and shrivelled peas, they would fling down their tools, slink into a dark corner, and not come out unless they were carried. Success is a cruel goddess. If she holds out a laurel wreath in one hand she has a huge bloody hammer in the other. Everyone thinks he will get the wreath on his head, but most get the hammer: not deserving it perhaps; but what ox by his own conduct deserves to be pole-axed?[31]

The pessimism is as total as that of Hardy or Conrad, and unmitigated by their feeling for man's dignity.

John Trevena is one of England's lost novelists. Rich and disturbing though his talents were, his books are too inchoate and too dated to warrant resurrection. And yet if one can persevere through the self-conscious writing and relentless barbarism, there is a unique experience to undergo; and even his weaker later books like *The Vanished Moor* (1923) are told with a spirit that keeps them intermittently readable. But his work has gone under rather like the lost hamlets of Dartmoor which he so memorably describes. This closing passage illuminates the tragedy underlying the rural novels of this time.

> The map is well sprinkled with names which suggest that the country is thickly populated, but it is not. Many of the names are delusions, more suggestive of the past than the present. A century ago hamlets occupied the sites now covered by a name, but there is nothing left of them today except dreary ruins of cob standing in a thicket of brambles or in what was once an apple orchard. What was formerly the name of a good-sized village is now the title of a

farmhouse, or one small cottage which would not pay for repairing and which therefore must be destroyed when it becomes uninhabitable. It is a sad land to wander through. It suggests a country at the end of its tether which has almost abandoned the struggle for existence, a poverty-stricken country which cannot face the strong-blooded flow of food importations from foreign lands. Even the goods sold in the village shops are of alien manufacture. A hundred little hamlets have given up the struggle in the same number of years, and been wiped, not off the map, but off the land. The country of Devon is like a rosy-cheeked apple which is rotten inside.[32]

III

Had all Trevena's writing been as good as this he would have been the finest rural novelist of his time. But it was not, and it is easy to grow impatient when one considers the talent misapplied and run to waste. It does not need melodrama to make the lives of isolated communities arresting, but both Trevena and Phillpotts seemed to consider their worlds significant *because* they were primitive. Ultimately their rural universe is one of fantasy.

It is true that naturalism as such is to be found in it – meticulous observation of domestic detail, a comprehensive treatment of physical experience. But the imagination ordering the detail is essentially literary, and tends, in the case of Phillpotts especially, to the stock situation and the stock response. The result is a subtle kind of falsehood. It is interesting in this context to consider the early novels, set in Cornwall, of Ruth Manning-Sanders, now better known as a writer of books for children. *Hucca's Moor* (1929) and *The Crochet Woman* (1934) portray primitive people with an evident wish to understand them. But the very restraint of the prose, the refusal to wallow in melodrama, leads, by an ironical paradox, to a sense of patronage. Instead of being treated with the relish and gusto of Trevena's work, her characters are kept at a distance dictated by literary good manners. Violence in literature needs to be realised and analysed, as in the novels of Dostoevsky, or enjoyed, as in popular melodrama and detective tales. The mere *exhibition* of violence serves little purpose; and a rural setting does nothing by itself to add significance. The reduction of primitive communities to a miniature world without the force of a microcosm indicates the place of the rural theme in popular consciousness in this period: its appeal, for all its pretensions, was to those who wanted to see in country life a conserved and shut-off world. Despite its claims to universality, the cult of the primitive ended up as a province merely in the literary imagination of its time.

5 Literary Regionalism: Hugh Walpole, Sheila Kaye-Smith

I

The popularity of the early twentieth-century regional novelists was not a new phenomenon. The description or evocation of particular localities had developed from the essentially pictorial art of Mrs Radcliffe – in whose novels the scenery gives rise to emotions which expand and elevate the sensibility of the beholder – into the more dramatic and historical function that the scenery performs in the novels of Sir Walter Scott. The opening up of the Highlands as a tourist attraction owes much to the popularity of the Waverley novels: not for nothing does the Scott Monument dominate Princes Street in Edinburgh. Scott's great achievement was to endow the purely pictorial appreciation of landscape with an added dimension, the dimension of human association, the suggestiveness of historical context. The Highlands and Islands, and the less spectacular Border Country, became in the public mind not merely hills and valleys to be travelled through and looked at, but the scene of romantic or significant events from which henceforth they took their distinctive colouring. Another landscape was being superimposed upon the actual physical one, a mental landscape, a symbolic one. Literary England was being born: a whole pattern of sensibility and a number of industries grew up simultaneously.

The industrialisation of nineteenth-century England and the coming of the railways alike increased awareness of the distinctive configurations of the landscape. Increased mobility naturally led to increased knowledge and appreciation of regional differences, though it led to a decrease, or rather a shift of perspective, where actual observation of living conditions was concerned. The tourist is not the same thing as the traveller: he relates what he sees to his own state of feeling and his own physical needs; the objective, disinterested curiosity of earlier writers tends to disappear. The railroad age begot no Celia Fiennes, no Defoe or Young or Cobbett. Travel books were concerned more to celebrate than to analyse, and found their logical development in the guide-book, which is designed to 'sell' a region in both senses of that verb. The life of a region tended to be submerged in its appearance and romantic past, and the human element, when it did obtrude, did so in the form of ancient customs, folklore, handicrafts and dialect. The growth of self-conscious regionalism within an increasingly centralised society has produced a curious fragmentation. (The case of Eden Phill-potts is apposite here.)

By the end of the nineteenth century the literary tourist trade was in full swing: 'Dickens's London' had followed on 'Scott's Border Country'. The immense popularity of Blackmore's *Lorna Doone* (1869) was largely owing to its romantic Exmoor setting;[1] the romanticising of 'the Brontës' was already under way, for Elizabeth Gaskell's biography had laid great and justifiable stress on the importance of the Haworth moorlands to any understanding of the Brontë novels. Indeed, Mrs Gaskell was to perpetuate more than one element in the mythology: a whole style of book production and of tea-shop design may arguably be said to derive from *Cranford* (1853).

And there was 'Wordsworth's Lakeland'; but this was a rather different matter, for the literature was of a more demanding kind, as was the physical exertion needed to explore its background. More characteristic of the commercialisation of landscape is the cult of the Herries novels of Hugh Walpole (1884–1941). That these books have been financially beneficial to Cumberland one has only to visit the neighbourhood of Keswick to see; while the presence of 'Judith Paris's cottage' at Watend-lath has played havoc with the very solitude that her creator valued. The four books which comprise the continuous chronicle – *Rogue Herries* (1930), *Judith Paris* (1931), *The Fortress* (1932) and *Vanessa* (1933) – attempted to fulfil 'the only ambition I truly have – to be connected for some time to come with Cumberland;[2] and although Walpole was to return to a Lakeland background for *A Prayer for My Son* (1936) and the two historical Herries novels, the original four are the ones on which his popular reputation as a regional novelist rests.

At the outset of his career he was attracted to Cornwall; part of his schooldays were spent there, and he made it the setting for *Mr Perrin and Mr Traill* (1911) and other novels. But he was soon to create a county of his own, called Glebeshire, whose cathedral city (Polchester, an obvious capitalising of Trollope's Barchester) was to be the setting of several of his books. The creation of fantasy worlds with real streets and houses and people of their own, with cross-references from novel to novel, is in itself productive of reassurance: it induces a feeling of belonging somewhere, and Walpole was instinctively right about his market when in his novels he made play with superficial terrors in comfortable and identifiable settings. The wooden and predictable people in *The Cathedral* (1922) are of the essence of what can only be thought of as 'commodity novels', and the book itself seems merely a justification for a description of its setting. The same is true of *The Herries Chronicle*.[3] And since Walpole was the kind of novelist who, like Bulwer Lytton, tried his hand at various kinds of fiction, it is the more significant that topography and a feeling for landscape should be the determining factor in his choice of *magnum opus*.

The books are an account of the fortunes of an English family from 1732 to 1932. The opening volume centres on Borrowdale and the ramshackle old house which the raffish Francis Herries settles in to the scandal of his neighbours. Subsequent narratives are concerned with his daughter Judith (the most interesting and credible character in the saga: she dominates the two middle novels) and peter out rather tamely in *Vanessa*, which is little more than a repetition of motifs developed earlier. Throughout the series the love of Cumberland serves as the touchstone of moral and spiritual worth. Judith especially is a child of the hills, her mother a gypsy girl whom the Rogue takes for his second wife; and against the lawless or artistic streak in all these members of the family we have the grasping and materialistic Herries, whose feuds with the others provide what linking theme the novels possess. Perhaps the most effective things in the books are the accounts of solitude in which the characters' relation to the country is explored in terms of emotional affinity; the least memorable are the big crowd scenes in which the author took a delight but which he was unable to develop with any particular feeling for their significance. The local life of Cumberland plays but a secondary part: for all their apparent sweep these books are studies of private sensibility and conflict. They are conventional Hugh Walpole novels transposed into the past, and with a mountain background.

Undemandingly readable though they are, the books have a major weakness as a regional series: the Herries family are in effect outsiders. They are rarely if ever seen at work, and seem to have no necessary connection with Cumberland. Their residence there is, like Walpole's own,[4] fortuitous. That the landscape is repeatedly and determinedly described is not sufficient to integrate it with total persuasiveness in the novels as a whole: too much of a fuss is made for it to be convincing as the vision of a native.[5] The effects are gained by reiteration rather than by any narrative placing.

Walpole is most successful when he attempts a kind of analytical scene painting.

> It was a country . . . of *clouds* and *stones*. Stone walls, grey clouds, stone-coloured seagulls on dark fields like fragments of white stone, streaks of snow in winter thin cloth of stone, and above these stony crags pinnacles of stone, needles of stone, piercing a stony sky. He learnt to see a small imprisoned valley, wind-swept, as a living thing subject to growth and decay like himself. Through this vale twisted the mountain torrent, fighting with stones, letting its life be dominated by these piling stones, that heaped themselves on one another, that fell in showers down the hillside, that at length perhaps choke the life of the stream and form a stony pathway that leads at last to new shapes of grass and moss and fern. The clouds feeding the streams, the streams fighting the stones, life moving ceaselessly from form to form, from pattern to pattern.[6]

The passage in *The Fortress* where the young Adam Paris's tutor teaches him about the Lakeland landscape has genuine eloquence: it is an unforced outpouring of love for a country to which the author desperately wishes to belong. Indeed, as the novels develop, the setting increasingly takes over, so that when John and Uhland Herries engage in their fatal duel they are sent, more picturesquely than probably, to the lonely Skiddaw House to fight it. The author's feeling for the scenery is greater than his understanding of his characters.

Walpole's descriptive writing is often vitiated by a falsifying whimsy:

> Gable with its great rounded top is the least hostile of mountains, and the whole plateau with its stream and tarn is kind because it has been there for so long and is so sure of its passive power.[7]

He does, however, at one point touch on a deeper kind of experience than the rationalising of perception which is his normal mode. He was always, to judge from his novels as a whole, peculiarly susceptible to the imaginative suggestiveness of mist – *Portrait of a Man with Red Hair* (1925) is a good example of this – and in the following passage an almost Wordsworthian feeling is attained through a subtle alignment of inner and outer, of landscape and perceiver.

Advancing through the mist the watcher is suddenly conscious of a warmth that wraps him like a robe and a glow that comes, as it seems, from his own heart, making him one with the ground at his feet. He is drawn inward and is aware of a life so urgent, permanent and independent of time that, for a brief instant he fancies that he will snatch the secret of his own immortality.

But then the author's nerve begins to fail him.

Very swiftly he passes into the colder mists again and, returning to Cumberland ham, matrimony and the Income Tax, wonders at himself for a fool.

This sentence, with its deliberate jolt, reflects not only the characteristic consciousness of a materialistic age with its bashful and apologetic attitude to spiritual experience, but also the degree to which the author is himself immersed in it. And in the isolated sentence that follows he gives himself away.

The hills, of course, had not been aware of his solemn presence; they have so many real things to occupy them.[8]

The confusion here is total. The first part of the sentence with its half-playful 'of course' (always a tell-tale phrase) at once denies the possibility of any reality behind the experience: the second tries to grab it back, with a note of peevishness at the deprivation. The whole effect is one of muddle, of feeble yearning and resented solipsism.

Walpole's fiction is of considerable historic value as evidence of the ambiguity in contemporary attitudes to the world of nature. A would-be romantic himself, seeing himself as a literary successor to Scott and Hawthorne,[9] he craved to embody in his work a more imaginative and deeper view of life than that of Arnold Bennett[10] But he had neither the literary technique nor the imaginative boldness to do so. His novels, for all their narrative flow and obvious enthusiasm, collapse in almost every case into banality of plot and diction. An over-eager teller of tales, he was swallowed up by the bustle and chatter of the literary life,[11] and his love-affair with Cumberland (the trite phrase seems unhappily appropriate) only served to highlight the limitations of his art.

II

Hugh Walpole was also the author of a study of Trollope[12] which assisted in the popularity that the creator of Barsetshire recovered in the 1930s. That popularity, however, was largely owing to the fact that his mythical county embodied a dream of security for those distressed by the continuing process of social upheaval. Realistic in its own day, it has become a kind of worldly-wise Arcadia in ours. Similarly, George Eliot's early novels were, and possibly still are, as much valued for their evocations of early nineteenth-century Warwickshire as for their penetration into human nature. And the process of regional adoption reached its logical fulfilment in the popular transformation of Hardy into the chronicler of 'Wessex'. His tragic portrayals of a rural society in crisis took second place to the romantic fatalism that coloured his portrayals of individuals; and with that particular emphasis it was an easy step to transform his picture of rural England into a nostalgic and thus pseudo-comforting portrayal of the good times gone.

This process can be well seen in the *Wessex* volume in Blackie's 'Beautiful Britain' series, plump and profusely illustrated tomes that can still be found in second-hand bookshops. They were the coffee-table books of their time, and their illustrations – water colours in the Birket Foster tradition – perpetuate with no little charm the idea of rural England as most people would like it to have been. The author of *Wessex* already has Hardy placed in this nostalgic tradition :

this portion of England, which Thomas Hardy has so vividly described to the enchantment of thousands, invites attention and study like some beautiful low-toned picture. In its peaceful vales it is still possible to forget the town, the fret and fume of city life. What more can a modern pilgrim of the thoughtful type desire, when this same quietude is wedded to beauty, and much of old-world simplicity?[13]

The novels of Sheila Kaye-Smith (1887–1956) were in their day considered to be 'doing for Sussex' what Hardy had 'done for Wessex'. The Sussex Edition of nine of her novels, published in 1925, carried a notice that fortunately tells us more about the marketing of the books than about their character.

The folk who people her pages can be met with by anybody who roams round the delectable stretches of open country and sylvan woods of this region. The inner life, however – its problems, morality, customs and hereditary propensities – is not for parading before the eye of the visitor. But through the eye of Miss Kaye-Smith, herself a denizen of that sunny county, these things are seen in the love stories and struggles of her characters, whom she invests with life, life abundantly indeed, and in their native milieu, actuated by their native outlook and native freedoms.

But Sheila Kaye-Smith was taken seriously by several critics as an interpreter of country life, though Compton Mackenzie remarked of her that

> She seemed to enter the English novel in rather the same spirit as that in which land girls took up agriculture during the war, and she was one of the first women to assert her rights to masculine objectivity without at the same time assuming the name George in order to do so.[14]

There was nothing coy or possessive about her treatment of Sussex in her four best novels: *Sussex Gorse* (1916), *Little England* (1918), *Green Apple Harvest* (1919) and *Joanna Godden* (1921). The previous novels are uneven, a little crude, decidedly dated. The later ones run to the formula she had perfected. Her books sold well. A doctor's daughter, she spent most of her life in Sussex, becoming a Roman Catholic in 1928, and is probably best known at the present time for two informal but pleasant and perceptive books about Jane Austen written in collaboration with her friend and fellow novelist G. B. Stern.[15]

The early novels are historical romances, but *Spell Land* (1910), with its sub-title 'The Story of a Sussex Farm', shows where her real interest lay. It is a depressing book, melodramatic and full of moral attitudinising. *Isle of Thorns* (1913) is more determinedly modern, and embarrasses as a result – a note of high-pitched idealism (the hero ensuring that the girl he loves does a spell in prison for the manslaughter of his rival) being matched with a would-be sexual outspokenness – an uncomfortable mixture. These novels were, the author confesses, made up as they went along: the decisive factor in her literary growth was her friendship with the novelist W. L. George, who 'taught me to plan beforehand in great detail – almost down to paragraphs; then having got my blueprint absolutely clear, to follow it closely in a single script which would need only slight revision'.[16] This accounts both for the novels' readability and for their rather machine-made air. Impeccably paragraphed, each chapter subdivided into short sections, the books move forward simply, easy to take up and easy to put down. (The actual business of reading was never so simple as in the first two decades of the present century, when books were bound and printed well, and novels were assembled by their authors with the utmost neatness.)

But at their best Sheila Kaye-Smith's novels, though they do not surprise, have the merit of an honest and faithful reporting on experience. Her Sussex is realistically presented, her subject matter being for the most part the lives and ambitions of small farmers; and, although she has a love for old customs and traditions, she accepts the twentieth-century world without complaint (in this an exception among rural writers) though not without criticism. In *The End of the House of Alard* (1923), one of her more popular and more stereotyped novels, she portrays an ancient aristocratic family adapting to change through the various compromises and revolts of the younger generation. The eldest son, putting the estate before personal inclination, deserts his true love and marries money. The theme is Trollopian though the resolution – suicide – is not. One of the daughters turns down the man she loves because he is not good enough for the family, while her younger sister marries a local farmer and has to adjust her life accordingly. The youngest son becomes a garage hand and, later, a monk: on his accession to the title he decides to sell the estate. There is a constant stress on the stultifying nature of mere conformity to tradition, a serious questioning of such values as family loyalty. But in the sequel, *The Ploughman's Progress* (1933), Gervase Alard's altruistic action comes in for sharp criticism. As one of the independent farmers writes to him,

> You took the land away from the squires to give it to the yeomen, but I don't suppose you will be broken-hearted to hear that the yeomen have found your gift too expensive and have in their turn handed it over to the speculative builder (on the edges) and to desolation (in the midst).[17]

This book, a thoughtful treatment of the changing agricultural conditions of the time, is a characteristic rural novel of the 1930s; but the conventional incidents and characterisation make it compare unfavourably with the less obviously polished work of A. G. Street and Adrian Bell.

In other novels we find the invocation of a more intangible reality (the kind of reality at which Hugh Walpole more uncertainly hints).

> He looked out to sea, and saw the path that the light had trodden from the moon. The low soft roar, the blurred horizon, the phosphorescent break of the waves on the beach were a comfort to him in the strangeness of his disembodied town. His little refuge between the sea and the woods had betrayed him – his bit of time had crumbled – but its eternal boundary remained, the great whole of which Marlingate was a part, and to which its ghost, so restless and trembling tonight, belonged, the deep from which it was taken and to which it would return.[18]

This sense of an underlying physical order that can be spiritually apprehended is a feature of several of the novels, as it is of those of Eden Phillpotts. It is the final comfort of the defeated hero of *Spell Land*, and an abiding one to the ferocious protagonist of *Sussex Gorse*. The latter novel is the nearest that Sheila Kaye-Smith comes to writing the kind of work parodied and criticised in *Cold Comfort Farm*. It is the story of Reuben Backfield, a Sussex farmer who surrenders his life to an obsession, his determination to buy up and subdue to the plough the piece of upland called Boarzell Heath. To this he sacrifices everything – wife, children, honour and love. The story anticipates Mary Webb's *Precious Bane*, but, whereas Gideon Sarn is defrauded in the hour of his triumph, and his wrong-headed choice proved false, Reuben Backfield wins through. There is something satisfying about his refusal to conform to the expected moral pattern: throughout the book one waits for the apparently inevitable defeat, only to find at the end that he regards the havoc he has wrought as well worth while. It is an interesting departure from his creator's general approach (one which she again derived from the advice of W. L. George[19]) and a corrective to the relentless intensity of other parts of the novel. Reuben is seen as being almost a force of nature; and he has a good deal more vigour than most of Eden Phillpotts's characters in this vein.

In a short passage at the end of the book Reuben's achievement is discussed by his son Richard and a group of town friends, enabling the author to parody the kinds of literary movement with which her name was to be associated.

> 'He's a fine fellow, your father, Backfield,' said the man who was writing a book on Sussex commons. 'I can almost for-

give him for spoiling one of the best pieces of wild land in the country.'

'A magnificent old face,' said a middle-aged woman with red hair – 'the lining of it reminds me of those interesting Italian peasants one meets – they wrinkle more beautifully than a young girl keeps her bloom. I should like to paint him.' . . .

Richard felt almost proud of his parent.

'He's certainly picturesque – and really, there's a good deal of truth in what he says about having got the better of Nature. Thirty years ago I'd have sworn he could never have done it. But it's my firm conviction that he has – and made a good job of it too. He's fought like the devil, he's been hard on every man and himself into the bargain, he's worked like a slave and never given in. The result is that he's done what I'd have thought no man could possibly do. It's really rather splendid of him.'

'Ah – but he's never heard of Pan's pipes,' said the youth in the open-work socks.[20]

This passage is not as simple as it seems. Reuben's observers are placed in a satirical light; but the treatment of Reuben's own achievement is ambiguous. He has got the better of nature in more than one sense – all natural affection has been subordinated to an impersonal ambition. His reward is a sense of communion with the impersonal world of natural elements and forces.

He learned to love the moving shadows of clouds travelling over a sunlit view – to love ridged distances fading from dark bice, through blue, to misty grey. He used to watch for the sparkle of light on far cottage windows, the white sheen of farmhouse walls and the capped turrets of oasts. But he loved best of all to feel the earth under his cheek when he cast himself down, the smell of her teeming sap, the sensation that he lay on a kind breast, generous and faithful.[21]

Sheila Kaye-Smith's writing has the merit of evoking not only a contemplative's feeling for landscape but also the actual feel of working the land. *Joanna Godden* is a faithfully drawn picture of a young woman farmer; indeed, it contains more than the portrait of Joanna herself, and portrays a whole community, the other marsh farmers, the clergy, the labourers, the squires, as well as the impact of the world of the town, above all the world of social fashion as mediated through Joanna's younger sister Ellen, whom she succeeds in educating into a way of thought and feeling hostile to all that the farm stands for. The world of the farm is the world of honesty, of work as a source of life and not simply as a means towards it: it represents the positive in the author's scale of values. In a characteristic passage she portrays both Joanna and that for which she stands:

> Father Lawrence came to see her one April day when the young lambs were bleating on the sheltered innings and making bright clean spots of white beside the ewes' fog-soiled fleeces, when the tegs had come down from their winter keep inland, and the sunset fell in long golden slats across the first water-green grass of spring. The years had aged him more than they had aged Joanna – the marks on her face were chiefly weather marks, token of her exposure to marsh suns and winds, and of her own ruthless applications of yellow soap. Behind them was a little of the hardness which comes when a woman has to fight many battles and has won her victories, largely through the sacrifice of her resources. The lines on his face were mostly those of his own humour and other people's sorrows, he had exposed himself perhaps not enough to the weather and too much to the world, so that where she had fine lines and a fundamental hardness, he had heavy lines like the furrows of a ploughshare, a softness beneath them like the fruitful soil that the share turns up.[22]

This is beautifully done: two worlds of experience are here related and shown to be complementary. Sheila Kaye-Smith's own Christian convictions are, however, subdued to a more general concern with the values of a Christian humanism – her study of religious fanaticism in *Green Apple Harvest*, for example, has more to do with its effects on her pitiful protagonist than with the rights and wrongs of his belief.[23] Where her own specific convictions obtrude they are ecclesiastical, as in the portrait of the young Anglo-Catholic priest in *The End of the House of Alard* and of the older one in *Shepherds in Sackcloth* (1930), which are sympathetic accounts of the impact made by the Oxford Movement in the country districts.

It is, however, in the study of farmers and their families that Sheila Kaye-Smith excels. Her Sussex is a place where people work, their lives making for health and sanity in spite of the complications wrought by human temperament. In *Iron and Smoke* (1928), a story of the marriage between the daughter of a northern industrial magnate and a southern squire who loves his land more than his wife and family, industrialism is seen as the enemy, and the book ends on a note of triumph with the breaking of the General Strike. The author clearly has sympathy with the magnate's rebellious son when he says,

> The trouble's deeper – in the earth itself. She has set her curse upon us for digging into her heart for our wealth, when she gladly gave us her surface for our necessity. It's the work itself that's impossible, apart from any housing or wages. If we paid our miners sixty pounds a week and gave them palaces to live in, they would still be a rebellious race, because they live and work at enmity with nature.[24]

But this is a superficial distinction; and one has only to read Lawrence's account of the miners in *Sons and Lovers* to perceive the limitation. When Paul has to leave home to go to work he sees that 'the valley was full of corn, brightening in the sun. Two colleries, among the fields, waved their small white plumes of steam.'[25] The juxtaposition is not a contrast; and seen like that it shows up Sheila Kaye-Smith's opposition between mining and farming as being, however humanitarian in impulse, an artificial one.

In the straightforward portrayal of men and women at work she is on surer ground. One passage from *Joanna Godden* may be cited as an example of her ability to realise a physical scene and fuse it with its emotional significance.

> Joanna flounced off, and went to find Socknersh at the shearing. In the shelter of some hurdles he and one or two travelling shearers were busy with the ewes' fleeces. She noticed that the animal that Socknersh was working on lay quiet between his feet, while the other men held theirs with difficulty and many struggles. The July sunshine seemed to hold the scene as it held the Marsh in a steep of shining stillness. The silence was broken by many small sounds – the clip of the shears, the panting of the waiting sheep and of the dogs that guarded them, and every now and then the scraping scuttle of the released victim as it sprang up from the shearer's feet and fled off to where the shorn sheep huddled naked and ashamed together. Joanna watched for a moment without speaking; then suddenly she broke out:
>
> 'Socknersh, I hear it's said that the new lambs will be poor in wool.'
>
> 'They're saying it, missus, but it ain't true.'
>
> 'I don't care if it's true or not. You shouldn't ought to tell my gel Martha such things before you tell me.'

Socknersh's eyes opened wide, and the other men looked up from their work.[26]

Here the carefully recorded, rather Hardyesque picture of the sheep-shearing prepares, by its very nature, for the account of Joanna's infatuation for Socknersh. He is the man of the land whom she regards (with some justice in view of the hierarchical nature of marshland society) as socially unsuitable to marry. Later she aspires to, and nearly attains, marriage within the landed squirearchy; deprived of this by her lover's death she finally falls victim to a cockney fortune hunter. Her love affairs are thus an implicit parable; but the parable is never underlined. Events take their course and the points are made dramatically. Joanna herself, with her high spirits, her impulsive affections, her ambition and love of property is a characteristic early twentieth-century heroine, a type that begins with Bathsheba Everdene and ends with Scarlett O'Hara. The feminist movement had as one of its principal literary results these portraits of a capable but feminine woman in a man's world.

A more familiar style of farming family is portrayed in *Little England*. The fortunes of the Beatup family and their neighbours in the First World War is coloured by a vein of patriotic fervour that is, however, commendably restrained. As an observant, sympathetic, unpatronising picture of very ordinary people it is among the most likable of Sheila Kaye-Smith's books, and is representative of all her best qualities. The account of old Mrs Beatup's feelings on her son's conscription is genuinely moving; and her reaction to Tom's death is itself a comment on the conventional responses.

'Proud' – that was the word they were all throwing at her now. . . . They said 'You must be very proud of Tom', just as if all the age-old instincts of her breed did not generate a feeling of shame for one who died out of his bed. Good yeomen died between their sheets, and her son had died out in the mud, like a sheep or a dog – and yet she must be proud of him![27]

This novel is the author's least romantic book, a straightforward chronicle of an English hamlet. Its virtues – skilful balancing of incidents and character analysis, humanity and credibility are characteristic. Its weakness is more a matter of limitation, a deficiency in imaginative force, so that situation tend to drift into storybook resolutions; and in any great sense of change and history. But limitations can be more deadly than faults. As Edwin Muir observed, 'Her imagination is loose and general, she lacks that intensity which is the same thing as exactitude.'[28]

Sheila Kaye-Smith's Sussex labours under a particularity that limits its relevance; and her own powers were insufficient to overcome that limitation: the novels remain provincial in significance while metropolitan in presentation. Sussex is simply the place where the stories happen; and, lovingly described though it is, and evocatively as its place-names are used, it does not seem to have any particular meaning in itself. (The account of Romney Marsh in *Joanna Godden* is so vivid, however, as almost to cancel out this criticism.) The author's kindly if ironical understanding flickers over her characters, but it needs a mind of the rare warmth and sympathy of a George Eliot to combine this with intensity of feeling. Ultimately the work of Sheila Kaye-Smith, however workmanlike and humane, fails to kindle the imagination; its tendency is less to heighten its subject than, very slightly, to belittle it.

But only very slightly. And it is a novelist worthy of respect who composed the following letter from a village youth who has deserted from the trenches.

Dear Father,

By the time you get this I will be out of the way of troubling you any more. I am in great trouble. Mr. Archie said perhaps not tell you, but I said I would rather you knew. It is like this. I kept away in —— last time we went up to the trenches, with a lady friend, you may have heard of. Beatup says he told you. Well, I am to be shot for it. I was court-martialled and they said to be shot. Dear Father this will make you very sorry, but I cannot be helped, and I am not worth it. I have been a very bad son to you, and done many wicked things besides. Things always were against me. Mr. Archie is sitting with me tonight, and he says he will stay all night, as I am feeling very much upset at this great trouble. I am leaving you my ring made out of a piece of Zep and my purse, only I am afraid there is no money in it. Please remember me to Ivy Beatup, and say if it had not been for her I should not be here now. I think that is all.

ever your loving son,
Jeremiah Meridian Sumption

P.S. – The pardry says Jesus will forgive my sins. Thank you very much, dear father, for those fags you sent. I am smoking one now.[29]

This is an object letter in the achieving of simplicity without condescension.

III

Sheila Kaye-Smith was the first twentieth-century English novelist to attempt an entirely naturalistic picture of the rural community. In comparing her novels with those of Eden Phillpotts and John Trevena one is aware not only of her greater literary proficiency and tact, but also of a fundamental difference in approach. Sheila Kaye-Smith's Sussex is far less isolated from the contemporary urban world than are Phillpotts's and Trevena's Devonshire and Cornwall. Partly, of course, this is a matter of geography: the landscape configuration produces a different kind of peasant type. But it is also a matter of the way in which the rural community are presented. In the novels of Phillpotts and Trevena the peasant figures are drawn more than life-size, but Sheila Kaye-Smith's farmers and labourers are part of the same social world and moral world as her squires and parsons. And this difference is reflected in the technique, style and presentation of her novels, which are indistinguishable from others of the same period on more urban or psychological themes. As Katherine Mansfield shrewdly observed, reviewing *Green Apple Harvest,* two hands were at work:

> One is the country hand, scoring the dialect, and the other is the town hand, hovering over the wild flowers and pointing out the moon like the 'blown petal' of a cherry tree.[30]

Whereas Phillpotts and Trevena, and even Walpole, have a sense of inner purpose, of private vision and creative obsession, the world of Sheila Kaye-Smith opens out to nothing beyond itself. Balanced, likable, observant within limits, and highly readable, her books in the end fail to put the rural theme to more than a local and particular use. They remain regional in interest just as they are regional in setting.

6 Town and Country: Francis Brett Young, Winifred Holtby

I

One conspicuous paradox of twentieth-century cultural life has been that, while the growth of cities has led to a nostalgic valuation of the country (the word 'countryside' seems to embody it), this very love has tended to be self-defeating. Just as Hugh Walpole's celebration of Watendlath assisted towards opening up that solitary valley to the motor car, so the yearning for what was thought of as a simpler life led to the gradual complication of that life. (Sturt's comments on the settlers from the town in *Change in the Village* will be remembered.) The enormous increase in motor traffic and the accompanying building speculation led to the kind of widespread ugliness attacked in such influential books as Clough Williams Ellis's *England and the Octopus* (1928) and C. E. M. Joad's *The Horrors of the Countryside* (1931); and it was at this time that the shanty town of Peacehaven erupted upon the Sussex cliffs. The abandonment of all considerations of taste and design, let alone ordinary amenity, in the development of working-class areas in the nineteenth-century industrial cities was, by a nasty if appropriate logic, taking its toll of the rest of the country. As a result there arose a new, defensive relationship between town and country. The rise in population and a more widespread distribution of wealth and property were leading up to the now-familiar concern with the preservation of natural scenery and of amenities. Ultimately it was a question of government, its scope and function; but it is also a matter of philosophy. What is the true human scale of values? By what does a man live? That issue was raised in connection with the rural theme by two popular novelists of the period, Francis Brett Young (1884–1954) and Winifred Holtby (1898–1935), and the difference in their treatment of it is illuminating. Both were prominent figures in the literary world of their time, and both exemplify in an interesting way the relationship between personal self-expression, social conditions and literary convention, those several elements out of which the major artist makes a harmony.

Brett Young belonged to the literary world of Compton Mackenzie, Hugh Walpole, Edward Marsh, J. C. Squire, Charles Morgan, with all of whom he was friendly.[1] He also, on account of several years residence on Capri, became acquainted with Axel Munthe and D. H. Lawrence. (The relationship with Lawrence proved, as relationships with Lawrence usually did, mutually revelatory.) He was the son of a doctor, and practised as one himself before retiring to become a full-time novelist. Accounts of his experiences are to be found in *The Young Physician* (1919), *My Brother Jonathan* (1928) and *Dr Bradley Remembers* (1938), and his knowledge of human physiology lends a quality of robustness to novels that otherwise tend overmuch to the refined. It colours too his apprehension of the industrial age in which he lived. Here is one account among many of Birmingham (called North Bromwich in the novels):

> In the heart of the city the sense of power, impressive if malignant, is so overwhelming that one cannot see the monstrosity as a whole and can almost understand the blindness of its inhabitants. Go, rather, to the hills beyond Halesby, to Uffdown and Pen Beacon, where, with a choice of prospects, one may turn from the dreamy plain of Severn and the cloudy splendours of Silurian hills, to its pillars of cloud by day and its pillars of fire by night; and perhaps in that remoter air you may realise the city's true significance as a phenomenon of unconquered if not inevitable disease. If you are a physician, you will realise that this evil has its counterpart in human tissues, where a single cell that differs not at all from other cells and is a natural unit in the organism, may suddenly and, as it seems, unreasonably acquire a faculty of monstrous and malignant growth, cleaving and multiplying to the destruction of its fellows – a cell gone mad, to which the ancients gave the name of cancer.[2]

The rejection of industrialism here is absolute; and the recurring contrast between town and country in Brett Young's work is not a dynamic one. His own working experience was urban; and his most vivid and convincing writing comes when he is describing the work of a busy doctor or the conversation and outlook of the great industrialists, the conventions of late nineteenth-century suburbia and all the outward trappings of social change in the period between the Diamond Jubilee and the First World War. His knowledge of the country, on the other hand, is a knowledge born of leisure, a walker's knowledge and, later, a resident novelist's knowledge. The town and the country were experienced by him in different ways and thus do not effectively relate in his novels. The country is seen in them as the place of romantic escape, of the fulfilment of dreams. It is a townsman's view, like the view, so frequently referred to in the novels, from Pen Beacon and Uffdown – the Clent Hills in Worcestershire, between which and Birmingham lies Halesowen, Brett Young's birthplace and the Halesby of the novels. This contrast between two worlds, as seen from the Clents, is the central image of the 'Mercian novels'.

The latter title was his own for the seventeen books he wrote about his native region. They do not account for the whole of his work, but they form the principal part of it. He also wrote about Africa,[3] Ireland,[4] Egypt,[5] and Capri.[6] From Brixham, the setting of *Deep Sea* (1914) to the contrasted worlds of Birmingham and Italy in his last novel, *A Man About the House* (1942), he was always intensely interested in the spirit of place.

This is readily apparent in his first book, *Undergrowth* (1913), written in an undetectable collaboration with his brother.[7] It is the story of the construction of a dam in the Welsh border hills, and of the effect upon the men building it of the haunted and lonely country in which they work. Both in setting and treatment the novel recalls the work of Arthur Machen, with its heavily luxuriant portrayal of natural scenery, its preoccupation with mysticism and pagan rituals: a sense of claustrophobic oppression is ably maintained. There is a suggestion, never fully formulated, that the building of the dam is an interference with nature; and it is the main weakness of the book that this idea is left undeveloped. In a later novel, *The House under the Water* (1932), Brett Young used the theme again, but this time in a more muted key, and the flooding of the valley is here seen as something temporarily pathetic but ultimately good. The symbolism now relates to the necessary passing of an old way of life. The later book is a far more accomplished piece of work than *Undergrowth*, but it is far less interesting. Later, in *Cold Harbour* (1924), the author returned to the theme and in a short but disturbing account of a haunted house explored the interaction between psychic influences and material environment. Here it is a failed industrialist who pits his enormous energies against the powers that infest Cold Harbour; and his participation in the rites of Astarte, together with the siting of the house on the very edge of the

D

Black Country, aligns the new industrialism with the anti-human activities which have infected the haunted house. Both *Cold Harbour* and *Undergrowth* have an intensity lacking in Brett Young's other work, and suggest a seed of imaginative vision that might, had it been allowed to develop, have given his work that force and energy which it so disappointingly lacks.

A further hint of where his creative gifts might have led him is found in *The Crescent Moon* (1918), another tale of Astarte worship, this time set in Africa. Remarking that Africa is not in fact mysterious, he elaborates this by saying,

> Mystery is a thing of man's imagining, and springs . . . from an air which generations of dead men have breathed, emanates from the crumbled bricks with which they have builded, from the memory of the loves and aspirations of an immemorial past.[8]

This was to be the world of John Cowper Powys; but, in his introductory letter to Martin Secker, Brett Young disclaims the intention of proceeding further and describes the novel as 'the last shocker I shall ever write'. In fact the book is, for a shocker, decidedly tame; but its cross-evocations of Shropshire, the Isle of Aran and Africa are highly effective and add a dimension of aesthetic pathos to an otherwise ordinary tale.

In common with other of the early novels *The Crescent Moon* employs the dramatic narrator, the tale within the tale. In *The Dark Tower* (1914) this technique is elaborated by the device of two narrators, together with the reported speech of two others, a literary feat that bears comparison with the achievements in this line of Conrad and Ford Madox Ford. But *The Dark Tower* lacks both the subtlety and intellectual gifts of Ford, and the physical actuality of Conrad's world: its Pelleas and Melisande story in a modern setting (a half-ruined castle in the Black Mountains) is rarefied and remote. The book is written, however, in a style of quite remarkable grace. Something of a *tour de force*, like the later *The Tragic Bride* (1920), it shows that Brett Young had gifts of poetic intensity that suggest a tragic vision of life very different from the urbane sprawl of the later Mercian novels. That vision is not wholly lost, but is accommodated within a more dispassionate outlook. Brett Young's talent is a case of the good being the enemy of the best.

Two other novels of this early period deserve mention: *The Iron Age* (1915) and *The Black Diamond* (1921). The former is a critique of industrial society in terms of the money values of the manufacturer Walter Willis and the romantic discontent of his son Edward. The planning of the book is straightforward: the setting, the old hall now taken over by the new industrial landlord; the story, love versus money and conformity; the upshot, the father making huge profits out of armaments while the son enlists. But the dramatisation is weak, for the whole conception of Edward Willis is vitiated by the vague nature of his particular longing. He is fatally without the energy of Lawrence's rebels – fatally, not because he is a weak man, but because he is a man weakly imagined. The novel is too much of a parable for its author's powers.

The Black Diamond, on the other hand, is one of the best of Brett Young's books. It is longer than most of the earlier novels, developing at the leisurely pace characteristic of the later ones. It is the story of Abner Fellows, a working-class boy who migrates from a miner's life westwards into the Brett Young country of romance to become a navvy on the pipeline that is to convey the water from the reservoir in the Welsh hills to Birmingham. The novel moves from a quiet but carefully recorded picture of the mining community to a lonely pastoral world, where Abner becomes passively involved with two women, drinks, brawls, finally enlists when in his cups, and disappears. This fade-out is a feature of many of the early books – Edward Willis, the young physician Edwin Ingleby and the tragic bride Gabrielle Hewish are all left facing limbo, a complete unknown; they are defested idealists. The epitaph on Edward Willis is characteristic:

> He welcomed anything which should bring the current valuation of human life into line with that which was suggested by his own depression. . . . He didn't really mind whether he lived or died as long as life or death offered him a chance of escape from his own misfortune. It pleased him to think that he might be in at the finish, when the people of his age were shattering to bits the civilisation which had deceived them, leaving them, for all its flatteries, discontented. . . .[9]

A deep pessimism about his time informs all Brett Young's early work; and uneven though it is, it is this early work which most deserves to survive. In the later books, for all their inventiveness and smooth efficiency, the tragic issues are shirked.

The Black Diamond is perhaps the author's best study of country life, the remote life of shepherds and farmers in Clun Forest. The impact of the navvies upon the local people is described more realistically than in *Undergrowth*; and there is no sentimentalising of the country scene such as we find in a late novel like *Mr Lucton's Freedom* (1940). Above all, the book abounds in that feeling for men as workmen which is a distinctive feature of Brett Young's outlook:

> The old labourer was as hardy as the knotted oak that he resembled. His day's work began before dawn; he had more than three miles to walk to the farm on which he was employed, but when he returned in the evening after trudging the fields all day, he could never rest, but must be putting his strip of garden in order so intently that he scarcely had time to answer Abner's questions, staring up at him with those patient over-burdened eyes. His wages, which were regulated by his age rather than his capacity for labour, were only twelve shillings a week, so that his garden produce was really essential to his life. When he had finished his gardening, or when the light failed, he would retire to his kitchen and drink a crude, sweet spirit that he distilled from turnips. Sometimes at night they would hear him singing to himself the innumerable obscene verses of Devonshire folk-songs. Then, when he could sing no longer, he would drag his twisted limbs upstairs and sleep like a log in the certainty of waking before dawn to set out on his labours again.[10]

The quiet, closely observant detachment of this is characteristic; and it compares interestingly with John Trevena's account of old Barseba, quoted earlier. Brett Young always seems a little remote from his people; but there is little that he does not notice. Here is a country doctor at work:

> The doctor was leaning over Gladys, and breathing heavily through his nostrils. His hands, lean, brown, and slightly stained with iodine, were placed firmly, yet tenderly upon the pink and white of the child's thigh. His fingers moved like tentacles, searching, soothing the spastic muscles under the skin. Gladys gave a sudden frightened, 'Oh . . . *mam* !' – and the fingers tightened like bands of steel. All the man's mind was in his fingers; his eyes gazed vaguely out of the window to the cascades of fading laburnum blossom in his shrubbery, the billowy outline of lilac against the white sky.[11]

With the successful publication of *Portrait of Clare* (1927), which at once put Brett Young on a popular footing with Walpole and

Mackenzie, he embarked on a whole succession of novels set in the country between Birmingham and the Welsh hills. All the books are long, and appeared in handsomely bound and printed editions, large and spacious as the books themselves – and as elegant in appearance. But the intensity of the earlier books is lacking: instead, we have a leisurely series of chronicles, impeccably written in a style that at its best is clear and swift-moving, and at its worst is as bland as cream. Brett Young novels had become commodities as predictable as those of Phillpotts. He had found what he could do; but in finding it, it is hard not to feel, he lost something else – that constant search for self-knowledge, and for the further experience of exploration, that is a feature of the greatest novelists. In these later books we are moving in the world of the already known. One comes out of a Brett Young novel the same person as the one who went in.

But there is much in them to admire. The industry that went to their making: the 140,000 word *My Brother Jonathan* was written in four months, the first 95,000 of *Jim Redlake* (1930) in three,[12] and yet neither book shows traces of such speed. He was simply a born storyteller, though his very fluency can make him dull: the raconteur was stronger that the dramatist, and the authorial voice can be insidiously lulling. In addition, the books are rich in finely drawn landscapes – the farmhouse in *Far Forest* (1936), the hill country of *The House under the Water*, the desolate no-man's-land of the Black Country:

Over this slagged waste of carbon and dead metal a network of narrow-gauge mineral-lines spread, as it seemed, haphazard; and on them, like derelict engines of war, stood strings of trucks, some empty, some loaded with tawny iron-ore, coal, coke, china-clay, stone and sand – the prime materials of the district's merchandise, abandoned, apparently, in this phlegraean desert. Sometimes, with a sudden rumble, the train crossed iron bridges, spanning straight lengths of canal whose dense, stagnant waters, sterilized by the acid effluents of factories, reflected a low sky bronzed with eternal smoke.[13]

The writing here is as carefully orchestrated as if the author were describing a lyrical landscape such as those evoked in *Clare* or *The Dark Tower*; indeed, the Black Country exercised a romantic fascination over him, as if the industrial revolution had been a tapping of some occult power.

Its heat and fierceness corresponded with some element hot and fierce in his own dark nature, and called to it. The spectacle of this vast reservoir of smouldering heat and simmering power, the thought of the wealth surpassing all dreams that flowed from it, excited and challenged him. . . . Aware of his own strength and power to endure, he had an almost prophetic confidence in himself and his future.[14]

But such a reaction to the industrial scene is ultimately a reaction in terms of the old aesthetic values which industrialism contradicts. It constitutes not a step forward but a step back: the final feeling is negative. The values which determine it are the values which allowed the Black Country to come into being. To look back is simply to create the same conditions all over again.

One sees this evidenced unconsciously in *White Ladies* (1935), in Bella Pomfret's obsessive love for the old house which she restores with the money gained from the family works, a love which blinds her to the real needs of her son and yet which is regarded with a kind of admiration by her creator. The idyllic beauty of the old manor contrasts with the hideousness of the desecrated Stour valley; but ultimately it is parasitic upon it. An awareness of this tragic paradox might have enlivened the even pages of the book; as things are, the smooth prose amounts to a deception.

She was coming round, gradually, to Hugo's way of thinking – to the way in which generations of Pomfrets had thought. . . . And meanwhile, in the delicious suspension of these months of waiting for the birth of her son, and above all in this season of early summer, when the sweet mowing-grass in the park made a shelter for corn-crakes and above the green acres cuckoos flew calling from one wood-land verge to another, then white jasmine and old-fashioned roses pervaded the air with their vagrant perfume, and the house stood brooding, as it were, over its own warm beauty reflected in the mirror of the moat – in these lavender dawns and blue twilights and golden noon-days, there was surely beauty enough to assuage the most hungry heart.[15]

For all the *literary* skill there is a lazy sensibility at work here. Ulti-mately the effect is banal.

The same blurred vision is to be found, differently manifested, in the rather patronising *Mr and Mrs Pennington* (1931), an attempt at an English *Madame Bovary* which, lacking the anguished sharpness of

Flaubert, succeeds only in being belittlingly playful. But it is *Portrait of Clare* which is the key to Brett Young's achievement. This enormously long novel is the story of an ordinary upper middle-class Englishwoman, of her romantic marriage with the son of an industrial magnate; his death in the Boer War; her second, unhappy marriage, to the family solicitor; her obsessive love for her son; her son's marriage; and her love for the father of his wife. The book ends with the impending death of Dudley Wilburn, the solicitor, and a chance of final happiness for Clare with her highly conservative middle-aged lover, Robert Hart, who voices with almost embarrassing precision the kind of patriotic conservatism which Brett Young's work appealed to and which he knew so well how to express – as in his poetic epic, *The Island*, published in the Second World War.[16] Innumerable readers must have felt themselves speaking in the words of Robert Hart:

'This is my religion, Clare, and I thank God for it. Humbly, I assure you, in spite of all the pride I have in it. The earth that bore me and all my forebears. Its own beauty; the courage, the patience, the goodwill, the piety of the men who have lived in it. When I think of England that is what I mean. . . . That shadow – yes, only a ripple, North of Cotswold – is Edgehill: Shakespeare was born beneath it. And even today. . . . There's Elgar, Housman, Masefield. Small names but greatly English, whatever else they may be. . . . No man who isn't a patriot deserves to have a fatherland. What's more, in a larger sense we *are* the people. The day when our race goes under will be Europe's Götterdämmerung. Because . . . because the things we stand for, even if we don't always achieve them, are all that matters. The cult of liberty, mercy, justice, gentleness. Ben Jonson knew what he was talking about when he called the author of King Lear gentle !'[17]

What gives a novel like *Portrait of Clare* its particular interest is the way in which it so exactly supplies the ingredients of middle-class romance – gracious pictures of a peaceful landscape for Paradise, red-brick suburbia for Purgatory, industrialism for Hell. The hero is a true knight; there is a witch figure in the person of Lady Hingston, the imperious wife of a newly-created industrial baronet; two ugly sisters in the persons of Clare's stepdaughters; and a charmingly wicked magician in the person of Dudley Wilburn's brother Ernest. And flowing through everything goes the prose – supple, rhythmic, rising at times to a Meredithian intensity. It is the prose which carries the book along, and which gives it its distinctive quality. The characters are, like most of Brett Young's people, out of stock – faithful to type and bounded by it. It is the externals, the gardens and houses and street scenes which convince: as his wife admits in her biography of him, 'Places to Francis were much more complex than people, and, to him, more moving.'[18]

Brett Young's reasons for writing *Clare* are revealing:

> At this time he talked a good deal to me about 'the D. H. Lawrence and James Joyce obsessions.' He thought there should be a swing of the pendulum: 'I am determined to write a book about normal people with normal reactions, and if I can't make it beautiful I'll eat my hat.'[19]

Normality is a dangerous category to invoke, but in this instance it was to prove a profitable one – *Clare* at once commanded a public that never thereafter forsook its author. In 1931 Compton Mackenzie was able to compare him to a swan 'swimming for a long time in the tranquil lake of his success'.[20] The comparison is apt.

Lawrence, however, characteristically got closer to the point:

> He had been reading one of Francis' books: 'splendidly written,' he said, 'but I always feel there is something between him and It.' When I told Francis this he smiled. "Well, one thing is certain, there's nothing between Lawrence and It, and I do like to leave a little to the imagination!'[21]

The failure to see the point of Lawrence's remark is more important than the rather cheap sneer at Lawrence's expense, but both reveal an obtuseness. In every one of Brett Young's novels something intervenes between himself and It. He never pauses long enough to reveal the essence of his subjects.

In *This Little World* (1934), for instance, his portrait of a village community, the characters are stereotyped, and assembled mechanically to give a cross-section of conservative England faced with change: we have the squire in love with his land, the acid-tongued spinster, the feckless labouring family, the philistine rich neighbour. The comparison of this book with Constance Holme's *The Lonely Plough*, or *Joanna Godden*, or even *Widecombe Fair*, is a damaging one. The whole course of the novel is predictable from start to finish, well done so far as it goes, but going nowhere interesting. It is the reproduction of an already painted picture. In other novels, however, the very distance at which the author stands is an advantage: the panoramic method can highlight things that a more involved treatment cannot. In one of the best of the later books, *Far Forest*, he describes

> those minimal creatures of whom, unless they were 'known to the police' the Law took no cognizance: indistinguishable units in the horde of shifting labour which, since the middle of the last century, has moved slowly to and fro over the face of Industrial England – from the sordid back-to-backs of Lancashire (where the mischief began) to the Potteries and the West Midlands, and from the Midlands, again to South Wales – seeking work and food wherever these became plentiful, very much as their remote nomadic ancestors sought pasture – with the result that it was as easy for a man to be lost in the heart of the Black Country as in that of the Black Continent.[22]

In the same novel there is a description, of women manufacturing iron chains, that might have come from the pages of a piece of nineteenth-century social-realist fiction.

Far Forest is among the most successful of the novels for several reasons. Like much of Brett Young's best writing (and like much of that of Sheila Kaye-Smith and Eden Phillpotts) it is set in the last century, and is largely a chronicle of a bygone way of life rather than a tale of human passions; it abounds in descriptions of the Worcestershire fields and woods, notably the Forest of Wyre; and its characters are for the most part aspects of the landscape they inhabit. Brett Young's interest is in physical detail, with the way in which people live, what they eat, how they dress, how they move and talk – they are thus extensions of place. His country people, unlike his country scenes, are more striking than his town characters because they are drawn from the deepest springs of his imagination; though at the other end of the scale the portrait of the speculating adventurer Tregaron in *The House under the Water* is full of vigour – Brett Young never drew anyone else so vivid and true to life. He seems to embody the forcefulness that his creator denied himself.

The novels of Francis Brett Young continue to be read, and have been frequently reprinted. His appeal does not seem to lie as a regional novelist, however hard he tried, and his publishers tried, to establish him as one. His cultivated detached mind, his sympathetic sense of irony, played too far above the world he was describing. He was aware of the problems underlying the age in which he lived, without, apparently, being deeply concerned with them – at any rate in his art. But as a social historian he takes an honourable place among our novelists (if by historian one means recorder) and not the least interesting thing about him is the way in which his not inconsiderable body of work raises the question of what constitutes the really living novel.

II

The same question arises in connection with the rather different work of Winifred Holtby. As left-wing in sympathies as Brett Young was conservative, she was deeply concerned with the condition of England, acting for a number of years as a director of *Time and Tide*. An accomplished journalist, she was a prominent figure in the literary scene of the early 1930s; and her fiction was well timed. This period of the 'pylon poets' (as Auden, Day Lewis and Spender have been so glibly called), of the emergence of George Orwell and Graham Greene, of the rise of *Scrutiny*, and of the sedate literary heyday of Charles Morgan was not friendly to the romantic presentation of things bucolic. Winifred Holtby had in fact heralded the shift in tone in rural writing as early as 1923, when she published her first novel, *Anderby Wold*. This is a matter-of-fact account of a farmer's wife. What distinguishes it from most others of its kind is its employment of satire. Mary Robson is the kind of quietly self-infatuated female familiar from the contempory novels of 'E. M. Delafield';[23] her insistence on playing lady bountiful is shattered by a farm labourers' strike. The novel is unexpectedly subdued in tone for a young woman's book, and its ending is inconclusive: the author is reluctant to take sides. The picture of her native Yorkshire, to be taken up subsequently in *The Crowded Street* (1925), a chilling picture of a girl's submersion in a conventional upbringing, and *The Land of Green Ginger* (1927), is notably disenchanted. No mystique is attached to the countryside as such: it is merely a way of life, and less rewarding than many. Winifred Holtby was the daughter of a county councillor, and had a practical knowledge of how rural affairs were managed. Her early work contains a good deal of sharp, if somewhat brittle, writing, as in the description of Sir Wentworth Marshall, whose

ownership of a considerable portion of the surface of England enabled him to experiment with afforestation, small holdings, and sugar beet, but [whose] lack of any suitable strip of sea-coast somewhat cramped his style with international frontiers and the tides. . . . He continually exploited his position as landowner to attempt the impossible, and passed his time very pleasantly accomplishing nothing but a reputation for eccentricity. His wife, on the other hand, passed her time in a succession of small sensible accomplishments. She was a round ball of a woman, with immense energy, and the unshakable complacency of a mother of seven, conscious of duties numerically fulfilled – after all, the least ambiguous way of fulfilling anything. This achievement had influenced her whole career in the direction of numerical successes. She sat upon ten committees; she was a justice of the peace, a voluntary worker for Lindersdale district under the Ministry of Pensions, the organiser of a Girl's Friendly and Mother's Union. She rejoiced in quotations like 'Do the work that's nearest though it's dull at whiles,' or 'God's in His Heaven, all's right with the world,' and used them with effect when opening bazaars and new Church Halls. She was continually engaged in helping Lame Dogs over Stiles, though mildly resenting the tendency of lame dogs to be independent rather than submissive. She had a fine sense of property, which affected her attitude towards servants, pensioners, villagers, and 'Friendly' girls, and she enjoyed the unquenchable optimism produced by an assured income, good health, and small imagination.[24]

This is amusing, informative, and pointed; but one is more conscious of a clever mind than of a sensitive one, as the author herself would have agreed: she wrote to a friend a few weeks after *Anderby Wold* was accepted for publication that 'I want to write an epic about modern civilisation . . . and the duty of creating happiness in the world . . . and I write like parish magazines.'[25] The epic, or the nearest she got to it, is the posthumously published *South Riding* (1936).

Winifred Holtby's premature death prevented her from enjoying the success which that death, however, probably increased. Fortuitous or not, the success was earned. *South Riding* is a novel one can wholeheartedly respect, even if it is not one to be wholeheartedly admired; and it is one of the very few novels to portray country life in genuinely social terms. The book is a study of the work of a county council, and is based on much first-hand experience: authenticity of background is its keynote. In it Winifred Holtby draws not only on knowledge of her home county (for the South Riding is patently the East Riding, its principal towns clearly recognisable under their pseudonyms) but also on

her work as a journalist. As her close friend Vera Brittain records, the
pages of her note-books were

> crowded with paragraphs for stories; suggestions for articles, notes
> and editorials; descriptions of people and places scribbled in trains or
> buses as she passed by; jottings for speeches; lists of books to be read
> or reviewed; schemes for lectures and classes; observations on schools
> visited; summaries of Bills to be put through parliament; little
> vignettes of travels abroad.[26]

In view of this continual industry it is not surprising that *South
Riding* should read less like a novel evolved than like one assembled.

Its method is panoramic. Grouped into five books, each one centring
round the activities of a particular department of the council's work,
it portrays a wide range of people – a county landowner, a headmistress,
an innkeeper and his wife, a labourer's family, and so on. Their
various problems are sketched in with skill and understanding, and
related subtly to each other with a sure sense of how society is composed of interlocking events as well as of interlocking people. The
novel, compellingly readable, does succeed in being a coherent and
elaborate portrait of a world.

Much of its strength comes from its meticulous observation of small
details. This can serve to pinpoint actual cultural changes:

> Like most of her generation and locality, Elsie was trilingual. She
> talked B.B.C. English to her employer, Cinema American to her
> companions, and Yorkshire dialect to old milkmen like Eli Dickson.[27]

Or it can serve as a basis for direct social criticism:

> In a chest on the front landing known as the glory hole they stored
> the harvest of bazaars and birthdays, of raffles, bridge-drive prizes,
> bargain sales, and even presents which they had themselves received
> at former Christmasses. Into the glory hole went blotters, pen-
> wipers, and painted vases, dessert d'oylies, table-centres and imitation
> fruits of wax or velvet, lamp-shades, knitted bed-jackets and em-
> broidered covers for the Radio Times, all the bric-a-brac of civil
> exchange or time-killing occupation. The indictment of a social
> system lay in those drawers if they but knew it – a system which
> over-works eight-tenths of its female population, and gives the re-

maining two-tenths so little to do that they must clutter the world with useless objects.[28]

This one passage contains the substance of her earlier novel *The Crowded Street* – originally to have been entitled *The Wallflower*.[29]

Although Winifred Holtby avoids what she calls 'the Shakespearean tradition of finding the lower classes funny, whatever tragedy touched the kings and nobles',[30] she does all the same devote the centre of her picture to the tragic figure of the landowner Robert Carne, with his mad wife (an aristocrat) and neglected daughter. Carne represents the old values of hierarchy and benevolent squirarchic domination (he might have stepped out of a novel by Constance Holme), a domination that inevitably has to pass, just as, equally inevitably, his way of life ceases to be economically profitable.

He worshipped the God of order who had created farmers lords of their labourers, the county and the gentry lords over the farmers, and the King lord above all his subjects under God. He worshipped the contrast of power and humility implied in his religion, and on Sunday evenings, in the pew which was his property, sang that God had put down the mighty from their seat, and had exalted the humble and meek, with no effect upon his social principles.[31]

Carne is sympathetically drawn, with something of the mournful Jacobite about him; even his exasperated opponents can see in him one of those men

who profited by injustice, who perpetuated anarchy, who had never risked one hour's discomfort to relieve oppression [but who] could yet by a feeble anecdote, a trick of laughter, do something that Astell, who had given health, ambition, happiness and half his life to man's service, could not do.[32]

In Carne's conflict with his fellow councillors over land development we see the tragic theme of the book: the theme that the necessary work of change is often the fruit of greed and opportunism rather than of ideals. The devoted socialist Astell is mortally ill; it is the hardheaded Councillor Snaith who helps to bring about reform. Carne, like Astell a man of honour, goes under in the process. But the novel does not recount this conflict in terms of simple black and white; and the characters of Snaith and Carne, together with the attitudes to life for which they stand, are skilfully conveyed in the verbal exchange between them after a hunting accident caused by Snaith's unannounced wiring of his land.

'Do you know who put up that wire?'

'Certainly,' said the little alderman. 'Stathers, my tenant. He did so on my suggestion.'

'At your suggestion,' repeated Carne, breathing hard, his hand still automatically fondling the ears of the dying mare. 'I see. Good of you to acknowledge it.'

'Not at all. Why not? I am sorry you have had an accident, but I always said that hunting was a risky game, even for others beside the fox.'

'It's not marked.'

'No? Any compulsion? You weren't asked, you know, to come galloping over my land.'

Snaith was still in the best of tempers, mild, superior.

'My God,' half whispered Carne, 'Don't you see your bloody carelessness has cost the life of a beautiful mare and hurt a man, and you haven't even got a gun so that I can put her out of her suffering?'

'I realise that this is hardly an appropriate moment to discuss the ethics of fox-hunting. But if fifty grown-up men will amuse themselves by riding after one little animal to watch it torn to pieces by dogs, on other people's property, they must accept the consequences.'[35]

Here the balance between the reasonableness of Snaith and the humane passion of Carne is made further complex by the implied criticism, or qualifying, of liberal attitudes in the absence of the gun, and also by the fact that, while one's emotional sympathies are engaged on the side of Carne (both in this particular incident and throughout the book), reason is on the side of Snaith. The general optimism about human good intentions that pervades the book is never sentimental.

Winifred Holtby repeatedly checks her own point of view within the novel by subjecting it to criticism from other characters. If Carne and Sarah Burton, the headmistress, are the main objects of her sympathy, she never, at any rate in the case of Sarah, indulges it by allowing them a monopoly of persuasive talk. Thus even Sarah's honest impatience can receive a salutary check.

'We need courage, not so much to endure as to act. All this
resignation stunts us. We're so busy resigning ourselves to the inevitable, that we don't even ask if it is inevitable. We spend so much
time accommodating ourselves to other people's standards, we don't
even ask if our own might not be better. We're so much occupied in
letting live that we haven't begun to live. . . . We've got to have
courage, to take our future into our hands. If the law is oppressive,
we must change the law. If tradition is obstructive, we must break
tradition. If the system is unjust, we must reform the system. "Take
what you want," says God. "Take it and pay for it." '

'Ah,' said Mrs. Beddows quietly, 'but who pays?'[34]

Sarah's voice is the author's, and her optimism the optimism of the
inter-war years when hopes of rebuilding society ran high. *South Riding*
is an interesting novel historically, portraying a world in which town
and country could still be seen as part of a single social complex; it is
one of the very few novels of rural life which does not depend on
contrast between town and country to gain its effects. The landscape
of the Riding, its wide fields, low cliffs and extensive marshes are more
often indicated than described directly. But here too we find the natural
order as a norm of moral worth. Snaith the councillor is a man repressed and stultified in his emotions, more interested in cats than in
human beings. He dislikes the spring.

He saw the fierce needles of fine green corn, the young savage lambs
knocking and thrusting at their mothers, the swelling reddish buds
on the hawthorn hedge, combine in the monstrous battle for rebirth,
and it angered him that so fragile a creature as a wren, a mouse or
daffodil should renew its lusty life while he moved through the earth
without desire of increase.[35]

The rather limp and automatic writing ('monstrous battle', '*through the
earth*') indicates however that this is not the author's principal concern :
it is in particular, sometimes isolated, incidents that the novel's strength
resides, incidents especially affecting the weak and afflicted. Winifred
Holtby was already dying of Bright's disease when she wrote the book,
and ill health is treated with sympathetic attention. The predicaments
of the poor and lonely are constantly before us. The chapter about the
ineffective schoolmistress Miss Sigglesthwaite is genuinely moving. But
the name of the woman and the title of this particular chapter ('Miss
Sigglesthwaite Sees the Lambs of God') indicate also the novel's short-

comings: a tendency to seek the stock situation, the readily recognisable 'character', and with this rather archly to instruct and enter-
tain. The motives which led Winifred Holtby to write *South Riding*
are not to be impugned; but they were not, on the evidence of the
book itself, in the last resort the motives of art.

Ultimately the book's purpose is didactic. The didacticism can be
embodied ironically in the minds of the characters, as when at the
outset the young reporter Lovell Brown oversimplifies the council's
work, seeing it as

> World Tragedy in embryo. Here gallant Labour, with nothing to
> lose but its chains, would fight entrenched and armoured Capital.
> Here the progressive, greedy and immoral towns would exploit the
> pure, honest, elemental and unprogressive country.[36]

Or it may be introduced with quiet humour, as in Sarah's reaction to
the children's concert: initially repelled by the children's songs about
'spooning, moonlight, triplets, ripe cheese, honeymoons and inebriation',
it occurs to her later that

> the songs about drunken home-comers and bullying wives which she
> had found so gross dealt after all with common-places in the lives of
> these young singers . . . were not these [songs] perhaps necessary
> armaments for defence in a world besieged by poverty, ugliness,
> squalor and misfortune?[37]

At other times the message of the book is presented more frontally, as
when Astell, the idealistic socialist, declares,

> 'I want a great co-operative commonwealth of free peoples, all over
> the world. . . . I want to see them controlling their own lives, what
> they do and how they do it. . . . And that isn't going to come by
> working as I've worked here. Oh, I know that all this is useful – so
> far as it goes. But it's not changing men's values. It's not destroying
> their destroyers.'[38]

South Riding at times resembles the social dramas of the early years
of the century – it belongs to the school of Galsworthy and Granville
Barker, and looks ahead to the work of Arnold Wesker. It is certainly
one of the few rural novels to be written from a left-wing angle, muted
though the radicalism is. It is, however, conventional enough in the

manner of its narration, presentation and language; and conventional (though normative might be a better word) in its resort to feeling as a resolution. Sarah, at the novel's end, mourning her hopeless love for Carne in the derelict grounds of Maythorpe, his ancestral home, knowing that 'all her life she would love him and all through her life she would fight against him', comes to feel that 'she was not entirely alone, not arrayed against him; for he was within her'.[39] There is deep personal tragedy in the end of the novel, for Sarah left alone; and it is described with a restrained rhythmical eloquence reminiscent of the style of Constance Holme (with whose work this book interestingly contrasts). But it does have a slightly forced air about it, or, if not that, a too great predictability. This is how this kind of novel ends, one feels. It is the whole difference between high literary talent and creative genius.

One would not wish to end on a cavilling note, however. *South Riding* is an honourable book, sincere and hard-headed, free of clap-trap and sentimental posturing. Its scale, ambition and subject matter all tended to a contemporary overvaluation; but if today it suggests an Everywoman's *Middlemarch* this is still to remember that George Eliot's masterpiece is one of our touchstones of social literature, and that Everywoman, not a coterie or clique, was the audience Winifred Holtby set herself to reach. Her success is, as much as her limitations are, an ironic comment on the relationship between literary taste and popular culture. Compared to Brett Young's detached good manners, her work has a refreshing urgency; and her success as a rural novelist may well lie in the fact that *South Riding* as one reads it does not appear to be a rural novel at all. Her love of the country, obvious in this and the earlier books, was not dependent on the exclusion of the town. Whatever her shortcomings as an artist, her attitudes to her subject matter were of the kind out of which the most universal art arises; and the inclusiveness of her approach highlights the limitations of so much rural fiction of the period – its lack of imaginative courage.

III

Brett Young and Winifred Holtby differ from the other novelists considered so far in that their methods were essentially panoramic: they were intent on placing the life of the country alongside that of the town, and their books have a breadth of outlook and comprehensiveness of treatment that make them well worth reading as social history.

Moreover, they both attempted to draw a representative cross-section of society, and were free from any taint of literary peasant-spotting. Their novels treat country people with respect, make a restrained use of dialect to point up social or regional differences, and are aware that country life is bound up economically with the town. Both writers were conscious of the forces of change, and were interested in what was happening around them. But, whereas Brett Young offset an observant awareness of the material life of his time with a rather too attenuated and individualistic response to natural beauty, Winifred Holtby was conscious of life as being essentially communal – her picture of rural society therefore has much greater cogency than his. But as rural novelists both suffer from a certain detachment. Brett Young's aesthetic romanticism has affinities with that of Walpole, and Winifred Holtby recalls Sheila Kaye-Smith in her recourse to conventional fictional methods to convey her understanding of reality; in neither case do we find a sense of close personal engagement with the rural theme as such. The balance between the response of the man leaning over the gate to admire the view and that of the man riding the tractor is hard to come by; but it is the latter whose feelings need to be understood by the novelist if the presentation of the former's viewpoint is not to be felt as sentimental. Luckily there were a number of farmers who were also novelists, and in the 1930s they were there to provide the right perspective.

7 Farmer Novelists:
H. W. Freeman, A. G. Street,
Adrian Bell

The rural fiction that emerged in the 1930s was, like so much other literature of the decade, concerned with economic problems. The more romantic treatments of country life gave place to first-hand and practical accounts of farming methods. The precise nature of the change in tone can be illustrated by comparing a passage from Thomas Moult's *Snow Over Eldon* (1920) with one from *Down in the Valley* by H. W. Freeman (b. 1899), which was published ten years later. Thomas Moult (1895–1974) a Derbyshire novelist and poet, was the biographer of Mary Webb.[1] His prose style has affinities with hers.

> Then did we drop silent at our work, and take our fill of the music of our heart's contentment – the sounds at milking time in that warm-smelling Red Oak farm shippon. Immortal sounds, changing not through the years or through the seasons of the years; whether in the seasons of sunsets that are like some huge dusky flagon of old wine, flooding through the low doorway across the rich silk of the cattle; or in the season of young swallows twittering in a nest amid the cobwebbed rafters when their mother flashes in with food and out again for more, and wondrous graceful, moreover; or in the season of white snows drifting up the outer wall even as they drifted about us that Sabbath white afternoon. Changeless sounds always. . . . More priceless, withal, in their simplicity than empires.[2]

Now Freeman:

> He looked down at the narrow trench in which he was standing,

dug deep because the land was wet – and indeed, the water was already oozing up around his feet. . . . A useful piece of work it would be. Next winter the field would grow a good crop of turnips which those ewes of theirs would be able to eat without sinking up to their knees in mud; the ewes would tread the soil firm and enrich it with their excrement, so that the following summer it would bear a good crop of barley; the barley-straw would come back, perhaps, to shelter the ewes at lambing in the winter (though Bob Kindred might have told him that barley-straw, as litter, always breeds vermin), and the grain would be ground to feed the pigs; the muck from the pig-styes would go to fertilize some fields across the valley and grow a crop of mangold to fatten the lambs which the ewes had borne; they in their turn would enrich another field; it was a cycle without end and he, too, had his place in it.[3]

This is something more than the shift from an emotive relationship with material things to one activated by a sense of function; it carries with it a shift also in literary tone and purpose. The passage from Moult seems designed for an audience which does not share in the life described; a work of mediation is going on, and of lazy incantation (the archaisms, the inversions, the pat moralising). Rural life is being de-vitalised. In Freeman's work, however, we find an absorbed interest in fact. *Joseph and His Brethren* (1928), his first novel, is the story of a Suffolk farm – and really of the farm: those who work on it are secondary to it. It is interesting to compare his treatment of Crakenhill with Sheila Kaye-Smith's use of her farms as backgrounds to individual dramas. Superficially there is much in common between *Joseph and His Brethren* and *Sussex Gorse*; but in the latter it is the character of Reuben Backfield which holds the stage, in the former the interaction of those who run the farm with the communal work of the farm. Different social perspectives inform the two books. Crakenhill is not only the creation of the Geaiter family, it is also their continuing mode of personal expression. When at the end of the book the dis-possessed brothers are warned off the land by its present owner they retort, 'Your land! You've only got to look at it to see it ain't ourn.'[4]

The novel, convincing in its detail, is as a story a mechanical affair; and the early chapters introducing the ferocious old farmer (called, in a manner characteristic of much rural fiction, Benjamin) and his six sons, seem contrived and wooden. However, with the arrival on the scene of the spirited village girl (called, again characteristically, Nancy), and her eventual marriage to Benjamin, the novel comes to life. Freeman is an adept hand at portraying a woman's point of view and he traces Nancy's career with sober sureness – from her early happy confidence; through her second marriage, to a wastrel; to her final degradation into listless indifference. Freeman's view of rural life is quite unsentimental; there is nothing picturesque about his portrait of Suffolk and of the local villagers, no quaint humours, no rhapsodies, no horrors. It is all very honest, if all a little dull. Later novels like *Fathers of Their People* (1932) and *Pond Hall's Progress* (1933) are equally pedestrian: fidelity of setting and carefulness of style does not compensate for the absence of any human beings in whom one can, as such, take much interest. In *Hester and Her Family* (1935) and *Andrew to the Lions* (1938) part of the story is set in Italy, which, by way of contrast, enhances the particularity of the Suffolk scenes. But both novels are rather shapeless and seem to have no very pronounced inner compulsion.

Freeman is alert to the changes in farming conditions, and *Pond Hall's Progress*, like Winifred Holtby's *Anderby Wold*, is in part a critique of paternalism in rural affairs. The climax of the novel occurs when Dick Brundish, who has inherited his farm, Pond Hall, is confronted by Major Hannay of the Suffolk Industrial Farming Syndicate, and finds that his neighbours have not shared his opposition to the case put before them so convincingly.

'It's a matter of votes. We've a population of some forty millions, and just about one million of them are on the land. If the rest want cheap imported bread – well, they'll get it. And then, of course, wages are three times what they were, with wages-boards there to keep 'em up, and all your other costs of production have gone up, and you've got feed bills and tithe and mortgage interest to pay, and its damned hard making ends meet. . . . Farming is an industry like any other, and must be carried on by industrial methods. What we want is mass-production of corn on fields of not less than a thousand acres. That's the only way to make farming pay. The small capitalist farmer, Mr. Brundish, is doomed.'[5]

In that passage the present-day transformation of the east Suffolk landscape is prefigured. Freeman, like his contemporaries A. G. Street and Adrian Bell, is much concerned with the lot of the small farmer, who in the work of all three novelists, Bell's especially, becomes an emblem of the individual Englishman beleaguered in the modern world. And Freeman is aware of the necessity for change. He may be attracted to the independence of a Benjamin Geaiter – 'he did not go to church, he owned his own house and all his land, he employed no outside labour; there was no quarter from which he could be attacked'⁶ – but he is also aware that Benjamin's independence is secured at the cost of his humanity, and by the end of *Joseph and His Brethren* he shows the family opening out their lives to include trips to the town and participation in the social life of the neighbourhood.

In the same novel he reminds us that

> those were the days when bread was baked once a week and eaten stale to prevent the children from being too hearty with it, when wages were a shilling a day and meat seldom or never seen in a labourer's cottage.⁷

His work is a deliberate corrective to earlier sentimental presentations of country life; and it is an undeserved irony that his first novel should have been introduced by his fellow East Anglian novelist R. H. Mottram⁸ in words arch enough to recall that very school from which his book rebels.

> After all you had better read this book, whether you think you will like it or not, just as you had far better refresh yourself with joint, dumplings, greens, 'taters, a bit of cheese and what pseudo-ancient inns miscall a tankard – but which Mr Freeman and I still call a mug – of draught ale, all of which this book strongly resembles, rather than with any cocktails ever concocted.⁹

Freeman deserves better than this: at his best he writes with simplicity and warmth, qualities which the rural novel can supply with a naturalness denied to much urban fiction. In *Hester and Her Family*, for instance, there are many scenes of quiet tenderness, scenes in which the Lawrentian sensuousness is achieved without effort or self-consciousness.

> [Charlie] and Hester were sleeping quite literally in each other's arms. It was only a few weeks since, almost by chance, they had been initiated into this new and profound pleasure. It had happened one Saturday night, just when it was time to blow the candle out.
>
> 'That do fare a pity,' said Charlie with a sigh, 'that I can't keep my arms around you all night long.'

'That wholly do,' agreed Hester, 'but I wonder why you can't.'

'Well, they do say,' said Charlie, at last bringing to light the old male superstition that was at the bottom of it all, 'they do say that all married folks want to do that, but they never can – they get cramp or sweat too much, or something.'

'Well, I should like to try for myself, anyhow,' said Hester quickly, with her eager, Athenian curiosity.

The next morning, to their extreme surprise and delight, they woke up to find themselves just where they had started the night before, and curled up so close to each other that you could hardly have slipped a knife between them.

'Well there,' said Charlie blinking drowsily, 'you do sleep wonderful quiet, and no mistake.'

'Oh, darling,' whispered Hester ecstatically, 'all night long in your arms! Just think of that!' and for the whole of that day, which was Sunday, they could think, could talk, of nothing else.[10]

The faint suggestion of humour in that final phrase gives the passage just the detachment that it needs, but there is no betrayal of the characters to the reader. It is this directness which makes Freeman a writer to respect; and as a recorder of farming life between the wars he is surpassed only by Adrian Bell and A. G. Street.

II

A. G. Street, (1892–1974) a Wiltshire farmer, had an immediate success with his first book, *Farmer's Glory* (1930). This was written at the suggestion of another Wiltshire writer, the novelist and biographer Edith Olivier, who urged him to follow in the wake of Adrian Bell's just-published *Corduroy* with an account of a farmer's life written to complement it 'from the inside out'.[11] It is an autobiographical account of country life in the author's boyhood and later, the central part describing his work on a farm in Canada. The book, unassuming and robust in style, led to a succession of novels and essays, all about country life. Street has a marked sense of history, and all his work is concerned with the practicality of farming, with its social aspects, and above all with the effect of farming upon character. His writing, unassuming and without obvious literary graces, is singularly faithful to its subject and full of shrewd comment on rural psychology.

Of his four pre-war novels, the first, *Strawberry Roan* (1932), is a tentative affair, centring around a calf and the vicissitudes of its various owners: it has a slightly naïve, informative character. Towards the close we are told of a young mother, whose baby is saved by the strawberry roan's milk, that 'she had not the faintest conception of all that had taken place . . . during the previous three years, which had made it possible for this particular bottle of milk to be available for her baby's feed that evening'.[12]

Three novels later Street is ambitiously essaying an equally didactic story about the future, in which a farmer, who is clearly the author's mouthpiece, acts as a rural Joseph in a national food shortage. But *Already Walks Tomorrow* (1938) lacks the kind of narrative propulsion necessary if this kind of book is to be rendered plausible. The two intervening novels, *The Endless Furrow* (1934) and *The Gentleman of the Party* (1936), are more authentic in tone and critically intelligent in what they have to say; and they abound in local detail, the central character being a focus for a more general portrait of a particular way of life.

Both novels cover a long period, and record change as it occurred over the early years of the century. Street has little of the townsman's aesthetic approach to scenery: *The Gentleman of the Party* portrays the landscape of south-west Wiltshire as it impinges on a simple labourer, being seen in terms of familiar shapes and colours, and above all in the nature of the crops. This novel is a valuable account of the various farming methods practised over thirty years, the urban theorists being repeatedly proved wrong in the light of the wisdom of the old labourer George Simmons, of whom it is said that 'The Land's his God'[13] At the end of the novel Street comments on this long chronicle of experimentation:

Alone in the party of folk who had had dealings with Sutton Manor during his lifetime he had served the land without expecting commensurate material gain in return. . . . He had given his whole life to Sutton fields with no thought of ambition or money gain; with no other desire than to obtain enough to satisfy his belly and provide a humble roof over his head. So much he had given; and so little, so very little he had received in return. Alone amongst them he had always put the land first and himself second.[14]

But Simmons is not sentimentally presented: Street is writing not for the delectation of townspeople, but, one senses, for the country people to whom he himself belonged. He wants to vindicate their struggles and way of life and to celebrate the world they recognised and loved. He is under no illusions, either, as to the hardship of conditions at the end of the previous century: *The Gentleman of the Party* celebrates the virtues of the agricultural labourer as virtues that exist in spite of the conditions imposed upon him by his employers. (Sheila Kaye-Smith's *The Ploughman's Progress* is a not dissimilar account). And Street has a nice line in mordant comment. Thus, writing of one labourer he remarks that, though he had only ten shillings a week on which to feed his family of ten,

> his wife was a wonderful manager, so he supposed there would be something for the Christmas dinner, although the Earl of Ashton's Christmas-box of a couple of rabbits had been eaten two days before.[15]

Of the groom–gardener, Shiner, he writes that his appearance

> was an eloquent illustration of England's curious habit, either in town or country, of always paying those who work for its sport and pleasure more highly than those who work for its food or its trade.[16]

Elsewhere George Simmons learns that 'a tired employee was much to be preferred to a tired horse'.[17]

> He thought how queer it was that even Farmer Martin, who had cut at him with his whip because he had let a waggon wheel go over a sheaf during the previous harvest, would ride over his own wheat field after hounds without caring.[18]

And at times he turns the familiar observation as to the naturalness of a rural upbringing to surprisingly bitter purpose.

> His work in the lambing-pen was also his initiation into the mysteries of birth and death. He learnt that the former entailed pain, and that the latter seemed to be quite pleasant by comparison; which, he decided, was according to his remembrance of the smile on his father's face just before the coffin had been screwed down, and the terrifying shrieks of his mother when his younger sister was born.[19]

This might have come from the hand of T. F. Powys.

Street not only describes: he analyses. In *The Endless Furrow*, the story of a young grocer who takes to farming, he writes of one village that

> there was not a sufficient number of any one social class of people to contrive a self-sufficient life among themselves, with the result that the whole of the population, owing to the poor transport facilities at that date, were forced to live together intimately as a friendly community.[20]

And his attitude to the village poor is compassionate, without a trace of fake emotion, treating them with a dry detachment that is the fruit of genuine respect.

> Their parents were very little affected by the tidings of the disgrace and death of Sally and Fred. They had bred their children; they had brought them up; and subsequently these children had disappeared. Dolly could not read, and George could spell out large print with difficulty, so any letters bearing bad news or good had to be taken to the Rector to be read; and, not being continually buffeted by news of their children's doings, the old people considered their little world at Sutton far more important than anything outside it. If children chose to leave it, as they made their bed, so they must lie on it. The garden by the cottage, the well-being of the cows, the life of Sutton Evias, all these things were real and vital; the outside world was an unknown quantity.[21]

It is of Dolly that Street comments, 'How could she not save? She had no experience of spending.'[22]

Street is characteristic of his time in that the aristocracy no longer command the romantic allegiance granted to it by earlier novelists. The Earl of Ashton is treated with genial satire as being limited as much as privileged by his position. The very friendliness of the author's approach makes it more deadly.

> 'The trouble is that the farm's too big for the men to tackle. Would your lordship consider splitting it into several holdings?'
>
> 'No, I'm damned if he will, Hayward. You ought to know what that'll mean. Bloody little buildings all over the place, the shootin' spoiled, and the countryside lookin' like a lot o' blasted allotments.'[23]

At other times he can strike a gentler note, while losing none of the edge of his irony. Farmer Morley has quarrelled with his wife:

He got up, threw some more logs on the fire, and crossed the room to his desk. There he played with some papers, rustling them busily. He filled and lit his pipe. The silence continued. . . . He crossed over to her chair.

'Sorry, missus. I have been a bit short sometimes I know, but I'm sorry. You're right about it, and I'm right as well, I expect, but don't 'ee take on.' He kissed her clumsily, told her that he had something to see to over in the farm buildings, patted her shoulder, and left the room with a sigh of relief.[24]

Not a remarkable novelist himself, Street is a valuable corrective to more original artists, providing a sound norm from which their achievements can be assessed. Its lack of affectation makes his work attractive: he is the least self-conscious of country writers, free from the rather limited provincialism of Freeman's early novels (the town may not concern him but he is no self-appointed ruralist) and devoid of fake heroics. It is true that as much as other rural writers he sees the land in terms which lend themselves to sentimental exploitation; but he is not afraid to take the feeling to its very unsentimental conclusion.

Farming waited no man's pleasure and similarly no man's grief. A realization of the everlasting quality of the land by comparison with all other things came to him with sudden force. Here was something which he could see, and which he could understand and respect. What mattered it if his son was killed, if countless sons of other parents suffered a like fate? The land never died, and its needs must be served.[25]

It seems a chilling message; but this Wiltshire farmer is here voicing a perennial fatalism which is the rural novelist's most consistent moral affirmation.

III

Corduroy by Adrian Bell (b. 1901) was published in the same year as *Farmer's Glory*, and together with *Silver Ley* (1931) and *The Cherry Tree* (1932) forms a trilogy that may well stand as the classic account of a twentieth-century Englishman's conversion to rural life. In spite of disclaimers in the second and third volumes, the work is clearly autobiographical,[26] and the characters and background have complete authenticity. Together the books describe their author's training as a farmer (*Corduroy*), his purchase of a farm of his own and his urban family's visit to him there (*Silver Ley*), and his marriage and final settling down to a rural existence (*The Cherry Tree*). *By-Road* (1937) forms a pendent, and Bell was to continue the series with *Apple Acre* (1942), *The Flower and the Wheel* (1949) and other books of a similar kind. He also published novels more deliberately fictional than the early work which elaborates his original theme, *The Balcony* (1934) reading like a spiritual autobiography. Bell's novels belong, in a way that Street's and Freeman's do not, to the English confessional tradition.

Essentially works of self-expression, they are free from the country writer's frequent tendency to write down, or (worse) coyly up to his readers: they are a matter of honest statement. But the *Corduroy* trilogy gains force from the way in which it is presented from an ex-townsman's point of view; and its opening paragraph is also its summing up.

> I was upon the fringe of Suffolk, a county rich in agricultural detail, missed by my untutored eye. It was but scenery to me: nor had I an inkling of what more it might become. Farming, to my mind, was as yet the townsman's glib catalogue of creatures and a symbol of escape. The true friendliness of the scene before me lay beneath ardours of which I knew nothing.[27]

The ardours are not unduly stressed: the tone of Bell's account of his apprenticeship is gently ironic and, more frequently, admiringly interested. He learns a new perspective on things, above all a feeling for beauty as bound up with function, finding himself

> touched always with a sense of things that flash and shine with use among the mire they move in; it is always a little miracle of transfiguration – ploughshares, iron toe-pieces of men's boots, fork-prongs, and chains.[28]

And accompanying this is a quiet austerity of language that gives to his descriptions a precise sense of things seen. In his early work the style is notably direct and plain.

> There is an air of fulfilment and rest in the landscape and brooding weather of October. It is like a ghost of summer evening all the time; the faint spears of shadow, the sun's shield tarnished and hanging low, and under the trees, instead of shade, pools of their fallen

colours. The fields, being mostly stubble, have still the straw-gold light of summer, but the ploughs move there, as in the very afterglow of harvest, and the earth is gradually revealed again that has not been seen since spring.[29]

There is a sensibility here akin to that of Edward Thomas.[30] The rhythms are flexible and sure, the effect of incantation barely noticeable. But above all, the three sentences contain a sense of continuing process: they do not depict a mere spectacle, but something lived with and understood. So, too, Bell can achieve an effect reminiscent of some Dutch landscape:

> After dinner the men were out in the village allotments. Their women stood at their doors gossiping with one another, their arms folded, their hands clasping their bare arms. One old woman was scratching at the earth with a hoe. The land drains had ceased to run, and the cottage people went again to the spring in the hazel coppice whence they drew their water all summer. They stood staring at the clear pool which moved slightly, like a creature newly born just stirring into life. Around, the hazel catkins caught the sun, swaying softly. There was an invisible warm presence in the air, uncertain, like a butterfly flitting to and fro, touching arms and cheeks, then gone again.[31]

Bell always conveys a sense of life going on, of the working of the landscape: he is not interested in mere aesthetics, and neatly catches the shallowness of those townspeople who know the country only at a literary secondhand. On his return to his family for Christmas the author of *Corduroy* finds that

> I was called 'Giles' or 'Hodge', and treated to enquiries of ' 'Ow be thoi mangel-worzels?' Either that or I was a courageous self-eman-cipator, the wind whistling through my hair.[32]

The passage is the more effective after the undramatic and selfless account that Bell has already given of the life at Farley Hall Farm.

Like Street and Freeman, he is concerned for the position of the in-dependent farmer, and, like the latter, introduces a syndicate into his account of change. In *By-Road* he describes an enterprising newcomer who starts a fruit farm on the unpromising Suffolk soil; and, while conservative by temperament, he is aware of the benefits of modern inventions. His work keeps a nice balance between old and new ways; his characters are never mere types or embodied attitudes: Mr Colville, for instance, the farmer in *Corduroy*, is quite prepared to sell up and move if it seems practical to do so. There is none of the passion for a particular parcel of land as such which motivates the plots of, for example, *Sussex Gorse* or *Joseph and His Brethren*. Bell has little time for the smallholder who 'bartered the pleasures of life for an illusory independence'[33] – though he was to modify this view in his most subtle novel, *The Shepherd's Farm* (1939). And he is quietly scathing about the shopkeeper Mr Jolman's 'suburban' garden, whose 'vegetable region was screened away'.[34] The 'vegetable region' and what it stands for is the real heart of Adrian Bell's world.

The incursion of the author's family in *Silver Ley*, however, with their excited adoption of a more primitive way of life, provides a delicate and amusing slant upon the 'back to the country' romanticism of the 1920s. The author both applauds it and them, relishing their vitality and company; but in the end he finds them an impediment to the kind of quiet farming life he seeks. He knows that the country 'wasn't an escape . . . it was a wonderful grappling influence, like love in its depths and darkness'.[35] And it is the coming of love, and the beautifully drawn picture of conjugal happiness, that makes *The Cherry Tree* the natural climax of the trilogy. It is, perhaps, the nearest to a genuine pastoral idyll that twentieth-century English literature affords: genuine because rooted in the present, not in the past. There is a perfect chastity of style and outlook.

Bell's achievement gains in depth from the way in which he weds the world of outward objectivity with an awareness of interior, spiritual life. *The Balcony*, which stands apart from the rest of his work, is an account of the traditional springs of vision in the life of a young boy, and written in a more elaborate prose than is the rest of his work. It is the record of the discovery of 'a touchstone of an inner freedom'.[36] If we take the story of Roland Pace as autobiographical, we have an extended understanding of *The Cherry Tree*. What Roland sees and finds in his childhood in Kensington and the village of Pabbleton is achieved definitively in the experienced life of a farmer. Farming is the most fundamental of all occupations, 'for ultimately the earth is our only sustenance'.[37]

Bell's romanticism is modulated by his awareness of historical process: all his work is concerned with a present that is accepted even when it is criticised. Nor is his absorption in farming such as to rule out of account a love for the arts and an appreciation of literature:

references to a situation being 'Strindbergian'[38] or the account of the harpsichord player in *By-Road* help to extend perspectives. Perhaps the most succinct account of Bell's balance between the idealism of the past and the practical concerns of the present comes in *The Balcony*, where he remarks of Roland's elderly aunts that 'Life viewed as spiritual opportunity was the excuse for much that darkened their age, but also the inspiration of that singleness of mind which is the individual salvation'.[39] Adrian Bell's vision of the farmer is of one who embodies in his very occupation that singleness of mind: he is a custodian of primal values in a changing, unsettled civilisation.

For the most part Bell is content to demonstrate this descriptively, in his accounts of the farmer's year, his part in the local community and the satisfactions and hardships of his physical lot. But in *Folly Field* he does to some extent dramatise it in the story of Dick Jevons. Dick is a farmer's son who, on his father's death, turns down the chance of going to Cambridge in favour of carrying on the running of the farm. His decision, taken during his father's funeral in a storm, is described in a manner that reveals the author's awareness of the inter-action between physical happening and spiritual response.

Dick was wrung, but not with grief. . . . His whole life and body seemed shedding away in the storm and music, the passionate accept-ance of a tree that sheds its blossom in a sudden gust, its fruit set. And after that a sense of bare, spare beauty, and a new germination.

The conflict that had been gathering in him ever since his brother's going, broke forth now, was broken up and decided; not in thought, but at the source beyond, where the hereditary being murmurs like the sea in its caves. Self is a bird that rides that sea. Association swayed him, unresisting.

The storm was the farm. Not thunder, but sown wheat storming up, and frost shattering clods. The eternal silent violence of earth gripped him. His father now was of the power behind the visible and individual. He felt the smallness, the straw-like lightness of himself, the smallness of that which dies. He felt in the music and storm the press of power about him. He was a little magnetised point, and power, a common power, accumulated about it. He knew in his heart what was being decided in him.[40]

Adrian Bell rarely writes with this degree of intensity, but the under-lying presuppositions inform all his work: there is an integral relation-ship between man and the natural order: man does not simply walk about on the surface of the earth, he is made out of it, is responsive at untapped levels to its life. Hence the essential rightness of Dick's comment about Sally, the village girl who he has loved and who has run away to be an actress – a comment that shocks his patroness, the 'cultured' Mrs Carter.

> 'I reckon it's like when you've got a pretty good animal, you think, at home in the yard; but when you see it beside others on the show ground – '
>
> 'Dick – how *could* you compare – ' she admonished, 'It's such a pity you've let farming blunt you like that.'
>
> He smiled slowly at her fining things into emotional shades within her walls.
>
> 'Sorry – I didn't mean it that way. Still, it wouldn't ever have worked, you know.'
>
> 'It would have, if you'd been as I'd hoped. But still, it seems to be reducing such a thing to the lowest terms, considering whether it would "work" or not "work". Such a yeoman outlook – as though it were a tractor.'
>
> 'I mean – ' Dick began to explain, but she stated with finality, 'Love between a man and a woman is the only thing that matters in life.'
>
> He could no longer bridge the gulf that had grown between her inward and his outward life.[41]

The matter, if not the style, is Lawrentian; and in the account of Dick's relations with his wife we have a sensuousness that reminds one of *The Rainbow*.

Similarly the image of the gull at the end of the novel suggests Lawrence, in the use of animal life for symbolic ends; but it is less integrated into the action than are, for example, the rabbit or the mare in *Women in Love*. Nevertheless it recalls the earlier statement that 'self is a bird that rides that sea'.

> In that patient yet half-voluptuous sufferance of the gale there seemed a sardonic recognition that this muscular parrying of death was all; that the halcyon promise of the distance was mere lure – the adventitious was the only beauty.[42]

Folly Field ends on a note of subdued pessimism as the charming Folly is pulled down to make way for a main road; but it is balanced by the birth of Dick's child.

In *By-Road* Adrian Bell portrays the new world and the old working side by side, sometimes in conflict and always qualifying each other. His own powers of self-criticism are such that he can embody them in a dramatised conversation between himself and the go-ahead farmer, Rayner. Rayner refuses to employ the older labourers on his fruit farm, on the grounds that 'They're individualists.'

'Craftsmen.'

'Well – yes, if you like. They won't combine. It would be hopeless, for instance, to try to explain to them the idea behind all this, to fire them with it. Each person of this organisation is a necessary part, but only a part, and is efficient in proportion as he is working for the good of the thing as a whole. And the thing as a whole is a unit of modern life, and a grasp of the idea sufficient to breed enthusiasm for it is only possible with a knowledge of the modern conditions of life into which it fits. Of course they can have no such idea. The village is their world : half the people they talk about are dead.'

'Yet their lives have been full and satisfying lives – even culturally : not narrow in the deeper sense.'

'Because traditional. They did not look beyond the limits of home; and their satisfaction in life was in the feel of things rather, the knack of handling tools, the judgement of the products of their native place. Individualist, you see.'

'But each one reflected the village as a whole.'

'Perhaps – but at any rate it was a life of the senses. They could never feel the reality of an idea as a thing to work for. But modern life has broken down the limits which allowed them contentment . . . the young men would never be satisfied with what satisfied them; it isn't natural. It's only educated people like you who have potentially been through the whole range of "modernity" . . . that grasp a body-and-soul satisfaction in – in a hand-made wheel. And even that,' he laughed, 'is half nostalgia.'[43]

Here the ideas associated with the work of George Sturt are placed in a historical perspective; and the tragedy of the decay of rural England is transformed into something more positive. The power of idealism is related to a way of life which gives to Bell himself a satisfaction that harmonises with his own particular ideal. If his own attitude provides a norm, he is not beyond portraying its opposite without recrimination. His view of country life is presented not so much in antagonism

E

to the modern world as being that world's origin and centre. Observing a swarm of bees he reflects that

> men, when they work in unanimous myriads like that, are no more than this multitude of bees, crawling on the face of the earth, building up they know not why. Only the individual is transcendent, sitting aloof with his faculties balanced and true to him, his instinct seeking the stars for touchstone, or sitting alone in his garden enjoying the godhead of observation of hurried lesser life.[44]

And in modern society only the farmer seems to be an acceptable embodiment of that individuality – more acceptable than the artist, because more obviously concerned with what makes for life and growth. And Adrian Bell succeeds in relating the farmer to the modern world in his own person and in his simple and yet sophisticated books. The man and his writings form a single whole, both in the way in which those writings express his life, and in their value as projections of a personal vision. His work is more than of sociological significance : it is the creation of an authentic artist.

IV

To say that Adrian Bell is the best writer about country life since Sturt is not to say that he is a major novelist. Indeed, it would seem that the split between town and country life on which fiction has thriven demands a complexity of treatment beyond the aim or scope of the genuinely rural artist. The fidelity to what they see and hear and know of country life leads in all three of these 'farmer' novelists to a turning away not only from complex psychological concerns, but also from symbolism and romance, away indeed from a large part of the concerns of fiction. The truth of fiction is not the same thing as the truth of documentary; and valuable as all three writers are as recorders of a particular phase of social history, only Adrian Bell creates, instead of merely recording, a world. It is a considerable achievement. Bell combines a steady, almost documentary, account of the social realities of country life with a deep aesthetic response to landscape; he has a personal involvement, both physical and spiritual, in the life he describes.[45] Without being a major writer, he indicates where, for the rural novelist, greatness lies.

All these farmer novelists have the merit of being single-minded in their work; whatever its limitations, it is firmly concentrated on its subject matter. In this they compare favourably with the novelists discussed earlier, most of whom are half-hearted or confused in their handling of the rural theme. Their drawback, Bell apart, is a certain dullness. They lack intensity; perhaps because their subject matter has so totally absorbed them. In them the artist subserves the countryman. For this reason they cannot be regarded as the most interesting rural *novelists*, though they are arguably the most satisfactory rural writers.

8 The Land of Lost Content: Henry Williamson, Llewelyn Powys

The lyrical note that sounds through the work of Adrian Bell springs from a profound and common apprehension: the sense that man, being animal, is himself a part of the natural order and is at home there. It is found in accounts of rural childhood such as Herbert Read's *The Innocent Eye* (1933) or Edwin Muir's *The Story and the Fable* (1940);[1] and the view of childhood voiced in Wordsworth's 'Ode on Intimations of Immortality from Recollections of Early Childhood' (which, however, combines this sense of belonging with a feeling of exile) has passed into the English imaginative tradition, apparently to stay.[2] The lives of country children are often described in the fiction of this period, Kenneth Grahame's *The Golden Age* (1895) and *Dream Days* (1897) being succeeded by such popular books as Arthur Ransome's *Swallows and Amazons* (1930) and its successors. The latter are in the tradition of Richard Jefferies's *Bevis* (1882), where a boyish interest in practical affairs offsets any tendency to precocious feelings. But the most remarkable of these books is Henry Williamson's *The Beautiful Years* (1921), where Jefferies's influence is felt in a more ambiguous manner.

The reputation of Henry Williamson is a good example of the divorce between academic and popular standards: a writer of manifest and serious dedication, he has received scant notice in literary history, while enjoying a steady reputation among educated readers as a major and neglected figure. He was born in 1895, and served in the trenches in the First World War, an experience which was to be the mainspring of his career as a novelist. But it would seem that the experience of war, directly recorded in his novel *The Patriot's Progress* (1930), only confirmed a prior pessimism and sensitivity to pain. His earliest published essay, reprinted in his first collection, *The Lone Swallows* (1922), but written in 1914, is a description of a barn owl hunting; and he was to adopt this bird as his own literary crest. The pursuit-and-prey theme dominates all his nature stories. These tales remain his best known and most generally successful work; and they are the natural background to the novels – natural in more senses than one. In all of them a detailed and loving absorption in animal and bird life is accompanied by an equal absorption in the ways in which nature renews her life through death. An extraordinary fidelity and closeness of observation is matched by an emotional intensity, an obsession with pain and cruelty, giving these books, the short stories especially, an almost hypnotic vividness. Williamson portrays a world in which men and women are only one breed among many other inhabitants: we see the familiar landscape through a falcon's eyes, a badger's, a wild deer's. And the effect is the more impressive from the almost total lack of sentimentality with which the animals and birds are depicted: there is no attempted humanising of them, no prettifying, no whimsy. Moreover, in *Tarka the Otter* and *Salar the Salmon* the greater length enables Williamson to portray a whole way of living that is at once strange and illuminating, and yet parallel to, and illustrative of, the perennial human struggle for survival. In these animal stories Williamson projects a genuine world of his own, self-contained and, if narrow, percussive in the mind from the force of a virtuoso in prose.

[The peregrine falcon] had seen the pigeons wheeling above Scarnell Court, a white house ten miles away, and standing in a wood on the slope of the River Taw, just before Barnstable. One hundred seconds passed, and he was half-way over the lonely sandhills and the wastes of the Burrows. Above the ribs of wrecked boats embedded in the flats he passed, losing height as he stepped downward like a hissing and shankless anchorhead of iron. One hundred and fifty seconds, and now he was passing a train and its tiny string of white steam, as it crawled beside the estuary and its fawn sandbanks. Two hundred and eighty seconds, and the pigeons saw what was hurtling upon them; they scattered like torn paper thrown to the wind; the terror was above them, and falling vertically in a relentless stoop. The scream of the tiercel rose in pitch; at over two hundred miles an hour he fell. Now the pigeons were dashing into the trees, all except one that was neck-limp and clutched in the tiercel's talons; now an old gentleman, dozing in a chair on the lawn below was alarmed by the blood-splashes that appeared suddenly on his book.[4]

In the compiler's note with which he prefaces *The Lone Swallows*, Williamson states the creed which is at the heart of his novels.

My own belief is that association with birds and flowers in childhood – when the brain is plastic and the mind is eager – tends to widen human sympathy in an adult life. The hope of civilisation (since we cannot remake the world's history) is in the fraternity of nations, or so it seems to myself, whose adolescence was spent at the war; the hope of amity and goodwill of the nation is in the individual – in the human heart, which yearns for the good and for the beautiful; and the individual is a child first, eager to learn, but unwilling to be taught.[5]

The passage is symptomatic of what was to follow: the faint note of (understandable) querulousness, the sense of deprival, was to emerge in the *Flax of Dream* tetralogy as a sustained bitterness of tone. It is this bitterness which gives its particular character to Williamson's otherwise traditional romanticism, just as it is his awareness of the in-built cruelty of nature which qualifies his acceptance of her as a teacher. But he is fully in line with that nineteenth-century English tradition that sees the child as the gauge not only of innocence but also of personal fulfilment. In *The Flax of Dream* Williamson gives a systematic presentation of this theme.

The tetralogy comprises *The Beautiful Years*, which tells of Willie Maddison's country boyhood and of his relationship with his widowed father; *Dandelion Days* (1922), which contains a mordant account of his education at a small local public school; *The Dream of Fair Women* (1924), which moves to the immediate post-war years and tells of Maddison's unhappy love affair; and *The Pathway* (1928), which recounts his final doomed bid for happiness and understanding, and his death by drowning. The four novels came out in a single, revised volume in 1936.

There can be no question of Williamson's intentions in writing them: together they form a considered and deeply felt critique of traditional English educational methods, and of modern industrial society. His master (as is made apparent by somewhat wearisome repetition) is Richard Jefferies, an author about whom Williamson is inclined to be proprietorial in his enthusiasm.

Had he not, like Jefferies, entirely and utterly rejected civilization – civilization that was worse than barbarism – since it chained a man to slavery in its factories and towns, and as compensation, released him so that he might mutilate or be mutilated in order to save that civilization?[6]

But industrialisation for Williamson is secondary to faulty education – and is the result of it. The imagination, fed by nature, is the only true guide; but Willie Maddison's schooling ends in

the summer of 1914, which was to see the apotheosis of ideas and methods which everywhere had crushed the imaginative tissues of childhood, as the young leaves of dandelions on the Gadarene slopes.[7]

The Great War is the logical consequence of attitudes such as those of Willie's father, who, failing to understand the importance to his son's inner being of his life among the woods and fields, dispatches him with the words, 'You're going to Colham Grammar School, to play football and learn to be a man.'[8] The irony is a cruder version of that met in E. M. Forster's novels.[9] Colham Grammar School is presented amusingly enough as a breeder of moral duplicity: the boys are forced to use their mental faculties not to learn wisdom but

to avoid unnatural mental and nervous stress. Lightly and easily they knew that they were liable, if detected, to be caned as cheats and hypocrites, never realising how their minds were being served by the protective instincts deeply rooted within their very beings.[10]

But the vitality of the boys does much to offset the folly of the system; and ironically these school chapters of *The Flax of Dream* are far healthier in tone and more tonic in effect than the over-intense and tormented childhood chapters. We are told that Willie liked to 'dream back into the ancient sunlight of his past happiness' but it is the *un*-happiness of his early days which the books most persistently portray. This may be because in the character of Willie's father the author has drawn a highly convincing study of a conscientious, emotionally in-hibited man, baffled by the unruly child for whom he is responsible and who is afraid of him; while the woodland scenes and boyhood adven-tures are frequently marred by overwriting and turgidity – a fault of which, to judge from his preface, Williamson was aware, but which he felt to be appropriate to the emotional age of the protagonist. The result is, however, sentimental and at times embarrassing.

> 'Oh Phil, can you see the moon?'
> 'Yes, isn't it beautiful. Do you like music, Willie?'
> 'Yes, only I seldom hear any.'
> 'Father's just bought a wonderful gramophone. It's glorious – it's – it's like the trees outside now; and the wind, and the lovely moonlit clouds.'
> 'Phillip, can you see the moon? I often think it's like a – oh, you'll think me soppy – '
> 'No I shan't, honestly Willie. Go on.'
> 'It's like a maiden walking in heaven, isn't it?'
> 'Yes, I understand. I love the moon, too.'[11]

The trouble is that this *is*, in effect, soppy – not on Willie's part but on the author's.

What makes these boyhood chapters memorable is their wealth of observation. Tree-climbing, bird-nesting, rescuing trapped animals, Willie and his friend Jack (who is to be killed at the Western Front) enjoy a series of constantly renewed adventures; calf-love intrudes, but nothing can displace the primacy of life in the open air. *Bevis* is not only cited but serves as a model. The descriptions of the woods and fields are meticulous, even laboured; the presence of wild life at times assumes the nature of a catalogue. And everything is pitched in a high emotional key.

> Over the dark outline of the beech wood hung a star, a lustrous globe of radiance, larger than any star Willie had ever seen. They watched it in silence. Slowly it moved higher, glowing with softer and purer blaze as it was lapped by the light now flowing into the eastern estuary of heaven. It was neither white nor golden nor would any colour describe it: the darkness paled before the spectral dawn. Looking up into the sky, he saw that the stars were keener than before. Light, mystic light, the life of the world, was flooding like an incoming tide into the dusked shallows of the dawn. Gradually the footpath through the field showed up; from among the corn a lark rose singing into the sky – he too had seen the Morning Star. Another and another fluttered upwards till it seemed that a dozen trickles fell from the overspilling font of sky. Then the church steeple loomed in the murkiness, and the vapour lying below in the

water-meadows assumed a wandering and phantom semblance before the risen wind. A thrush flung clear notes from an oak outstanding in the covert; a pheasant crowed sharply. Immediately it seemed that the world was one great melody. As it rose higher the light-bringer shone with whiter fire; one by one the stars in deeper heaven grew wan and sunk into the waters of day. Like a motionless sea, light swept up the sky, purging it of darkness, glowing in the lofty empyrean, bringing life and joy to living things.[12]

At its best Williamson's prose can attain great eloquence and beauty: the musical qualities of the above passage are obvious, and the imagery is finely controlled and apprehended. But with the eloquence there comes after a while a sense of over-contrivance; the simplicity of childhood vision is overlaid with literary words. Beauty is being asserted and presented, rather than evoked.

Significantly, Williamson's rhapsodic prose works better in the early chapters of *The Dream of Fair Women*, where Willie's love affair with Evelyn Fairfax (a convincing mixture of sympathy and selfishness) is set against the background of the north Devon coast, the setting of most of Williamson's nature writing. Such passion is more suited to sexual love than it is to boyhood – and the substitution of the one theme for the other indicates obliquely what is wrong with Williamson's portrayal of childhood: it suggests (in keeping, admittedly, with his central thesis that 'the hope of the world, of the human race, is in the child') a reluctance on the author's part to stand far enough away from childhood and to detach himself from too great an emotional involvement. Indeed *The Dream of Fair Women*, with its evocation of the hectic post-war world, provides a better theme for Williamson's temperamental and stylistic intensity to work on than does the boyhood world of Willie Maddison; and it also contains what is lacking in the earlier books, an effective internal questioning of the author's attitudes. Thus on the one hand there is the kind of language that Willie uses to Evelyn:

'Care for me for ever and ever. There is no other refuge for me. In you I lose all the broken past – my childhood, the war, all wretched things. You are true – all the while, Eve. You are sunlight. I just stumble trying to find Truth, ancient sunlight. Love me from everlasting to everlasting.'[13]

After a good deal of this sort of thing it is refreshing when Evelyn loses patience:

'I am tired of you following me about like a shadow, questioning my movements. When you're not doing that you're babbling about the resurrection or something of mankind by association in childhood with birds and weeds and wind, and other unintelligible weariness.'[14]

But although Williamson is able to imagine people reacting in this way, he seems insufficiently detached from his hero to take their criticisms further. And this self-identification is taken to oppressive lengths in *The Pathway*.

In this novel Maddison returns to north Devon and to a girl who has loved him from childhood and who tries to understand him: she is called, rather predictably, Mary. Maddison, threatened with nervous collapse as a result of his unhappy experiences in love and war, withdraws to lead an eremitical existence, preaching a kind of Franciscan gospel of love and peace. He becomes a source of social embarrassment and is finally asked by Mary's mother to leave her home. He is drowned crossing the estuary when the tide comes in. The ending of the tetralogy is not, however, entirely negative. Maddison's lesson has been learned by Mary, and he comes to be regarded as a Christ figure, a martyr and prophet. 'He was too good to live among us, and so he was taken away.'[15]

An intense melancholy informs *The Pathway*. As in *The Beautiful Years*, trapped animals are a symbol of universal pain.

'They trap ten thousand [rabbits] every year on the Burrows. And the trapping rent just keeps Bonnie at school. Ten thousand screams in the darkness every year. . . .'
'The story of the Burrows is the story of all the world.'[16]

And the novel is full of people unhappily in love: Willie and Mary, Mary's hoyden sister Jean, their friend Diana Shelley. And there is another repressed child, in whom Willie sees his boyhood lived again. The landscape, the vast lonely expanse of the Burrows, the tidal estuary, the distant moors, is in keeping with the prevailing mood. Whatever its shortcomings, Williamson's work has an unforgettable impact: one may resist it, but it is hard to shake it off. The impact, however, is that of obsessive art: it narrows one's awareness of life rather than expands it.

In the last resort what prevents acceptance of the claims for Williamson's early achievement is the prevailing element of self-pity to be found in it. And there is an accompanying luxuriance about the pessimism.

> It would seem, therefore, that all endeavour was futile: the species might have its guardian, its godhead; but there was no heavenly protection for the individual: from dust it came, whether man or weed, and to dust it returned, its life like a spark struck from flint. In the light of fact, how feeble and frighteningly baseless seemed the imagined creeds and religions of mankind, of black man, of brown man, of white man – all so certain of eternal happiness after death.[17]

The rhetorical enumeration of races smacks of self-indulgence: pessimism demands austerity in its expression. And this point can be illuminated further if we turn to the stark account of the sheep dying in the drought.

> They were scraggy, gasping in the heat, fixing their eyes upon him as though beseeching green grass. He saw that the flanks of several were crawling with maggots, that even now heavy-winged flies were laying the eggs which shortly would hatch. The sheep showed no fear of the dogs; they had come to him, who appeared as a godhead, for relief: while overhead in a sky blue and hard as a sapphire burned the sun. One lay down, a froth on its nostrils. Its sides were red and raw. Its woolly skin flapped on its side like stiff leather. Maggots had eaten it loose. He contemplated the agony of the dying animal. Was there a beneficent deity directing all earthly endeavour – caring for the things it had created? Six months since, and half the world was a shambles, men destroying one another.[18]

Here the points are made without any flourishing, and with that closeness of physical observation which is one of the author's strengths.

That Williamson is himself aware of this split literary personality (the author of *The Old Stag*, for example, writing 'A titlark in corant dive of joy fell behind them, in its bill a song-straw pulled from the sun')[19] is suggested by his analysis of the two styles of Richard Jefferies. 'One of them is straightforward and concrete, the style of a natural man.' That, with some elaboration, might pass for the style of Williamson's early stories, and for a good deal of *The Flax of Dream*, certainly that which went to the account of the headmaster of Colham school, the maid Biddy, the local Devonshire gentry, the villagers at Rookhurst, and, above all, the wayward, unpredictable Evelyn. But Jefferies has another style,

> a candent, often incandescent, flow of words driven from him, as he wrote, by his daemon (in Shelleyan language): the daemon being his repressed or mortified self.[20]

The daemon in Henry Williamson seems at times to be self-consciously invoked: indeed, that his writing is vitiated by posturing can be seen from even a casual extract from, for instance, *The Labouring Life* (1932), in which he refers to 'my winged relative the aerymouse – for we are related through the common ancestor God, which nowadays is confirmed by science'.[21] The whole tone here is uneasy, a man listening to himself rather than a man talking to others. Williamson does not seem to have had quite the courage of his conviction that the average man was denaturalised.

> The remedy is not to teach Shakespeare to children, but let the spirit of earth, arising naturally for each child, make him into a Shakespeare![22]

Such faith is, in his own practice, compromised by didacticism.

This may account for what must be, to contemporary readers of *The Flax of Dream*, its most disturbing element. Williamson's admiration for Adolf Hitler is a response in keeping with the sado-masochistic note that runs through the whole tetralogy. The constant harping on animal violence and psychological oppression, the tormenting of Maddison by his teachers, his father, his mistress, is balanced by a kind of repressed savagery that results in a rejection of ordinary human companionship. When Williamson writes in his preface of 1935, 'I salute the great man across the Rhine, whose life symbol is the happy child', one gets an unpleasant feeling that something repressed and then over-indulged is avenging itself; and the unease is increased by the statement in the body of the novel that

> there is an ex-corporal with the truest eyes I have ever seen in any man, now rousing the young men and the ex-soldiers, to save the nation from disintegration: a man who doesn't smoke or drink, a vegetarian, owning no property, living for the sun to shine on the living.[23]

The English rural tradition had come to a strange pass when it fathered that misapprehension.

Henry Williamson is certainly among the most controversial and curious novelists of his time. That his work cannot be assessed solely in terms of *Tarka the Otter* and *The Flax of Dream* is obvious in view of his long series of post-war novels about Willie Maddison's cousin Phillip, *A Chronicle of Ancient Sunlight*, which provides a corrective to the distortions in his earlier work. But, however high or low one ranks his ultimate achievement, he is a genuine novelist: that is to say, for him the novel is a necessary form of personal expression and of discovery; and he is, with Constance Holme, Adrian Bell and the Powys brothers, one of the few writers who shared Lawrence's ability, in however restricted a form, to make of the rural experience an authentic and exploratory means of self-expression. To question the value of what is thereby expressed is not to question the force and skill of its literary presentation. Williamson is one of those writers about whom debate is likely to continue, in view of the powerful way in which he plays on the rural theme; but the continuance of the debate is itself a witness to his literary vitality. In its anger and self-conscious-ness and idealistic fervour his early work is like an exposed nerve in the body of twentieth-century fiction.

II

For lyrical intensity of utterance Williamson is matched in this period only by Llewelyn Powys (1884–1939). A younger brother of John Cowper and T. F. Powys, he is a very different writer from either of them, though sharing in, and frequently celebrating in his essays, their rich and fulfilling family life. The Powys brothers were children of the parsonage. Their father was an ardent naturalist and their upbringing combined religious observance with freedom to roam the woods and fields of Somerset and Dorset. This blend of discipline and liberty was to prove a fruitful preparation for life. Unfettered access to a good library, a community of intellectual interests and passionate expressions of individual feeling made for an unusually close-knit family world – a world, however, that was to be liberating and not a prison. A country life in this case proved seminal for wider cultural achievements.[14]

Although markedly different as personalities, as writers the three brothers share a certain doughty grimness: it manifests itself in a style which can move from the homely through the bookish to the unaffectedly majestic. This Powys temperament is exhibited in a very pure form in the one published novel by Philippa Powys (1886–1963), that 'mysterious and singular girl', as her brother Llewelyn described her, 'who . . . would sometimes appear to be the embodiment of the wind she so much loved'.[25] *The Blackthorn Winter* (1930) is a simple tale of a farm girl's infatuation with a gipsy, and of her life with him on the roads; it has an unsentimental realisation of the hardships of such an existence. What gives it its especial distinction is its intensity and compression. The style is rather stiff, and knotty with inversions; but it is subtle in its use of rural imagery, is never inflated, and clearly arises from the world which it describes. This really is a 'rural' novel; the West Country lanes and fields and downs are felt not just as landscape but as territory worked upon and wandered over. Nor does the book give the impression of being written for an urban readership. The author is as aware as were her brothers of the changing moods of landscape and of the fact of pain.

> The young cow had calved, but the calf was dead. Cautiously Nancy peered between wild herbage upon them. The cow kept uttering low mournful blares as her heavy head bent over the wet form of the still-born, while its lifeless jaws flopped noiselessly under the strong cleansing tongue of the bereaved mother. Around, the ground was trampled and marked with blood. The cow was humped with pain; the afterbirth trailed behind as the creature washed its dead with zealous care. . . . It brought to her visions of the time when the animal, wild with excitement, was turned out with the bull; and now what was the end? Only pain and misery.[26]

The directness of this is akin to that of T. F. Powys; the slight clumsiness only goes to enhance the sense of desolation. At the end of *The Blackthorn Winter* Nancy returns to her faithful lover, but both of them are changed. The romantic vision has been followed at the cost of hardship and sorrow.

Llewelyn Powys, while equally aware of the ruthlessness of nature, also saw in it a force by which men needed to assess their own ideals and needs; his residence in East Africa, recorded graphically in *Black Laughter* (1925), taught him much in this respect. Of the three brothers he was the one most attuned to the modern world; but he was also the one who sang the praises of rural life most persistently. The woods and pastures of Willie Maddison's boyhood are not described more fervently than are the woods and orchards of Somerset and Dorset in *Love and*

Death (1939) and Llewelyn's numerous essays. Indeed, all his writings – they also include travel books and philosophical works of a fervidly anti-religious cast – have a strong personal reference; while his auto-biographical works are written in a dramatised form that makes them read like fiction – in this they resemble his brother John Cowper's great *Autobiography*. Like Lawrence, Llewelyn Powys had keenly developed sense perceptions, and again like Lawrence he fought off a wasting disease by a passionate celebration of the natural world. Although he is an altogether lesser writer (lacking Lawrence's width of interests, complexity and sense of dialectic), his single-mindedness is persuasive, and gives to his rather random and scattered writings an authority which they would not otherwise possess.

He was not an instinctive novelist in the way that his brothers were; and he himself had no high opinion of his one work of formal fiction, *Apples Be Ripe* (1930).[27] It is an attack on restrictive attitudes to sexuality and on social conformism. Chris Holbeech, an obvious self-portrait, marries a schoolmaster's niece, and leaves her for a tramp's life in the West Country, where he has two love affairs and dies of rheumatic fever. The last part of the book is curiously unreal, con-sidering that it takes us to the country of the author's happy boyhood; but the early chapters, modelled on his experiences of schoolteaching,[28] have a certain crude vigour. But Powys, unlike Williamson, caricatures his enemies instead of trying to understand them, though Adela, the wife, rings true enough, especially in her attitude to sex – 'Why do you always want to be horrid?' – and there is a genuine pathos in her efforts to come to terms with a frustrated and rebellious husband. On the whole, however, the novel has an amateurish air, nowhere more evident than in the dialogue. None of the Powys brothers was at home with fashionable society ladies, but only Llewelyn was rash enough to write about one.

'Why, Flo, how perfectly chic you look in that gown! You are a winter queen. I could say my prayers to you. You really are ravish-ing! I insist upon your giving me the name of your dressmaker. Have you seen Roland? The poor dear cannot be separated from that Tapsfield girl; he is simply tied to her.'[29]

The best parts of the book are those in which Powys's own knowledge of country life comes into play. He can anatomise a bad landlord:

He never indulged in self-analysis or self-criticism, any more than he investigated the origin of the fortune he had inherited. He took his position for granted, and the servants he employed and the tenants of his farms and cottages in his sight found their only justification for living in so far as they contributed to his well-being. . . . He was never tired of railing against his heavy taxation, and through the employment of a London accountant did all that was in his power to defraud the state of its rightful dues. . . . Actually he was the product of an artificial social efflorescence, but his assurance gave to his comings in and goings out the semblance of an absolute reality that only some bloody revolution or appalling catastrophe of nature could have shaken.[30]

But this kind of social approach is not habitual with Llewelyn Powys; more characteristic is his evocation of the past in such passages as that in which Chris and Adela on their honeymoon at Abbotsbury pick up prehistoric flints from an ancient burial mound. A sense of history shapes his imagination and gives perspective both to his stringent atheism and to his ideal of the happy life; but being so exclusively concerned with bedrock essentials and states of consciousness he lacked the imaginative range to make his vision dramatically convincing.

Although not technically a novel, *Love and Death* (1939) is therefore more representative of his true potential as a novelist. This 'imaginary autobiography', as it is sub-titled, is partly daydream. The author is on his sickbed, high on the Dorset cliffs; threatened with death from repeated lung haemorrhages, he recreates in his mind a boyhood love affair which serves as a distillation of his inner life. His own imagined death concludes the book. Powys here pushes life-awareness to its utmost pitch, the intertwining of life and art being absolute; and he executes his design without a trace of self-pity, with unfaltering realism where his sickness is concerned, and with unabashed romanticism as he describes the idyllic hours spent by the lovers in the countryside round his boyhood home at Montacute. The memory of love in its most fervent aspect is counterpointed by the realisation of death at its most painful; but the two are linked in the persons of the author's wife and sister, whose care for him constitutes a love bound up with death. Similarly, the presence of death conjures up the memory of Dittany Stone, the imaginary girl whose beauty is, for the young Llewelyn, the quintessence of romance.[31] But it is his love for her, rather than hers for him, which is the subject of the book.

Love and Death is at once an elegy for romantic love and a celebration of it. The long, hot summer days, the woods and hayfields and the lanes at night, are living forces in the story; the eroticism is both intense and delicate. Llewelyn Powys challenges Meredith in his sumptuous presentation of familiar country scenes.

> On we passed through the immortal night, like two long-separated souls at peace and reunited at last in the crepuscular spaces of Elysium. Often there would come to us hot puffs of air, sweet with the perfume of banks of bedstraw, and presently we would pass near some field-stream, so overgrown with tangled brambles, starred already with pale blackberry flowers, and the tall growths of budding willow-herb, soft and damp to the touch, that it was impossible to see the crinkling water to which, every night foxes, badgers, rats and mice would come to lap with parched tongues large and little; and where, in the day, frogs would hop and small birds stand to dip and prink their sleek feathers – to fly away a moment later in freedom.[32]

This particular note has not been heard since: *Love and Death* may be even more elegaic than it appears. Its final impression is less of the power of sexual love than of the landscape of the author's boyhood, of some Eden of lost summers where the world of responsibility and communal commitment can be forgotten. But the book is saved from triviality by its continual awareness of death, which is seen in terms of life and as life's negation.

> For age after age in solitary cells of dissolution hosts upon hosts of dead men lie silent and senseless in the cold clay. Their tongues will wag no more, there is mould in their nostrils, and their eyes are empty of light. There is gravel in their mouths and their ear-holes are waxed with the fat of worms.[33]

This macabre, Webster-like feeling for the physical actualities of death is a characteristic of the Powysian imagination: it is to be found especially in the work of T. F. Powys. In Llewelyn's it is balanced by an insistence on the healing power of happiness. The lovers in *Love and Death* are part of a total experience of life which, the author would persuade us, to have done without is hardly to have lived at all.

III

If intensity be the criterion of excellence, then Williamson and Llewelyn Powys are the finest rural writers of their time. However,

the public proclamation of a private experience needs a greater objecti-
fying power than either writer can command; for all the lyrical beauty
of their writing, both authors speak out of a world so personally in-
dividuated as to invite rejection through its very solicitation of assent.
There is something overinsistent about their work (one speaks here of
their fiction – Powys's essays, on the other hand, being notably objective
and historically informed) and in Williamson's especially the reader can
feel stifled by his enclosure in the author's personal world.

But the hectic quality of so much of the writing is indicative of
more than the urgency of special pleading. A deep affinity between man
and his natural environment is being posited. Henry Williamson and
Llewelyn Powys, through their record of deep emotional experience
aroused by boyhood memories, discover that relationship within the
fulfilment of personality. Powys is more stoical than Williamson,
tougher in his acknowledgement of the indifference of the natural order
to human suffering; but both writers celebrate the life of the woodlands
and fields and rivers of the West Country as emblems of a spiritual
awareness without which men and women are effectively dead.

Both are distrustful of society and of political and religious leaders,
and both stand outside the literary life of the time: in their work
the rural experience stands over against the world of ordinary human
contacts. From here it is only a step (a step neither author takes) into
a world of romantic fantasy, of daydream and magic. The nostalgia for
boyhood happiness which they voice was to be taken up into an
idealised awareness of rural simplicity. It is a shorter step than may
appear between the intense fervour of Henry Williamson and the
more didactic romanticism associated with the name of Mary Webb.

9 Romantic Landscapes: Mary Webb, E. H. Young

Mary Webb (1881–1927) is the most well known rural novelist of her time. Her work was popularly supposed to be the chief model for *Cold Comfort Farm*, and she has on occasion been derided for the praise showered upon her by Stanley Baldwin at a Royal Literary Fund dinner. The fame resulting from the latter came seven months after her death, and led to a collected edition of her works, the five novels being installed as classics of the rural school. But, although part of literary legend (as a romantically neglected author – to the pseudo-sophisticated a 'primitive' one) and an easy target for ignorant satirists, she had established herself as a rural novelist of repute without the aid of any non-literary publicity. She had won a steady body of admirers long before her death, and was awarded the Femina Vie Heureuse Prize for *Precious Bane* (1924) three years before Baldwin was recommended to read it by his secretary.

She was a native of Shropshire, the setting of all her novels and of many of her attractive, highly personal poems. Like Llewelyn Powys she grew up in a comfortable and bookish home (her father tutored boys preparing for Sandhurst and the University), and her novels, with their fervent tone and colourful prose, show affinities with his. She married H. B. L. Webb, a schoolmaster who published a trio of historical novels after her death, under the pseudonym J. Clayton. He proved a congenial and devoted husband in a union which, thanks to her highly-strung, impulsive nature, and to her persistent ill-health must have been more exacting than many. Her last two novels were written while she and her husband were living in Hampstead, but Shropshire remained her inspiration.[1]

Her novels, poems and essays are all propelled by the belief that the world of nature holds a secret not to be found in cities or communities. The opening chapter of her book of essays, *The Spring of Joy* (1917), has as epigraph the words of Sir Thomas Browne: 'We live the life of plants, the life of animals, the life of men, and at last the life of spirits.[2] Mary Webb took these words very literally: her belief in the presence of that life informs her poetry and novels alike. In *The Spring of Joy* she writes of it meticulously, in extreme and occasionally obfuscating detail; but this pedantry of the senses is the result of a seriously held belief, one she shares with Richard Jefferies and Llewelyn Powys.[3]

> Life – the unknown quantity, the guarded secret – circles from an infinite ocean through all created things, and turns again to the ocean. This miracle that we eternally question and desire and adore dwells in the comet, in the heart of a bird, and the flying dust of pollen. It glows upon us from the blazing sun and from a little bush of broom, unveiled and yet mysterious, guarded only by its own light – more impenetrable than darkness.[4]

For Mary Webb this inner life is realised in the blossoming of individual consciousness: thus she writes of Hazel Woodus in *Gone to Earth* (1917) that 'she was of a race that will come in the far future, when we shall have outgrown our egoism – the brainless egoism of a little boy pulling off flies' wings'.[5] Hazel is a creature of the wild, morally innocent because ignorant of the life of the herd. For the herd is the arch-enemy of individual fulfilment: the novels are insistent on the mindless cruelty of men and women in the mass, whether it be the huntsmen who chase Hazel to her death in the quarry or the superstitious villagers in *Precious Bane*, equally ready for a bull-baiting or to lynch Prudence Sarn for a witch. The most explicit condemnation of the herd mind comes in *The House in Dormer Forest* (1920):

> It is the mass-ego that constructs dogmas and laws; for while the individual soul is, if free at all, self-poised, the mass-mind is always uncertain, driven by vague, wandering aims; conscious, in a dim fashion, of its own weakness, it builds round itself a grotesque structure in the everlastingness of which it implicitly believes. . . . The whole effort of evolution is to the development of individual souls who will dare to be free of the architecture of crowd-morality. For when man is herded he remembers the savage.[6]

Mary Webb is rather more than a nature-mystic; she takes her mysticism (so to call this hypersensitiveness to physical shapes and currents) as the basis of a fuller understanding of human life, and all her novels have a strong didactic quality. (She might have been writing of herself when, in *The Golden Arrow* (1915), she remarks of Mrs Arden that 'she made the mistake of most people with intuition – she pulled so hard at her thread that she broke it.'[7]) Her gift lies not so much in simple perceptiveness as in a feeling for the correlation between perceiver and perceived. She writes that

> the personality of a man reacting upon the spirit of a place produces something which is neither the man nor the place, but fiercer or more beautiful than either. This third entity, born of the union, becomes a power and a haunting presence – non-human, non-material. For the mind that helped to create it once, it dominates the place of its birth forever. Hence came the troops of medieval saints and devils. Hence came folk-plays, nature poems, sonatas – the heights of vision, the depths of melancholy.[8]

This might stand as an epigraph for much of the work of John Cowper Powys.[9]

The Golden Arrow, Mary Webb's first novel, is the story of Stephen Underwood, a man of intense sensitivity who has no corresponding power of self-expression. Having lived all his life at second-hand until his meeting with the country girl Deborah Arden, he finds himself unable to love her with a strength sufficient to meet and overcome the pressures of uncongenial work and of a landscape which terrifies him. There is an absolute division between what he sees and what he feels; he is too immature in love for the kind of trust and self-forgetfulness of which his wife is capable. But *The Golden Arrow* is memorable less for the story of Stephen and Deborah than for that of the shallow Lily Huntbatch and Deborah's brother Joe, whom she marries; for the descriptions of the landscape of the Shropshire highlands; and for a certain terseness and vigour in the writing which Mary Webb was never to recapture. This shows itself not only in a command of rapid narrative, but also in a dry humour, as when she observes of Deborah's father that 'He was very sensitive about his business faculty, not having any.'[10] Or again, 'Lucy never gave an opinion of any kind. She called it "useless argufying".'[11] This humour can be extended into a more probing analysis, as of Lily's thoughts when first seeing the cottage which is to be her married home.

She thought how easy the work would be. She was not meant for the hardy magnificence of manual labour. She should have belonged to the professional or tradesman's class, and had a small 'general' to bully, and been able to say with pride to her friends, 'Oh, no, I never do any work, but I know how it should be done.' But here she felt a decided impetus in the direction of domesticity, because for the first time it was picturesque; for the first time she saw herself in a romantic setting of shelves, cupboards, clean paint and flowers. She had a vision of the vicar's wife alluding to her as 'Joe Arden's pretty wife who makes such good jelly.'[12]

This is neatly done. Lily is both exposed and yet given sympathy; the bleakness of her past with her tyrannical old father (first and most memorable of a line of such figures in the author's work) is evoked to show the attractiveness of her ideal – an ideal which is presented in all its obsequiousness by the remark about the jelly. Had Mary Webb been content to make her points by such strokes of observation and subtle humour, her novels would have been more persuasive than they are.

All of them have elements of the parabolic, *The Golden Arrow* especially. The two girls are sharply, at times crudely, contrasted in character, and so are their fathers, Eli and John. The latter, modelled on the author's own father, is rather sentimentally drawn; and his belief in the healing presence of Cariad the Flockmaster is a note struck repeatedly in Mary Webb's writing. Her obsession with the cruelty of life is balanced by a poignant awareness of its beauty; and the figure of the Flockmaster is an embodiment of that 'summat as there's no words for, as makes it all worth while'.[13] He remains a figure of John's speech, to become incarnate in later books as Michael Hallowes and as Kester Woodseaves, the Christ-like hero of *Precious Bane*; but the hope of an underlying benevolence is common to them all. In *The Golden Arrow* this hope is given external form through the use of landscape.

The pickers wandered to and fro, lost in distance, appearing out of hollows, passing round the white signpost like dancers in some strange ritual. They stooped for the small, purple fruit, wrapped in purple shadows themselves. Little box-carts, trundled by urchins, began to fill with berries, heaped in miniature replica of the hills. Shadows began to climb from the cwms, and clouds came faster. The signpost – so lonely in its ring of worn turf – looked, with its outspread arms against the dim reaches of heather, like a crucifix under the troubled sky. It stood with forlorn gallantry between the coming storm and its prey. It would be lashed by rain all night; lightning would play round it. The pickers, as with some mysterious sense of kinship, circled round it – so disconsolately consoling it seemed, so like their own destinies.[14]

Superficially this passage resembles the work of Hardy; but the whole tone is softer, the rhythms more relaxed; the human element predominates, even to the 'climbing' shadows and the 'troubled' sky. The scene interprets an interior state.

To say this is to indicate the difference between Hardy and Mary Webb. She is not simply a lesser writer in the same genre, but a novelist who is doing something altogether different. Mary Webb's Shropshire is a land of romance, a region in which her characters act out fantasies of her contriving which can embody more effectively than her highly personal poems her passionate conviction of the kinship between man and nature. In some respects she is closer to Lawrence than to Hardy, for, like Lawrence, she saw in sexual wholeness the proof of a man's capacity to live and to experience.

The point is further developed in *Gone to Earth*. Hazel Woodus, an attractively outspoken gipsy girl, is doomed from the outset, a victim of the insufficient humanity of man. Her seduction by the dissolute Squire Reddin is followed by her unconsummated marriage to the simple preacher, Edward Marston; and the book recounts his tragedy as well as Hazel's. His self-denying consideration is helpless in a world dominated by the ethos of the pack; indeed, his very goodness determines Hazel's unhappy fate. But, as is usual in Mary Webb's work, the male characters are only partially realised, and both Reddin and Marston seem to have stepped out of the pages of some twopenny romance. More successful are the lesser figures, most notably Edward's mother, 'who was one of nature's opiates, and . . . administered herself unconsciously to everyone who saw much of her'.[15]

No one ever saw her hurried or busy, yet the proofs of her industry were here. She worked like the coral insect, in the dark, as it were, of instinct unlit by intellect, and, like the coral insect, she raised a monumental structure that hemmed her in.[16]

The wit of this passage is marred by that intrusive attempt at explication, which is a feature of this and the succeeding novel: the point

could have been better made without the reference to intellect and
instinct. The book's message is hammered home with such insistence
that even its comedy is infected with didacticism.

Hazel is an embodiment of that in the natural order which the
'filthy, heavy-handed, blear-eyed world'[17] inevitably destroys. She is a
kind of earth-spirit, though real enough as a human being in all she
says and does. Edward, listening to her singing, becomes aware of something that lies deeper than his own religion:

> The wail of the lost was in her voice. She had not the slightest idea
> what the words meant (probably they meant nothing), but the sad
> cadence suited her emotional tone, and the ideas of loss and exile
> expressed her vague mistrust of the world. . . . It was the grief of
> rainy forests and the moan of stormy water; the muffled complaint
> of driven leaves; the keening – wild and universal – of life for the
> perishing matter that it inhabits.[18]

It would be pleasant to read Dr Johnson on Mary Webb; but, having
said this, there remains the salty tang of that 'probably they meant
nothing' – the overwrought solemnity, the essential fallaciousness of the
ensuing passage is offset by it, just as throughout her work the sentimentality and rhetoric are balanced by a gift for epigram. So even in
this, the most extravagant of her novels, she is capable of the blunt
statement that 'Life is a taciturn mother, and teaches not so much by
instruction as by blows.'[19] The central weakness of *Gone to Earth* is
that Hazel's story is too remote from ordinary human concerns, and
is forced to bear a burden of cosmic significance which it cannot really
sustain: in this it epitomises the limitations of the rural genre. Moreover, the anthropomorphising of natural forces recoils upon the human
protagonists, and all alike are rendered unbelievable. Even in the
relatively simple *Golden Arrow* Mary Webb can liken a honeysuckle
petal to 'the tongue of a faery hound in age-long chase of a deathless
quarry'; in *Gone to Earth* such similitudes are legion, all harnessed with
misguided consistency to the central theme of pursuit and chase. A
genuine and original sensitivity is being worked to death.

This shows itself in the descriptive passages. Compare the following
with the simplicity of the account of the signpost in *The Golden
Arrow*:

> The sky blossomed in parterres of roses, frailer and brighter than the
> rose of the briar, and melted beneath them into lagoons greener and

paler than the veins of a young beech-leaf. The fairy hedges were so high, so flushed with beauty, the green airy waters ran so far back into mystery, that it seemed as if at any moment God might walk there as in a garden, delicate as a moth. Down by the stream Hazel found tall water-plantains, triune of cup, standing each above the ooze like candelabras, and small rough-leaved forget-me-nots eyeing their liquid reflections with complaisance.[20]

Here proliferation of extravagant fancy and a lack of controlling imagery lead to a kind of clotted chaos of sense-impressions which conceals rather than reveals the objects described. The total effect is one of softness and self-indulgence, most clearly manifest in the sentimental transformation of God Himself into something suggestive of a pixy. But if such pieces of fine writing prompted Stella Gibbons's parody, it is also probable that they have been one reason for their author's continuing popularity.

However, there is more to *Gone to Earth* than this. It is swift and vivid, with at times a ballad-like quality. Hazel and her father, the bee-keeper, are not mild and simple creatures in the way that, for example, so many of T. F. Powys's 'innocent birds' are: they are tough, lacking in affection for each other, often violent, and only half-aware of their relationship with nature. Hazel's devotion to animals is more questionably handled: the taming of the wild hardly matches her own wildness, and her death, while protecting her pet cub Foxy from the hounds, is too obviously symbolic for entire conviction. There is an element of false picturesqueness about it, betrayed by the careful elaboration of the writing: however passionate the feeling that informs the passage, the catastrophe has been led up to so insistently throughout the book that its final incidence appears contrived.

Still more contrived is *The House in Dormer Forest*, which develops the conflict between the individual and the herd. Dormer Old House, with its hide-bound customs and rigid exclusion of the unorthodox and unexpected, is the symbol of a civilisation ossified. But, whereas the Darke family, conceived deliberately as grotesques (in the manner of the inhabitants of Mervyn Peake's Gormenghast), might have been successful as an image of the herd mentality, as presented realistically they are clearly the chief inspiration for the Starkadder family in *Cold Comfort Farm*. Their vitality is that of brightly painted marionettes. The most memorable of them is the grandmother. Her pat Biblical quotations, her greediness, her black nodding curls, her childish egotism mask something sinister:

There was a ghost hiding in Mrs. Velindre's eyes – a cadaverous, grisly thing which had looked at her out of other people's eyes when she was a child; slowly possessing her in womanhood; finally absorbing her whole personality – eating into it like a worm into a rotten fruit. . . . She had lived so long by fear and not by love, that her capacity for cruelty had grown in proportion to her capacity for panic. She had for so many years been trying to be like other people, that she was now like nothing in heaven or earth. For the more the soul conforms to the sanity of others, the more does it become insane.[21]

But Grandmother's liveliness is such that she belies this description; and the oppressed younger members of the family being drawn with far less conviction, it is in her rather than in them that one is interested. The moral and emotional elements of the book are imperfectly aligned.

The love story of Amber Darke and Michael Hallowes, a shadowy figure who appears as a kind of *deus ex machina* to rescue her from the miseries of home, represents the other side of Mary Webb's imagination. The passage describing their first meeting is an example of her writing at its worst.

They looked at one another, and their look was that of friends who have met a long while since, in other lands, to the sound of wilder music, but with the same remembered ecstasy. Dim thought came to them of primeval forests which it seemed that they two, wandering hand in hand, had traversed; of antique seas far away on whose loud shores they had, as childish playmates, slept; of huge, serrated mountains where they had climbed – mountains now worn to low green hills. Where were those forests and those roaring seas? They could not tell. In this world ages since; in other worlds; in the strange saharas of their own secret souls – it did not concern them to know.[22]

This kind of unbridled, high-pitched romanticism consorts ill with the tart accounts of life in Dormer Old House; moreover there has been no dramatic establishment of the lovers – one is presented with a *fait accompli*. And the account of Michael Hallowes is less reminiscent of Hardy or Phillpotts than of Florence L. Barclay.

His mind had the qualities of flame. He was one of those men who, passing through filthy places, burn up evil as they go. His face had the strong sweetness that belongs to a man who has been through the mire of human sin, and has come through with his spirit intact.[23]

The use of the words 'one of those' is usually a danger signal; it means that imaginative effort is being shirked. The reader is to be bludgeoned, not persuaded.

Although *Seven for a Secret* (1922) is more free from didacticism than its two predecessors, there are signs that the author is beginning to repeat herself. Gillian, torn between Rideout and Elmer, is a variation on Hazel torn between Marston and Reddin; Farmer Lovekin has features in common with Solomon Darke. Even Rideout brooding on the moor recalls Enoch Gale, the hired man at Dormer Old House.

> Day after day, in the early morning or after his work was done, he brooded upon the waste as it lay beneath his gaze, self-wrapped, conning its own secret, dreaming of itself and its dark history, its purple-mantled past and its future clothed in vaporous mystery. The colour that comes on the heather when it is in full flower, which is like the bloom on a plum, was in his dream. The rumour that runs, in warm, dark spring evenings, from the peering leaf down the veins of the stalk, to the waiting flower sleeping in the root – a rumour of rain and misty heat and the melodious languors of a future June; this, too, was in his dream. Wave on profound wave of beauty broke over him, submerged him. The wonder and terror of it came to his soul with a keenness that darted from the colours and perfumes like a sword hidden in roses.[24]

Although the language has more vitality than that of Phillpotts in similar passages, the sensibility is too soft to be convincing. Moreover, Rideout's feelings for the moor are not integrated into the plot; they are an addition to his character and determine nothing. Indeed *Seven for a Secret* would be a more satisfactory book had it attempted less. In essence a straightforward tale of abduction, murder and intrigue, it is invested with a spurious 'significance' through Robert's kinship with the moor. The final climax is oddly half-hearted, and out of keeping with the portentous references to it in the earlier part of the novel. As in *The House in Dormer Forest* one is aware of a disintegrated imagination.

Indeed, all four of these novels suffer from the same shortcomings of a sensibility divided against itself. On the one hand they reflect a brisk and humorous vision of human character and behaviour; on the other an ardent and almost anguished susceptibility to the forces of nature.²⁵ But this susceptibility is essentially a psychological affair. Except in *The Golden Arrow*, Mary Webb's Shropshire, although she was a native of the county, bears little resemblance to the Shropshire landscape as it actually is: it is an interior landscape, a projection of emotions, terrors, above all of a feeling of pity. Hazel's predicament with Foxy is a mirror of her creator's predicament with her own sensitivity. Mary Webb might have been a novelist of rural life and manners, for her knowledge of rural life was first-hand, her acquaintance with ancient customs and intuitive sympathy with them comparable to Hardy's; but alongside this straightforward human responsiveness there existed a fervent romanticism that knew man and nature as parts of a reality greater than either. Her rejection of orthodox religion did not, however, issue in pantheism, but rather in a clothing of the landscape with human attributes, and the belief in a spiritual presence within nature less akin to Pan than to Jesus Christ. And the tension between these two elements in her work, the realistic and the mystical, resulted in the uneasy see-saw between narrative economy and rhetorical didacticism which has been already noted. In part the problem was technical, and the two voices, those of the characters and of the author–commentator, were to be fused by the simple expedient of using a first-person narrative. In *Precious Bane* Prudence Sarn embodies both the homely wisdom of the countrywoman and the fervid romanticism of her creator.

The success of *Precious Bane* is also linked to another problem. In all the earlier books the element of fable had been predominant; but this had been weakened by the awareness that we were also in a contemporary world – or, more strictly, by a failure to imply that we were not. In *Precious Bane*, however, by setting her tale in the time of the Napoleonic wars and after, Mary Webb succeeds in distancing it sufficiently for it to exist in a world that is at once physically real and yet psychologically abstracted. To say that the book attains to the full grandeur of myth would be to praise it beyond its deserts or its intention; but the charm that it still has the power to exert is the charm of a tale which at once establishes its own imaginative world and which, both in the manner and the matter of its telling, illuminates that world's significance.

As a story *Precious Bane* is simple. Gideon Sarn, the young farmer brother of the narrator, Prue, sacrifices his youth, his sweetheart and his family in order to better himself in the world by getting rich – gold is the precious bane; but on the eve of his final achievement his ricks are destroyed by the father of the girl whom he has seduced. The girl's suicide and his own failure cause him to drown himself; and Prudence, with her hare-shotten lip, is nearly drowned also, by the neighbours as a witch. She is saved by the weaver, Kester Woodseaves, whom she loves. The novel is thus as much of an old-fashioned melodrama as is its predecessor; but the conventional plot is here an advantage. It reads like some country ballad, some story told by Hardy; and in its style of narration it evokes the kind of world in which its telling would be natural. Style is indeed the governing element in *Precious Bane*. Everything depends on Prue Sarn and how she tells her story.

Through the use of a deliberately mannered and artificial diction Mary Webb succeeds in combining the two elements in her imaginative world. Prue's speech is lulling and rhythmic, full of old-world turns of phrase, swelling up to periodic intensities, sinking down to quietness. It has the flow of monologue with the fluidity of free association; and the descriptive passages are mediated through the corporate consciousness by the use of local names, quotations of local proverbs, references to local beliefs. Thus even the more implausible people and events are presented with a leaven of worldly wisdom, of matter-of-fact physical detail. The world of the novel is self-contained and self-consistent; it is both factually and imaginatively persuasive.

The comparison of two contiguous passages may serve to illuminate this point. In the first, Prudence is describing a winter landscape seen on the way to the love-spinning at Wizard Beguildy's:

> We came out into the open fields, and I thought no day had ever looked so fair, yet knew not why. The hills Lullingford way were blue as a summer sky, a deep promising blue, and there was a richness on the world, so it looked what our Parson used to call sumptuous. There were the red ploughlands and the old yellow stubble in the sun and Plash Pool, glassy blue, and the mill roof in the valley, red. All the grassland was clear green like the green in church windows, or like the green hill far away where no herb grows but the Calvary clover. Even a summer day can seldom match such a day as that, when the snow is but just gone and the waters freed, and when there is a clear shining above and below.[26]

This has a notable simplicity and precision compared to the descriptions in the last three novels: at the same time it is informed by a strong idiosyncrasy. It is a landscape seen in a particular way, it is an aspect of Prue Sarn herself. The similitudes are no longer strained or laboured, but are an integral part of the world which they describe – they are apt to this particular experience. And it is characteristic of the rounded-ness of vision which Mary Webb achieves in *Precious Bane* that the next paragraph should turn quite naturally into humour.

> Missis Miller was a poor creature, like a mealworm, but very pleasant-spoken. Sexton's missus was just the opposite. She always made me think of a new-painted coach, big and wide, with an open road, and the horn blowing loud and cheerful, and full speed ahead. She was as gay in her dress as a seven-coloured linnet, and if she *could* wear another shawl or flounce or brooch, she would. She wore so many petticoats it was a wonder she could walk, and once Tivvy said to me that to watch her mother undress was like peeling a big onion down to the core. Tivvy wasna one ever to make a joke, so it shows what a great thing it must ha' been to watch.[27]

The attractiveness of *Precious Bane* is bound up with the attractive-ness of Prue herself. She might easily have been sentimentalised, being of the breed of the heroically long-suffering who are notoriously a trap for the romantic novelist. But Prue is spirited and stoical, with a vein of humour and no self-pity: her hare-lip is a source of wonder to her as much as heartbreak. Her love-on-sight for Kester is more convincing than that of Amber Darke for Michael Hallowes. Kester, however, remains the most shadowy of the characters in the book: he is seen with the nimbus of Prue's adoration. He is given Christ-like notations, as when he takes the place of the bull at the baiting, or, more speci-fically, when Prue refers to him as 'the very marrow of Him that loved the world so dear'.[28] Kester is indeed an embodiment of that benevolent presence in nature which Mary Webb invoked in her poem 'The Vagrant'.[29]

> Close by the water
> Wrapt in a dream, I saw a faint reflection
> Like a wayfarer, calm and worn of features,
> Clad in the brown of leaves and little creatures,
> Stern as the moorland, russet of complexion.
>
> Dark in the shadow
> Fathomless eyes met mine with thought unspoken,
> Wistful, yet deep within them laughter lingered.
> With sunburnt hands a wooden flute he fingered
> Under the thorn-tree, where the lights are broken. . . .

Over the meadows
Wild music came like spray upon the shingle;
Piping the world to mating; changing, calling
Low to the heart like doves when rain is falling.
Surely he cut his flute in Calvary's dingle?

This poem relates not only to the reference to Calvary in the account of the winter landscape quoted above, but also, and more significantly, to the meeting between Michael and Amber, and the former's Christ-like testing of his bride on their wedding night, with its overtones of the call to the disciples to forsake all and follow their master. Kester is a less sombre figure than Michael, and his final appearance when he rescues Prue from the villagers is more like that of St George than of the Jesus of the New Testament. But it is he, and Prue's love for him and his for her, which is the informing spirit of nature in *Precious Bane*. At one point near the end of the book Prue remarks that it seemed as though 'Sarn, all the live part of it, us and our beasts, the trees full of birds, and the wood ways with the wild creatures in them, had sunk to the bottom of the mere',[30] and it is when Prue is about to be drowned in the mere that Kester rides up to save her. She undergoes a kind of resurrection.

Precious Bane is the epitome of the rural romance as enjoyed by the early twentieth-century public. It is easy to account for its popularity. Apart from its compelling readability, it told of a vanished past, setting a high value on what was being destroyed. There is no social awareness in Mary Webb's novels, no knowledge shown of agricultural problems, no attempts at social criticism. Whether she would have developed further as a writer is doubtful. Her surviving fragment, *Armour Wherein He Trusted*, is set in the time of the First Crusade, but the voice of the narrator, Gilbert de Polrebec, is the voice of Prudence Sarn. This tale of a young knight's love for a witch maiden carries little imaginative vitality, and the author was disenchanted with it before she died.

The popularity of Mary Webb's novels in the 1930s and 1940s is understandable. She was a genuine original and her work, for all its extravagance, carries imaginative conviction: this is a world believed in, felt with, inhabited. She is an excellent story-teller and treats her characters with respect; and she is free from whimsy. But the rural world that she describes is remote not only in location but also in presentation. There is no real sense of an England existing outside her fictional Shropshire, no sense of that Shropshire being a part of something greater than itself. The world of the novels is entirely self-contained. Hence perhaps their appeal: they are a part, and a not inconsiderable part, of the literature of fantasy and dream.

II

The same charge (if it be a charge) cannot be levelled against the novels of Emily Hilda Young (1880–1947) a writer whose approach to the country resembles that of Mary Webb in certain ways, and whose novels were brought out in a collected edition with a format similar to hers. She is not strictly a rural novelist, though she has some claim to be considered a regional one. With two exceptions all eleven of her novels are set in and around Bristol, which is disguised in each of them as 'Radstowe'; and Clifton especially ('Upper Radstowe') and the Somerset country across the Avon play determining parts in the action. The rural element in these novels acts for the most part as an indication of the individual's quest and craving for personal fulfilment. In their themes and subject matter the books are a faithful but not uncritical reflection of feminine middle-class attitudes of the time. The period in which the best of them were published – 1922–37 – was one in which the shock of social change after the First World War was already being cushioned for the professional classes by the effects of economic recovery. In all of them there is an undercurrent of disturbance and unrest, manifesting itself in satire at the expense of the complacent and unimaginative bourgeoisie, coupled with a tender feeling for the domestic and a rejection, in personal and imaginative terms, of the materialistic philosophy that sustains the bourgeois attitude to life. In this respect the novels of E. H. Young may be compared with those of Mary Webb.

What gives them their especial interest in relation to the rural theme is the way in which, as they mature and deepen their concern with human problems and affairs, the theme diminishes. Between A Corn of Wheat (1910) and Chatterton Square (1947) lies even more than that thirty-seven years: to pass from the one novel to the other is to move from youthful idealism and extravagance to tolerance and considered wisdom. But common to both books and to all that lie between is a fundamental seriousness, reflected in a style of rhythmic deliberation and conveyed on an undertide of humour. E. H. Young's work, precisely because of its sober and traditional qualities, is an interesting

critique and exemplar of the place of the countryside in the early
twentieth-century popular imagination.

In the three early novels mountain and moorland scenery play a
leading part. *Yonder* (1912) moves between Radstowe and what looks
very like Wasdale in Cumberland; and the appeal of the mountain
landscape is the link between the two families whose relationship is
the main subject of the novel. Here scenery is an embodiment of a
mental world; and the rather Trollopian plot about a young girl who
breaks off an apparently desirable engagement in order to marry the
man of her romantic choice is given a very un-Trollopian colouring by
the way in which that decision is related to her inner imaginative life,
fed by her father's account of the mountain world from which her lover
comes. But the novel, although it contains the ingredients of a conventional love story, is more concerned with what links people to each
other at the deepest level. So Theresa can conclude that her rejected
lover 'loved the surface of her and would not look into the depths, that
a principle of his life was to avoid looking into depths'.[31] Alexander,
on the other hand, 'through nature . . . was half-consciously trying to
find God'.[32] and his idealistic character is portrayed as being consonant
with, as well as conditioned by, his mountain home. In later novels,
too, the North Country landscape is seen as conducive to spiritual
clarity and as a measure of character judgement. Thus Margaret in *The
Vicar's Daughter* (1928) finds that the 'calm spaciousness of that
country seemed to enlarge and quieten her own nature',[33] and Felix in
Chatterton Square brings his romance with a shop girl to an end because she would not form a part of the new world he had discovered
while rock-climbing in the hills. 'She would have hated those hills. . . .
and I knew, as soon as I saw them, that I never wanted to see her
again.'[34]

The emotional life centred upon a response to natural scenery and
processes comes to be replaced by an emotional life centred upon people.
The conflict between duty to neighbour and duty to the inner self is
the heart of all of the novels. The first three have extravagant and con-
ventionally 'romantic' plots, in which coincidence and melodrama play
a leading part; but the quietness of the tone in which they are couched
points to the more assured books that were to follow. In *William* (1925),
The Vicar's Daughter, and *Miss Mole* (1930) we have portraits of
people instinctively wise in the management of others because of a
quality of tolerance combined with an intense relish for life and nature.
Jenny Wren (1932), *The Curate's Wife* (1934) and *Celia* (1937), however, develop a critical attitude to such favoured ones, and are more

F

complex and interesting as a result – and far more interesting than their titles would suggest. In these novels the cult of individualism receives some hard knocks. All six, with the exception of *The Vicar's Daughter*, are laid in Radstowe, a terrain decisively annexed in the earlier *The Misses Mallett* (1922), which on its inclusion in the Collected Edition lost its original and more relevant title, *The Bridge Dividing*. The bridge is the Clifton suspension bridge, and the contrast between the two sides of the Avon gorge as it was in the author's time is used by her as emblematic of the conflicting claims of society and self. And it is the country which is the refuge for the self.

This is made explicit in *A Corn of Wheat*, an immature work excluded by the author from the Collected Edition. Its heroine has a passionate attachment to nature, which is far more to her than any human contact: 'she was a limitless receiver of impressions, with no connection pipes to the minds of others'.[35] But by the end of the book she has learned that 'she could not return to her old life of feeling, that she had now the necessity to act'.[36]

> She walked on until she left the open and entered a wood of red-trunked firs. Silent they stood, unmoved by the slightness of the breeze, and above their green tops the sky was spread. Judith was still as they, and she felt the arms of Nature put round her lovingly, wrapping her about with peace. . . . The old love had given her only personal happiness, the new had given her understanding; and she knew that unless she sought for further knowledge this world of lovely symbols would vanish like a wreath of mist, and leave the unreality of material things.[37]

This is the sensibility of a Mary Webb heroine. The writing has the deliberate cadence that is typical of all E. H. Young's work; but the descriptions of nature were to remain characterised by a slightly self-conscious lyricism.

Alongside this poetic streak is the dry, satirical quality that was with equal pertinacity to offset it. '[The vicar] was economical by nature, and never wasted words except, inevitably, in the performance of his professional duties.'[38] 'The village was as immoral as other places where amusement is restricted and opportunity frequent.' 'He had much to be thankful for, and that he had never said so to himself was a sure proof of his content.'[39] Perhaps it was phrases such as this, as much as the quietness of her settings, which caused some reviewers to liken E. H. Young to Jane Austen.[40]

There are Austenian parallels in *Moor Fires* (1916), the plot of which pivots on the contrasted characters of two sisters. But Helen and Miriam Caniper have more in common with Deborah and Lily in *The Golden Arrow* than they do with Elinor and Marianne Dashwood. The plot is, moreover, preposterous, the taming of a brutal young farmer by his marriage to one sister who agrees to it in order to save the seduction of the other. It is as if the moorland setting dictated an attempted tale of 'passion'; but the telling of the tale is so quiet and at times so witty that credulity is strained. It is clear that this is not the kind of book that the author should be writing. But in the relations of the two girls and their brothers with their stepmother we find a fore-shadowing of a situation to be developed further in *William* and *Jenny Wren*: the conflict between temperament and affection, and between both and filial duty. It is a psychological conflict parallel to that be-tween the love of solitude and natural beauty, and the demands of the community. The slightly priggish Helen wonders 'by whose law it had been decreed that no human being could have a destiny uncon-ditioned by someone else, and . . . also saw that this law was the glory as well as the tragedy of life'.[41] Helen communes with the moor in the rather self-conscious way that characterises the heroine of a novel of this type: again one is reminded of Mary Webb. What is a marked feature of such writing, a feature at once contradicted and encouraged by Hardy's hypostasising of Egdon Heath is the attribution to landscape of human feelings. 'The moor itself had the patience of the wisdom which is faith'[42] – this is a kind of shorthand, but it is a danger-ous one to employ, for the external world comes to be treated as a vehicle for the emotions instead of as a corrective to them. It is the weakness of all E. H. Young's writing about nature that, carefully depicted though her landscapes are, it remains a spectator's portrait merely. What saves it from sentimentality is the treatment and analysis of the spectators' attitudes.

In this respect as in others *The Misses Mallett* is the crucial novel in her development. Here at last she strikes her distinctive note. The story of Rose Mallett, her sentimental love for a rejected suitor and her subsequent rivalry with her young niece, is told with restraint and subtlety; and the quietness of the tone conceals a sharp insight into the defences thrown up by well-bred people against passion.

Restraint and a love of danger lived together in her nature and these two qualities were fed by the position in which she found herself, nor would she have had the position changed. It supplied her with the emotion she had wanted. She had the privilege of feeling deeply and dangerously and yet of preserving her pride.[43]

Rose marries her lover at last, having saved Henrietta from his attentions (the rivalry between the older woman and the younger is very shrewdly done), but she pays the price.

She could tell herself that something of her dead love had waked to life, yet when she tried to get back the old rapture, she knew it had gone for ever.[44]

Love in middle age is a recurring theme in E. H. Young's work: it figures in *The Vicar's Daughter*, in *Miss Mole*, in *Chatterton Square*, most bitterly in *Celia*, which provides a chilling picture of continuing self-delusion, not least because it afflicts a type of self-reliant, life-moving character who is normally the author's moral touchstone. Rose Mallett is one of these; and in her relation to the country in which she lives she provides a good example of E. H. Young's use of landscape to place her characters in perspective.

The world of *The Misses Mallett* is a small one. The three sisters are members of the prosperous middle class, living a life of sheltered routine, dependent on servants, and with a recognised and leading place in Upper Radstowe society. The pleasant stagnancy of the household and the backward-looking existence of the older sisters is beautifully described in a just blend of quiet criticism and humorous appreciation. Rose is no rebel against her world: reserved, dignified, aging with irreproachable decorum, her only emotional outlet is to ride to the country across the river. The following account of it indicates its significance in a number of succeeding novels – most notably in *Jenny Wren*.

She ought, she knew, to have kept to her own side of the bridge, to have ridden on the high Downs inviting to a rider, but she loved the farther country where the air was blue and soft, where little orchards broke oddly into great fields, where brooks ran across the lanes and pink-washed cottages were fronted by little gardens full of homely flowers and clothes drying on the bushes. There was a smell of fruit and wood fires and damp earth; there was a veil of magic over the whole landscape and, far off, the shining line of the channel seemed to be washing the feet of the blue hills. The country had the charm of home with the allurement of the unknown and, within sound of the steamers hooting in the river, almost within sight of the city lying, red-roofed and smoky with factories, round the docks and mounting in terraces to the heights of Upper Radstowe, there was an expectation of mystery, of secrets kept for countless centuries by the earth which was fecund and alive. She could not deny herself the sight of this country.[45]

This is writing obviously informed by love, but weakened by a certain softness – that 'veil of magic' informs too much prose of this type. And it is the *sight* of the country that is indispensable: with the exception of Hannah Mole all the leading characters of E. H. Young's nature novels are wistful visitors from suburbia. And the central theme in all of them is symbolised by the character of Radstowe itself,

an aged city [that] had tried to conquer the country and had failed, for the spirit of the woods and open spaces, of water and trees and wind, survived among the very roofs. The conventions of centuries, the convention of puritanism, of worldliness, of impiety, of materialism and of charity had all assailed and all fallen back before the strength of the apparently peaceful country in which the city stood.[46]

That linking of materialism and charity is the nearest that the author gets to any radical *social* criticism; but the other enemies to the human spirit are all targets for satire and are most conspicuously worsted by those who live by the kind of values that, for the author, the country-side embodies. The pathetic fallacy is reversed to good purpose here.

For all this, the country can prove dangerous to the emotionally restricted, like Rose Mallett, or to those who, like Jenny Rendell, are emotionally immature. Jenny, brought up in the country though she is, is seduced by the accepted hierarchies of rank, and falls disastrously in love with a weak-kneed young squire; while Rose acquires her feeling for Francis Sales largely from the nature of his home and from the background of his wooing.

Her intellect made no mistake about Francis Sales, but her imagination, finding occupation where it could, began to endow him with romance and that scene among the primroses, the startlingly green grass, the pervading blue of the air, the horse so indifferent to the human drama, the dog trying to understand it, became the salient event of her life because it had awakened her capacity for dreaming.[47]

In *William*, a quietly humorous study of the effect upon a respectable Radstowe family of the break-up of a marriage, the country cross-river in which the runaway wife takes refuge becomes the symbol of forbidden passion. In *Jenny Wren* and *The Curate's Wife* it has a not dissimilar notation. Louisa Rendall, the country girl who marries above her station, is an incarnation of the simple and spontaneous virtues that are overlaid by the conventionalism of suburbia, a woman

> uneducated, inarticulate . . . but incapable of meanness, tolerant, possessed unknowingly of a wisdom derived from the country in which all her days had been spent, where she had seen the seasons come and go, the crops spring up and fall under the reaper, bareness where once there had been woodland and fertility overcoming waste, while the rocks and the shape of the land, the wind and the rain remained the same.[48]

But Louisa is dogged by the memory of her adultery with the farmer Thomas Grimshaw, a love-affair of which her more highly educated daughters are ashamed. Throughout the action of *Jenny Wren* Grimshaw and his market cart crossing the bridge to Radstowe are symbols of a demanding physical feeling that is a threat to the carefully contrived standards of the town. There are similar notations in other novels. In *The Curate's Wife*, the sequel to *Jenny Wren* and a sharp study of the hazards attendant on a marriage where the two partners inhabit different imaginative worlds, Grimshaw's farm is described in terms that recall Richard Jefferies or the Lawrence of *The White Peacock*.

> The beauty had come, as it were, from rare moments of leisure, it had survived and increased and was all the greater for its subordination to homelier necessities. Inside the house there was the smell of stored sunshine, of a kitchen fire, chiefly fed by wood, that had been burning, summer and winter, for a century, of apples and baking bread and damp cloth under a hot iron. The threshold was worn by the passage of heavy boots, the kitchen flags were worn, too, and in places they had sunk a little so that only familiar feet could cross the room without uncertainty. It was the typical living room of a farmhouse built when there was no grudging of space or labour and the women were as little likely to complain of many yards to scrub as the men of broad acres to plough.[49]

Louisa belongs to the country in a way that the rest of E. H. Young's characters do not; and indeed, if the author herself seems to be a spec-

tator of the land she describes, she is well aware of the difference between Jenny and Louisa. Jenny is 'nostalgic' for the country in which
she has been brought up but from which her education and her father's
death has separated her; but

> Louisa's need of it was not a conscious emotion, to be assuaged by
> a temporary return: she was not aware of seeing beauty in trees and
> meadows and sky: they were a part of her life while she was among
> them and, when she left them, their separate existence gave her no
> satisfaction. . . . The things over which more sophisticated people
> grew ecstatic were commonplaces to her and had the importance of
> the commonplaces to which she had been accustomed all her life.[50]

The whole change from a rural to an industrial society is implicit in
that paragraph.

But the character who most entirely embodies the values of E. H.
Young's world is Hannah Mole, who belongs to both sides of the
bridge. She is by birth and upbringing a countrywoman, by education
a gentlewoman, financially a distressed gentlewoman, who ekes out a
precarious living as a lady's companion until she comes to act as
housekeeper to a Congregational minister and to sort out the problems
of his motherless children. *Miss Mole* is probably the author's most
well known novel: it is certainly the one with the most obvious ingredients for popular success. The heroine is one with whom many
deprived or lonely women could identify; her inner resourcefulness and
interest in little things are qualities on which it is both easy and grati-
fying to pride oneself. But the author makes Hannah Mole see the
dangers of such a self-compensating attitude to life: fundamentally her
own attitudes are austere, astringent but not bitter. Hannah wins only
a partial success in the Corder household; and, although she finds
romance in the end, it is in the highly prosaic person of a bank clerk
at whom she has been accustomed to poke fun. The book closes on a
somewhat rueful note.

Miss Mole's uprootedness, the more obvious in view of her rural upbringing, leaves her with no refuge but thought and feeling; but the
methods she employs to build herself a world are a countrywoman's
methods, born of a countrywoman's knowledge. Corder's eldest daughter
reminds her of a colt, and so she

> went on with her darning, behaving just as she would have behaved
> with the nervous colt, pretending she was not watching it and letting

it get used to her presence before she advanced, and she could feel Ethel gaining confidence though her fears kept jerking her back.[51]

The mountains of the north and the woods and fields of Somerset between them fill out the mental and spiritual background of these people's lives – the world of sex and romance represented by the country across the river, the far-off mountains signifying the endurance necessary if life is to be lived with honesty and courage. Indeed, in her final books a strain of didacticism comes near to the surface of E. H. Young's writing. This is appropriate enough in the two books she wrote for children: in *Caravan Island* (1940), for instance, we find the hills of the west of Scotland providing a setting for a tale about the growth of a group of children in unselfishness and mutual trust under the aegis of an aunt who is own sister to Miss Mole.

'The aunt always agrees to things, doesn't she?' Hugh remarked with appreciation. 'It's funny, that, in a grown-up person.'[52]

Childhood also forms a vantage point for moral assessment in *Chatterton Square*, which also contains, in the character of Caroline Spanner, the definitive account of the E. H. Young solitary female – wry, tough, but humorous and sympathetic at need. The book, in some ways the maturest of the novels, suffers, however, from a rather artificial use of the Munich crisis to make its points. It represents a failure at the last on the author's part to accept her limitations.

E. H. Young is a good example of the novelist who gets buried in the multiplicity of books: her virtues are not of the kind that make for landmarks in literary histories. As Graham Greene pointed out, reviewing *The Curate's Wife*, 'The critical reputation of novelists rests, perhaps unfortunately, to a large extent on other professional writers, and it is only natural that these should prefer an author from whom they can learn.'[53] But E. H. Young, if no experimentalist, remains readable and interesting. Her manuscripts show her to have been a careful craftsman, her published work an unostentatious one; she has a mastery of dialogue, a sensitivity to domestic life and an intrinsic wisdom. The novels create their own distinctive world, spiritually as well as topographically, and succeed, where those of Mary Webb fail, in integrating an aesthetic and romantic sensibility into the contemporary world of change. Intensely and narrowly feminine at times, her work is as historically interesting as it is satisfying for its integrity and wit. Wasteful neither of words nor of emotions, the novels of E. H. Young are a perfect example of that steady undertow of minor but honourable writing which helps maintain the tradition and the public which can support the truly great.

III

The aspect of the rural experience presented in the novels of E. H. Young is probably that most widely held in its day: it has a genuinely representative quality. The country in its visual beauty, its quiet and freshness contrasting with the urban world of noise and mechanisation, becomes a symbol, not so much of a communal Arcadia (that, as has been seen, is rarely present in rural fiction), but of an emotional condition resistant to social and personal pressures. It provides a mental background to daily living, an emblem of inner freedom, much as it is found in Brett Young's novels or, more inquiringly, in the work of Sylvia Townsend Warner. Less attempt is made to draw country life as it is lived than to relate it to contemporary human values. The country has been tamed.

But, whereas E. H. Young keeps her country in touch with the town across the river, Mary Webb distills her own romantic landscape out of a world that was genuinely remote. Nonetheless she too makes of it a vehicle for truths to be mentally apprehended; her mysticism remains highly individualistic in effect, if not in intention. In both writers the more specifically romantic element strains the fabric of their work.

And in both of them we are aware of a tension (one that is acute in Mary Webb's books) between a realistic and humorous response to human life and a desire to interpret and idealise it. In terms of rural fiction this points to the contrast between an awareness of what country life actually involved, and the place which the country, through literary heritage and emotional custom, had come to mean subjectively. The kind of balance attained by Adrian Bell was not easily achieved; and in Mary Webb and E. H. Young it is subjectivity which predominates. To right that subjectivity and keep it rooted in actuality, so that it could become in a human sense truly sacramental, it would seem that an absolute regional affiliation was needed, and there were few novelists to possess it. Phillpotts did not live on Dartmoor; Trevena came to it after a varied career outside; Hugh Walpole and Sheila Kaye-Smith were oriented to London literary life; Brett Young travelled extensively; and even Mary Webb, though much against her will, did not live exclusively in Shropshire. The native writers immerse themselves more thoroughly in their material (Street is an obvious example here) but at the cost of narrowing its range and appeal: even Bell's work, fine though it is, is more a record than a fictional re-creation. In the novels of Constance Holme, however, we do find a regionalism that is given a meaning of universal application, while in those of T. F. Powys the Dorset world he knew is used for fictional ends that transcend the limitations of his material. Both writers lived exclusively in the districts they describe; but what makes them the most satisfying rural novelists of their time (1913–31) is the fact that each possessed a methodology and an overall moral outlook which makes of their experience something more than a mental or a local one. They indicated to what dimensions the rural novelist might reasonably aspire.

10 A Land of One's Own: Constance Holme

I

The novels of Constance Holme (1880–1955) are set in the area of marshland and fell surrounding the head of Morecambe Bay. The youngest member of a family established there for generations with a long tradition of land agency behind it, she herself married a land agent, and lived for some years at Kirkby Lonsdale, a short distance inland from the Bay, before returning to her birthplace at Milnthorpe, closer to the shore.[1] There is a singular completeness about her work, and she appears to have had the unusual quality of knowing what she was able to do as well as what she wanted to do, and of confining her actual performance to that. She published eight novels between 1913 and 1930,[2] and a book of short stories as well as a few poems and one-act plays. She occupies a curious place in publishing history, having, on the initiative of Sir Humphrey Milford, had all her works printed in 'The World's Classics' series – the only twentieth-century author to have this distinction. Indeed, The World's Classics edition of her short stories, *The Wisdom of the Simple* (1937), is the only one.

Her attitude to her work was serious (she was a slow and careful writer) and her outlook conservative. In a letter to Humphrey Milford she decribed herself as 'one who tried to crystallise the loveliness of England before it departed',[3] but the prefaces written for her early novels when they were included in The World's Classics show her to have been aware of the inevitability of change. All three books describe a society on the brink of upheaval: horse-carriages and motor cars drive side by side down the lanes. As she wrote in her preface to *Crump Folk Going Home* (1913), 'Country life was at that stage which, it is said, may be seen in the sinking of a vessel when the water seems to pause for a second before it swamps the boat.'[4] This novel in particular, with its pierrot concert party and early ragtime songs, gives one the feel of a past era moving perceptibly into a contemporary one.[5]

Its theme is the power of tradition. The Lyndesays have owned Crump for centuries, and a younger branch of the family have acted as its agents for the same length of time. The novel is the story of Deborah, the last of the line of the younger branch, who, from her love of the place and its traditions, is prepared to marry into the older branch for that reason alone – an interesting variation on the love-versus-marriage theme. The death of her betrothed is followed by the humiliating discovery of his secret marriage to the daughter of a local horse-dealer. Deborah finally marries the younger brother, after prolonged misunderstandings, and Nettie, the horse-dealer's daughter, pairs off with the farmer whom she has always loved. Thus the novel's resolution establishes a balance between classes once again – the world of Constance Holme is as stratified as Jane Austen's. But it is not rigidly stratified: class is seen in terms of function, and to know one's place is presented as knowing one's place for service in the community. Indeed, Dixon the farmer is every bit as proud as the Lyndesay family; and Nettie has to be forgiven for leaving her sphere as much as 'the county' feels that Deborah needs to be forgiven for aspiring beyond hers.

Crump Folk Going Home is an extremely vivid, fast-moving book, written very much from within the society it portrays, yet with a sharp eye for that society's follies. It proceeds almost inferentially by a narrative method which was to be developed further in the later novels. The landscape is beautifully evoked, and the book is full of local life and events – a sheep-dog trial (extremely well described), a wrestling match, a hunt, all of them highlighted cinematically. The style is often terse, a shade elliptical, though with an unerring sense of rhythm.

> Deb turned from earnest contemplation of a window of tinned fruits to find the Hon. Mrs. Stalker's carriage at the grocer's steps; that august personage herself enthroned therein, wearing a fur garment of such dimensions as to send all the Crump cats scuttling for shelter to the nearest drain.[6]

Here the quickening of pace with 'Crump cats scuttling' serves to emphasise the high-spirited irreverence; while in the account of the sheep-dog trial the very phrasing and accompanying change of tempo help to convey the actual movement of events.

Dixon dropped his hand to the dog's head, and she cowered to the very ground. He repeated the experiment until she stood up confidently under his touch, and the two looked into each other's eyes. Then he jerked his own head sharply, and she was gone like the wind up the edge of the slope, to be checked by a sweet, clear whistle before she was upon the fresh prey, who raised innocent eyes, unafraid of the harmless black and white patch so near. presently there was another whistle, a languid wave of a thin ash plant, and the quartette was ambling unconcernedly towards the first of the flags.[7]

In *The Lonely Plough* (1914) Constance Holme gives her most comprehensive picture of the society into which she was born, and the book is a celebration of its values. It is her most well known novel, her most conventional and technically the least interesting. More deliberately than the others it sets out to portray a way of life, to show, in the words of the preface, that

> the need for loyalty remains – for honesty and straight dealing and confidence in our fellows. . . . 'Be honest with the land,' say the farmers, 'and it will be honest with you' – and while we have the land we shall have the lesson.[8]

Loyalty and honesty are here tested against the background of a great flood on the marsh at the head of the bay. A huge sea-wall is built to withstand the tide and reclaim acres of farmland; and doubts are cast on its strength. Itself a creation of the father of the present land-agent, it becomes a symbol of the esteem in which the Lancaster family are held. An old man moves into the cottage behind the sea-wall as a gesture of confidence in the Lancasters: but the wall gives way, and he and his wife are drowned. The whole conception of loyalty is thus questioned.

The picture is avowedly that of 'an ancient system working at its best under the most ideal conditions, a triangular relationship which needed the right men in each department to keep the bearings smooth',[9] but there is no idealisation: the farmers are each sharply characterised, the landlord is somewhat ineffectual, and the main burden falls on the land-agent, Lancaster. He has chosen to back his father's faith in the impregnability of the dike: when it breaks it is himself and not his father whom he blames.

I'm not of the class that judge their fathers. I was brought up to see mine as the standing emblem of right thinking, and right doing. . . . My father *had* the right to take the risk, both for himself and for posterity. . . . It isn't that I don't believe in inheritance, in reaping and sowing from one generation to another. I've seen the dragon's teeth come up too often for that. We're bound both before and behind – I admit it all the way. . . . We've a hand in more fates than one. But, in spite of that, I hold that a strong man wins out on his own – wins out or goes to the wall. There's no other self-respecting creed. This thing fell to me. Judgement is due on me. I wouldn't have it otherwise.[10]

The Lonely Plough depicts a vanished world, but it does so with a simple conviction that remains valid, and with a dignity and warmth of feeling that it would be hard to produce today. Not that the novel is entirely successful : the sub-plot concerning the singer Cyril Wigmore, 'the great Quetta', and his visit incognito to the new family from Manchester, who have taken over one of the local country houses, is far-fetched and rather silly; nor are the businessman and Lancaster's hare-brained aunt more plausible as characters. Indeed, the whole part of the novel concerning the Shaw family and Lancaster's 'Green Gates of Vision' is shot through with whimsicality. What stays in the mind is the account of the marshland landscape, the farming families, and the stubborn old man Wolf Whinnerah, who is the pathetic victim of his own obstinate trust. And the portrayal of Harriet Knewstubb, the awkward, bossy, mannish young farmer, is as touching as it is humorous and unpatronising. Harriet's portrait is a success because she is presented as part of a total social world – she is not just a 'character', but a product of her environment and a part of it.

Both these first two novels are full of the sense of what it means to belong to a particular region. As the author wrote to Humphrey Milford, 'How lucky "regional" writers are, to be able to give people a breath of home.'[11] Home : a place where one lives as oneself. These early novels are an analysis of what that means; and the last of them, *The Old Road from Spain* (1915), subjects the community to more critical attention. Here, Rowland Huddlestone is literally worked to death by the imperious Mrs Garnett, who uses his love for her to push through her endless social projects. In this novel we find a wariness about social activity coupled with a sympathy with contemplation and a celebration of personal ties; and the author uses legends and traditions from her own family to tell a haunting story of a man's conflict with his ancestry. In doing so she draws freely on the supernatural. To use supernatural motifs in a serious, as distinct from a purely diversionary, novel may be to beg questions; but Constance Holme integrates this element firmly into her plot. The sheep doom hanging over the Huddlestone family, whereby the herd of sheep descend from the fell into the park to warn the master of impending death, is a matter of local consciousness and thus an essential part of the life of the community. Luis Huddlestone accepts his part in the family tradition and lays the curse by himself retravelling the course taken by his Spanish ancestors washed up on the shore after the Armada has sailed round the north of Scotland. Within the book's total context this is plausible: it is shown as the reassertion in him of the sea-faring strain of all the 'Spanish' Huddlestones. The story can be read as a parable of the nature of tradition.

Whereas death is feared by the Huddlestones, to the Faussett family it is a welcome fact of life. The portrayal of the Faussetts, however, suffers from the same kind of weak prettiness which disfigures the account of the Green Gates of Vision (the capital letters are themselves a warning sign of affectation) and represents a side of the author's writing which is elsewhere held more firmly in check, a side that is the result of her own social situation and which she is insufficiently detached to control. At this point her work suggests the Florence Barclay school. But Constance Holme can put even her most irritating characters into perspective. One of Rowly Huddlestone's affectations is to run his house for the benefit of a frequently invoked but never present Lady of the House. This is as bad as Bill Faussett's talk of his Dear Old Mother: that is until, after Rowly's death, it is revealed that the Lady of the House is the vigorous Mrs Garnett, whom Rowly had refused to marry because of the family curse, and who has ever afterwards resented his refusal to allow her to share his fear. 'I had a right, a supreme right, and he took it from me without my leave – the right to suffer if I chose.'[12] Mrs Garnett voices a just criticism of Bill's and Rowly's worlds: she thinks Bill sentimental 'with his pretty-pretty world of dreams'; she despises Rowly for being 'too stupid to see that he thrust upon me the harder cross, too soft-fibred to dare to trust either my strength or my love'.[13] But this attitude is not endorsed by the author, and the concluding paragraph suggests that her real sympathies are with the Faussetts. There is an uncertain balancing of moral values.

II

Constance Holme's central achievement is the quartet of novels in which she explores the lives and life-illusions of those whose work maintains the great families in being: *Beautiful End* (1918), *The Splendid Fairing* (1919), *The Trumpet in the Dust* (1921) and *The Things Which Belong* – (1925). These books are interesting and valuable in more than one way. They are effective character studies of elderly people, itself an unusual choice of subject; but what is peculiar to them is the manner in which they explore their theme. Each novel takes place within a single day, and the action is interrupted by continual flashbacks, conducted largely through the medium of the characters' thoughts and feelings. Four years before *Jacob's Room* appeared, Constance Holme had anticipated the method of Virginia Woolf. Dorothy Richardson had, it is true, published the first instalment of *Pilgrimage* in 1915, but her narrative methods are different. Constance Holme does not employ any of the mannerisms of the stream-of-consciousness technique; unlike Joyce she makes no attempt to imitate the processes of thought. Rather, she uses the device of free association, the reminiscent style exemplified at its best in Ford Madox Ford's *The Good Soldier* (1915), published three years before *Beautiful End*.

These four novels embody a philosophy, a comment on human experience and a definition of tragedy. Each book centres round a dream and the nature of its fulfilment and as such comments obliquely on the rural novelist's confrontation of change. In *Beautiful End* Christopher Sill, penned up in his shrewish daughter-in-law's slatternly home, old and unwanted, dreams continually of returning to his marsh farm, sold up through his own incapacity for business; at last he does return there, as the cherished guest of his other son and daughter-in-law – only to find that the new reality is destroying the dream by which he has lived. He is too old to adapt, and voluntarily returns to his life with the hateful Marget. In *The Splendid Fairing* Simon and Sarah Thornthwaite have consoled themselves for their wretchedly unsuccessful life on the marsh farm with the thought of the return from Canada of their feckless son Geordie. Geordie does return, on the day that Sarah learns that she is going blind and Simon agrees to become his younger brother's hired man; but, feckless to the end, he pretends to be his cousin Jim, son of the hated and overbearing sister-in-law Eliza; and Sarah, broken by bitterness, sends him to his death on the sands as the tide comes in. This, the most Hardyesque of the novels, seems at first to play too much on coincidence to be effective; but the action is rendered as the result of character – Geordie's, Sarah's, Eliza's. The dream is destroyed through Sarah's disloyalty to the spirit of the dream; but that very disloyalty is itself the result of personal misfortune. This is the darkest of the author's books, a tale of total defeat without any alleviating circumstances.

In *The Trumpet in the Dust* the central figure is Ann Clapham, an elderly charwoman. On the day that she acquires the almshouse on which she has set her heart, she hears of her daughter's death and voluntarily surrenders it in order to take care of her grandchildren. In *The Things Which Belong –*, the shortest and simplest of the group, Constance Holme portrays a gardener's wife who has for years lived off the hope of following her children to Canada : when at last the dream is about to be realised she finds that she is too old to go. In every case it is the past which determines the present: the characters of Kit, Sarah, Mrs Clapham and Mattie Kirkly have been formed without their knowing, and they find that the dream they live by cannot be achieved without adaptation to circumstances. Only Sarah fails to learn the lesson: in *The Splendid Fairing* the external tragedy coalesces with the internal tragedy of the non-fulfilment of the dream. This is because Sarah interferes with the course of events. Goaded by the smug and patronising Eliza into boasting that Geordie is coming home and that Jim is dead, she is compelled to follow her lie through, so that when the real Geordie does turn up she is unable to see through his disguise. Her outward blindness is the token of an inner one, and although her deepest self knows who he is, her fatalistic despair joins with her desire to hurt Eliza in allowing him to walk out in ignorance to his death.

The tragedy is caught poignantly when Sarah succeeds in convincing Eliza that Jim is dead. Eliza breaks down at the sight of Jim's photograph.

There was no doubting the sincerity of her grief, and the big sobs shaking their way through her shook Sarah too. Her own lips trembled, and her eyes filled; her hands quivered on the arms of the chair. She could not see the pitiful fingers stroking the child's face, but she who had offered that worship herself needed little help to guess. She had her revenge in full as she sat and listened to the passion that never dies, forcing its way upward even through Eliza's leathern soul; but the revenge was a two-edged sword that wounded herself as well. All the generosity in her that was still alive and kind would have sprung to the surface instantly if the story had been true. She would have groped her way to Eliza's side in an effort to console, and perhaps the lifelong enemies might have drawn together for once. But the story was not true, and she had nothing to offer and no right of any sort to speak. She could only sit where she was and suffer and shake, hating herself more in this moment of absolute conquest than she had ever hated Eliza in her darkest hour.[14]

The tragedy in *The Trumpet in the Dust*, on the other hand, is a surface matter only. Mrs Clapham's whole nature is bound up with her work, and it is the weakness of age which makes her seek out the almshouse. The scene in which she visits it and comes up against the prim old ladies who are to be her fellow inmates is a piece of comic writing worthy of Mrs Gaskell – the novelist with whom Constance Holme has most affinities.[15] Both writers had the rare gift of portraying simple kindness without slipping into sentimentality. Whatever lapses there may be in the early novels, Constance Holme does not falter in the later ones. Mrs. Clapham's dream house is in keeping with Mrs. Clapham's nature; life in the almshouse is not. In the end her renunciation is an act of self-affirmation.

This novel and that which succeeded it are full of evocations of domestic life, of much-loved household furniture and of all the routine and impediment which go to make up the undertide of life. It is this undertide which, in *The Things Which Belong –* , ultimately rises up to flood the dream. As Mattie realises,

They would plant another hedge for her, if she wanted it . . . but they could not ensure her another forty years in which to watch it growing. They could not make each leaf and twig speak to the memories of a whole life. They could not give her back the English soil which she had salted and watered with her tears.[16]

The measured cadence of these three sentences, their dying fall and almost Biblical intonations are characteristic of Constance Holme's later style. The sharp, rather mannered idiom of *Crump Folk* gives way to a more simple and flowing measure, handled at its best with consummate ease. It is this style which more than anything else gives their sense of timelessness to these brief tales of tragedy, loss and healing. But the serene movement of the sentences is balanced by the use of dialect and realistic speech, as in this scene from *Beautiful End* as Kit sits, lost and bewildered over his tea, on his arrival back at his old home:

'You're a good lass,' the old man said suddenly, looking her in the face, and for the first time his voice sounded warm and strong. Their eyes met in full and happy accord, and their smiles mingled like the smiles of intimate friends. Their natures, each kindly and beautiful in its way, reached out one to the other and were enriched. Just for a moment she saw him as he had been when he was young; the affectionate, dreamy soul whom so many had helped and loved. He in his turn saw her as the future of the place, the soul that was making the new dream for the house. The beauty of kindness and good humour and happy work, she was bringing it all these, just as his own wife had brought them long ago. But it was a new beauty, and there was no place in it for him; he had his own, and his own was quite complete. Now he was beginning to see what he had done – how he had wandered into another's dream of home. There was no room for him here unless he was ready to renounce his own, a thing which he had not thought possible even with death. Already he was being punished as those are punished who are false to their dreams: he could neither look forward happily nor yet behind. Suddenly he was conscious of being stifled by the pleasant room, oppressed by the fire and the sun and the smell of the food. His eyes dropped wearily from the girl's face, and age and blankness came back to his own. 'It's terrible warm,' he said, in a fretted tone, and pushed back his chair sharply, and got to his feet. 'I'll gang out,' he added, looking towards the door. 'I partly what think I'll be easier outside.'[17]

The transference of style here is very telling. And the tragedy is not only Kit's but that of Agnes as well: for all her kindness she is, in her determination that she knows what is best for Kit, potentially as much a tyrant as is Marget.

Marget, who makes no bones about finding him a nuisance, and does all in her power to make his life a misery, nevertheless has an odd but definite relationship with him.

They had come too close . . . to slip apart with ease. The hatred on both sides had its mixture of fascination and fear. He felt a helpless dread of a power that beauty could not touch; she, an angry terror of genius out of reach.[18]

Beautiful End is the most subtle of these four tragedies. The poignance of Kit's return to the farm is intense; and yet the dream must be its own justification.

Comfort, position, peace in his last days – all must go into the fire
to serve the fine flame of his dream. He was only a vague old man
who had made a muddle of life, but firmly and fightingly he was
sure of that. There was nothing here for him but lovely things
grown strange. That which he had made for himself he might have,
but nothing else. 'For what we take we must pay, and the price is
cruel hard.'[19]

This is the theme of all four novels. Mattie is saved from Kit's mistake,
Mrs Clapham finds her dream in voluntarily surrendering it, Sarah
loses it through falseness to its spirit; but in each case the same austere
law holds good: 'no matter what you paid, there was always something
to pay'.[20]

This awareness of moral law is furthered by the close-knit fabric
of the narratives: everything holds together, there are no loose ends.
In *Beautiful End* especially there is a fine use of linking imagery.
Agnes, waiting for Kit to arrive, and watching the slow progress of the
trap which is carrying him across the marsh, is reminded by it of a
yacht she once watched sailing across the bay, and of how it seemed
as if it were about to sail right into the farm beside the sea-wall. Later
on we are told of Kit, riding in the trap as Agnes is watching him, with
his fiddle on his knee, being reminded of how once he had sailed across
the bay to the farm and had thought that he was about to sail into
the house, and of his bitter disappointment when the ship came to rest
at the usual landing place. All these images are caught up in the following passage, which, however, occurs before one is given Kit's recollec-
tion of the ship, so that it is only on a re-reading that one is made
fully aware of its significance. It in fact interprets the whole theme of
the novel.

She began to sing as she went about, and her voice escaped through
the open windows and fled away through the door; yet it was in the
house all the time as well. Down on the shore a man looked up as
he stepped on the sands, hearing the voice that was both within and
without. The house looked empty, he thought, with all its windows
wide, and the voice that sang seemed a bodiless voice, making the
house the emptier for its song. It followed him as he went leisurely
out, making for the channel and the farm across. He did not hurry
for the tide would not be ready to turn for over an hour. Presently
he was on the bank, hailing the farm for a boat; and his voice, shrill
and lost-sounding in the open space, broke like a cry for help across

the joy of the song. Thomas, down by the gate, heard both the song and the cry, but the old man coming in the trap heard only the fiddle singing on his knee.

She sang so long that she did not know when she stopped, but Thomas, down by the gate, felt as if a fiddle-string had snapped. He had the same sense as of something wounded and ceasing to be. It was just at that moment the trap checked at his side . . .

The wife in the house looked out and saw the marsh roads empty north and east and south. The crawling speck she had watched so long must have reached its stopping place at last. She thought again of the yacht, swinging so eagerly over the tide, only to turn so suddenly, at the end. Even the highest hopes, it seemed, met barriers they could not leap . . . But the trap, when the time came for it to turn, trundling over land that had once been sailing ground as well, would leave something behind it when it went away.[21]

This passage is as shot through with complex meanings as a poem. The disappointment of both Kit and Agnes is identified by the use of the image of the yacht; the man on the shore is in one sense Kit, since it is his cry for help which cuts Agnes's song; while Kit himself, whose life is bound up with his skill as a fiddler and with his music, is, through the man's cry and its effect on Thomas, linked once more with Agnes so that his tragedy is seen to be in one sense hers. The apparent emptiness of the house, in part the effect of the song, looks forward to Kit's own sensations in fact of Agnes's triumphant welcome to a house that has been renewed beyond his powers of recognition. The final note about the trap is an added irony: it will carry away rather than leave what Agnes had hoped: 'a heart in haven, a spirit released, a wanderer come home'. What it will leave for Thomas and Agnes we are no more told than we are what Simon and Sarah's future is to be: all we know is that they 'had taken, and would have to pay'.[22]

This passage also exemplifies another aspect of Constance Holme's writing, and one which can produce irritation: her use of a row of dots to conclude a paragraph or single sentence. (In the above passage, for instance, none of the dots signify omissions.) This was a device of the time – one finds it repeatedly in the novels of Hugh Walpole and Osbert Sitwell – and was frequently employed in order to load a sentence with a significance which it might not otherwise possess.[23] But in Constance Holme's case they are put to a more specific use. The resemblance of her technique to that of the moving picture has already been noted: scene dissolves into scene in accordance with internal

association, there are fade-outs, long-shots (as in the above description
of the man on the shore), linking symbols; and the 'cuts' from scene
to scene are frequently made by the resort to the method of punctuation,
in which authorial comment often appears as if actually lighting a scene,
giving it its particular proportion or significance. A good example comes
in *The Splendid Fairing*, after the description of Eliza's gate-crashing
of Simon and Sarah's quiet wedding by arranging behind their backs a
joint one with Simon's brother Will. Her wedding finery and noisy
guests ruin the whole affair for Simon and Sarah.

> They stood in the grass among the rose-bushes on the graves, and
> watched Eliza drive triumphantly away. The parson followed them
> out to make a kindly speech, which they were far too angry and
> humiliated to hear. He wanted to tell them that God had certainly
> liked them best, but he knew they would not believe him if he did.
> They were so certain that it was Eliza who had had the beautiful
> hour. They were too simple to know that it was only they who had
> any of the beauty to carry home . . .

This fade-out, so to call it, both modulates and concludes what had
gone before; and it is followed by a change of key or scene:

> All their lives Simon and Sarah had been the victims of Eliza's
> Method. Nothing they had, horse, cow or cart, but was sooner or
> later measured by Blindbeck standards and condemned.[24]

The description of Eliza's Method, one of insidious and denigatory comparison between the fortunes of the two families and their farms brings
us back from the past to the narrative of the events of the pivotal day
round which the novel is built, with a presentation of that method in
action, resulting in Sarah's fatal lie – itself seen as the inevitable consequence of the wedding day long years ago. And the phrase about the
beauty carried home is echoed bitterly at the end of the book when
Sarah thinks of the fairing that Geordie would bring her from Martin-
mas market, and when she calls out to herself, after sending Geordie to
his death, 'There'll be a bonny fairing for Eliza when the tide comes
in !', and later still, in the last words of the book, 'Gang out and seek
our fairing, master – mine and thine !' It is this close density of image,
this superimposition of scene upon scene which gives body and reality
to these otherwise simple tales, and which makes them permanently
rereadable. Less extended in formal scope than the early novels, they

yet present a fuller and more satisfactory picture of the life of the region, perhaps because in them the human element interprets the regional and not the other way round.

Nevertheless the background plays a crucial role. The deep love with which Constance Holme writes of her native country is based on the awareness that the landscape does itself become a part of character. In *The Splendid Fairing*, for instance, she remarks that

> it is the landscape itself which holds the eye, and from which comes the great, silent magic that is called memory, and mostly means youth. It is the little events of every day life that obsess a man at the last; the commonplace, circular come-and-go that runs between the cradle and the grave. Not public health problems, or new inventions, or even the upheavals of great wars; but marriage, birth and death, the coming of strangers destined to be friends, the changing of tenants in houses which mean so much more than they ever mean themselves. Binding all is the rich thread of the seasons, with its many-coloured strands; and, backing all, the increasing knowledge of Nature and her ways, that revolving wheel of beauty growing ever more complex and yet more clear, more splendid and yet more simple as the pulses slow to a close.[25]

It is this feeling for the sacredness of daily routine which gives the novels their Wordsworthian quality. Moreover, there is a unity of symbolic reference underlying them all. The sea is the bringer of tragedy, the land the place of security and peace. In *The Things Which Belong –* , it is Mattie's fear of the water which ultimately stops her going to Canada. In *The Old Road from Spain* Ireleth Hall faces inland as if to ward off the curse on the sea-fairing Huddlestones; and in *The Lonely Plough* and *The Splendid Fairing* too the sea is hostile. However, it is the marsh, where land and sea meet, which is the main focus of attention; only in the last two novels does it play no part.

In her final novel Constance Holme turned to the life lived inland, in the dales. *He-Who-Came?* is a quiet and charming tale of white magic on an inland farm, told with a ritual repetition of motifs and phrases. In this little fantasy there is an element of the parabolic. Aunt Martha, with her happy ability to make the butter come and her second sight and friendship with the birds and animals, is an idealised extension of the typical good farmer's wife, herself a part of natural forces and mistress of her environment. Under her care the four motherless children grow up in an idyllic world, the magic unquestioned and accepted as normality. But Aunt Martha overreaches herself, indulges a personal whim; and the spell whereby she compels the Prince (of Wales, presumably) to pass a night in the farmhouse spare-room makes the children self-conscious and unhappily aware of a magic that is on the verge of becoming black. Innocence has gone:

> One by one they were creeping out of the charmed circle of their childhood. . . . They . . . had crossed a boundary. Henceforth the merest buttercup magic would smack of 'fetching Samuel'.[26]

There is a breath of genuine tragedy, in *He-Who-Came?* in spite of its lightness and humour: more than any of Constance Holme's other novels it celebrates a world that is forever gone, the English pastoral ideal in an austere North Country setting, but ideal nonetheless. Even the formidable Mrs Walker, the children's mother, a robust comic creation with a touch of Mrs Poyser, is an aspect of it; her very death partakes of its beauty and fitness.

> Whatever world she had gone to before the sun had set, she must have taken with her delicate yet sharp pictures of a crystalline, coloured earth and sky; of Box Tree, white as a Leghorn hen against its screen of shaded greens; of clean flags and mossy slates, shining windows and blue smoke. Scents, too – of sweet-briar somewhere in the garden hedge; the warm, kind smell of the shippon, and the cheerful smell of her own baking. And sounds – of running water; of cattle feeding; of children's voices; of the whole busy stir of nature life about her; and of her first-born son, whistling to his dog on some high spur of the opposite fell; whistling sweetly and yet so piercingly that it seemed as if in no part of the universe could she be too far away to hear him.[27]

This was Westmorland as Constance Holme knew and loved it. The presentation of its world naturally has its limitations: her very familiarity with it, her acceptance of it, mean a lack of dramatic tension; but she is aware of the distinction between a settled way of life and a good and properly human way of living it. Against the happy picture of Box Tree and of Agnes's home-making in *Beautiful End* must be set the fact of Eliza's Method, whereby even in the prosperous farm of Blindbeck can become a hell on earth. Indeed, Eliza in her use of Blindbeck to further her own spite and desire to bully, suggests an exploitation of the traditional and old-world not unrelated to the cheap deception of a travel agent's poster.

'Sally, my lass, you'd best see about mashing another pot. There'll be a deal of folk sending up for more in a brace o' shakes, and we can't have them saying they're not as well tret at Blindbeck as they're used. Not as anybody's ever said it yet as I've heard tell, though you never know what folks'll do for spite. Most on 'em get through their three cups afore they're done, and me like as not just barely through my first. Eh, but I used to be terble bothered, just at the start, keeping folks filled and their mugs as they rightly should! You barns wasn't up then, of course, but we'd farm-lads in the house, and wi' a rare twist to 'em an' all! Yon's a thing you've never been bothered with, Sarah, wi' such a small spot and lile or nowt in the way o' work. You'd nobbut a couple o' hands, at any time, had you, and not them when you'd Geordie an' Jim? You've a deal to be thankful for, I'm sure, you have that! You've always been able to set down comfortable to your meat, instead o' fretting yourself to skin and bone seeing as other people had their wants . . . Nay now, Mrs. Addison, there's a cup in the pot yet! . . . Pass Mrs. Addison the cream, Mary Phyllis, and waken up and look sharp about it! Blindbeck tea's none the worse, I reckon, for a drop o' Blindbeck cream. . . .'28

This embodies a criticism of something more than Eliza herself. As with all Constance Holme's work, it is the expression of something deeply and thoughtfully felt.

Her achievement, while not of the very highest kind, is a fine and authentic one. Integrity, craftsmanship, a seriously pondered scale of values, compassion, humour, a feeling for human dignity and for the elements which go to make up human life, and a knowledge of her own creative limitations, all entitle her to an honourable place among the novelists of her time. That she has, despite the tribute of the Oxford University Press (though perhaps, in view of its inflationary nature, because of it), been almost totally neglected by literary critics is perhaps to say more about the state of literary society and politics than it is about literature: it certainly reflects on the status of the rural novel. The occasional softness of phrase and sentimentality of conception, the occasional facetiousness and banality of language rightly tell against her; but they are small flaws beside her virtues. It is more probably her virtues that do her disservice, for the gentleness in her work is currently out of fashion. Her portrait of Westmorland, with its bustling market days, its choral societies and hockey matches, bazaars and wrestling contests, rent-audits and poverty, feuds and household sales, goes deep. It has a quiet unemphatic insistence upon the continuing presence of goodness, a goodness of a simplicity in which it is no longer easy to believe. But the continual awareness of fell and sands and marsh creates a moral landscape, austere and beautiful, which is more pervasive than the visible one. In the last resort it is this extra dimension of meaning which gives the novels of Constance Holme their strong and enduring appeal. For all the limitation of her gifts and outlook, she is in the tradition of Wordsworth and Coleridge:

> we all create the land we love and which we look at with our eyes, since the soul by which it breathes and speaks is drawn for each one of us from his own.[29]

That is the definitive justification for the regional novel; and the recognition of the artist's vocation and nature which the words imply is the proper measure of her own achievement.

11 Rural Symbolism: T. F. Powys

I

If Henry Williamson is an example of a novelist esteemed by a large body of educated readers but ignored by critics, T. F. Powys (1875–1953) is a clear instance of the opposite. He shares with Mary Webb the doubtful distinction of being one of the targets of *Cold Comfort Farm*; and, indeed, the kind of bucolic world which he created was to have many, not necessarily satirical, successors, the most notable of these being Dylan Thomas's *Under Milk Wood* (1954). But in Powys's case the attribution is more of a compliment than a slight. Far from being a formally 'realistic' writer, he is, in his handling of rural material, deliberately mannered, even to distortion. Those who mock his work have failed to see the point: like his brother John Cowper Powys (in this if in nothing else) he had a predominantly ironic vision; and also like his brother he produced work that was eccentric to contemporary taste. That eccentricity has denied him a wide public; but there is no other rural novelist who can match him for originality.

Theodore Powys was for a short while a farmer in Suffolk; but he soon retired to a remote part of Dorset and devoted himself to writing. The centre of all his novels and short stories is the downland village of East Chaldon, where he lived in a red-brick villa reputedly designed by Thomas Hardy.[1] All his novels are set in similar small villages, grouped together and related to each other in his last full-length novel, *Unclay*. The various villages have different symbolic qualities. Those of the earlier novels – Shelton, Norbury, Dodderdown – are on the whole places where human wickedness proliferates and where there is no benign Mr Weston or Tinker Jar to intervene and save the innocent from their persecutors. The villages of the middle period – Mockery Gap, Madder and Folly Down – are places of more comprehensive society, a mixture of good and evil. Tadnol, the setting of Powys's one comic novel, *Kindness in a Corner*, and of many of the lighter tales, is the one place that approaches the idyllic, a village where innocence flourishes and the amiable ghost of the virgin saint Susanna appears upon the green. That the inhabitants of these villages were distinct in the author's mind is evident from the various cross-references which are to be found throughout his work. That work is thus a coherent whole, and it has a significant development.

This is a point worth stressing in view of the fact that Powys is generally known only as the author of *Mr Weston's Good Wine*. That *Mr Weston* is his most successful novel is demonstrably true, and it alone would justify his claim to serious critical consideration; but to view it in isolation from the rest of his work is to underestimate his achievement. His range is wider than might at first appear; and there is a good deal of diversity in style and method. To read *Mr Weston* in conjunction with *Mr Tasker's Gods, Mark Only*, the *Fables, Kindness in a Corner* and the stories in *The Two Thieves* is to realise how his craft and attitudes progressed.

The novels did not appear in the order in which they were written,[2] and when the three tales published in *The Left Leg* appeared in 1923 Powys already had a good deal of work in manuscript. 'The Left Leg' itself had been preceded by *Mr Tasker's Gods*, written as early as 1916, but not published until 1925, and by *Black Bryony*, written in 1917 and published second. *Mark Only* (1924) was written in 1922. Thereafter, the order of writing follows the order of publication, except for certain short stories which appeared in various collections. It is notable that once publication was achieved the tenor of the writing decreased in bitterness. The early novels are harsh and savage in tone.

Of these *Mr Tasker's Gods* is the most interesting. It posits hard-and-fast attitudes that are to be modified in Powys's maturer work, and it is told with a certain crudity; but it is forceful and has a dourness that is effective. It is the most socially conscious of the novels, and in it the author establishes antinomies that are to be the central element in his work. The contrast between the rich and the poor is overlaid by that between the weak and the strong, and still more notably by that between the greedy and the meek. A fierce, almost Swift-like irony plays over much of the book. It appears on the first page, when Powys remarks that 'It must be remembered that servants like a room with scant furniture: it means less work and it reminds them of home.'[3] This is a kind of social perspective that is carried further in his portrait of the worldly young curate, John Turnbull:

He went forth every afternoon, like a hunter, and followed respectable rich families almost to their bankers' doors. He was polite and
genial, the sort of young man who gives cigarettes out of a silver
case to tramps.[4]

But this kind of easy satire is less characteristic of Powys's attitude to
the clergy in this book than the unrelenting hatred with which he
pursues the character of Turnbull's father. His main charge against
the clergy is that they have betrayed a trust, have become part of a
world which it is their mission to redeem. He is under no illusion as
to the wickedness of his rural world:

> in the village, there were human beings of divers kinds. There were
> full-fed, greed-haunted, soul-starved farmers; work-worn labourers,
> scraped almost to the bone by their toil; mean-mouthed women,
> whose tongue rudely garnished their homes, and poisoned the beauty
> of the village; and children, who from the very first, even from the
> breast, were taught to hate all thoughts that are noble. They were,
> the people down there in their mud caves, shut out from all the fair
> gardens of wonder, of life, shut out by their own hands . . . all their
> lives they were ruled and dominated by the greed of getting, longing
> always to get, never to be; the under ones waiting, like gaunt cattle
> with starved eyes, for their chance, for their chance of rising from
> stealing broken bits and sticks and cinders, to openly putting money,
> pulled from the already wasted souls of other labourers, in the
> bank . . . they were ever ready to cast dung upon any shining spark
> of heaven-sent light that fell amongst them.[5]

The disenchantment here is total. It is this relentless insistence on
human limitations which makes Powys's world so unpalatable: his
innocents are helpless before the oppressors, because the power of the
world is with the oppressors. The only lightening of this grim vision
is in the words of Mr Neville, the saintly parson of Maid's Madder:
'It is horrible, it will always be horrible, but it is also divine, because
the Son of Man suffers here too.'[6] In these early novels Powys contents
himself with presenting the terrible dilemma of man, but in his later
work he seeks for a resolution.

The gods of Mr Tasker are his pigs. This novel is really about
religion. Powys's attitude to the Christian faith is ambiguous. On the
one hand he has scant respect for the worldly established clergy, while
filling his pages with amiable, ineffective parsons like Mr Dottery of
Tadnol or Mr Hayhoe of Dodder, who had God Himself for his only

penitent;[7] on the other hand he has an austere sense of judgement, and a sophisticated awareness of what religion is in its psychological aspects. Mr Tasker's love of gain, which brutalises and dehumanises him, is both mirrored in and furthered by his pigs – they are at once the means to his wealth and the gods which control his life. It is an ugly picture of certain aspects of modern society.

The ironies and bitterness in this novel permeate the narrative. An old housekeeper is presented as 'unpleasantly human';[8] a mother observed with her offspring on the highway, is described as being 'surrounded, almost eaten into, by three or four children'.[9] Even the landscape is depicted in sinister terms: the hero watched 'the angry summer clouds, like mad black sheep, racing each other across the heavens, and . . . the tortured movements of the green leaves of the elm tree that resented being beaten by the wind'.[10] In places the bitter tone is overdone, as when one woman's footsteps 'quickened with joy' at the prospect of rain preventing her neighbour's washing from getting dry. There are times when Powys's earlier work, in its bucolic exaggeration, does indeed suggest *Cold Comfort Farm*. What saves *Mr Tasker's Gods* from self-parody and morbidity is the terseness of the language, conveying a firmly held sense of injustice and a tartly tragic view of life that rests, not on any sentimental upbraiding of a postulated Providence, but on a stark though unreconciled awareness of man's inhumanity to man. Its grimness has a certain bracing quality, its pessimism a trace of health.

In these early books rustic society has no romantic qualities. 'Hester Dominy', the second story in *The Left Leg* volume, is especially concerned with the sheer boredom of much village life (a boredom reflected too in the flatness of the writing and the listless nature of the tale). It is a classic statement of futility. Religion has become a matter of listening to the church-bells: with a quiet effectiveness peculiarly his own, Powys anatomises the stultifying effects of conventional Christianity.

> The bells had taught Hester so much wisdom; they had, by dint of their monotonous ringing, made her tire of her own prettiness, they had coated her soul with an iron substance. The bells had led her into a blind alley from whence there is no turning. They had dimmed her light, they had increased her darkness, they had only left a little opening in her heart for love.[11]

There is no denunciation of man or fate, only weary resignation. What lightens the tale is compassion, nowhere in Powys's work so touchingly

evidenced as in his treatment of the old village women. The chapter
called 'Old Feet', besides anticipating his later use of mythological
elements, is notable for the tenderness with which he treats the willing
victims of that living death symbolised by the message of the bells.

> The nearer the farm the slower the two old women walked. They
> walked limply, dejectedly; the gleam of glory was gone, they were
> now eternally themselves.
>
> But slowly, too, there crept back into their hearts their old order
> to comfort them.
>
> 'Perhaps we had better use the new table-cloth to-night for tea,'
> Grace said. 'It will be nice to see something new, and we might try
> to make a new covering for the arm chair.'
>
> These homely plans rose up like ancient servants to comfort them.
> They had been driven out of the courts of love by the weight of their
> years, and now they returned as true old maids would return to the
> little pieces of furniture for comfort. . . . They had tried the sunshine
> for a moment, but for a moth the brightest sunshine is the deepest
> gloom.[12]

There is a touch of Tchekhov in this; and that stress on the regular
and ordinary which is a feature of the English rural novel at its
best.

Black Bryony is similarly pessimistic, and its title contains an unpleasant pun, since the bryony refers not only to the weed of that
name – a symbol here of sexuality – but also to the baby who is burnt
to death in the fire at Norbury Rectory. This is the poorest of the
novels, disjointed in construction and implausibly motivated; but it
has its moments of intensity, as in the strange opening when the
Salvation Army girl binds the black bryony wreaths about her head, or
when the kind old rector, Mr Crossley, watching the flames devour his
house, learns to love his flock – fire, in this novel, being a symbol of
purging, though it is also one of destruction. In Powys's world the
two concepts are usually the same.

Mark Only is the last and most accomplished of this early group of
'dark' novels. It is the life story of a ploughman, a quiet, simple man
born to be cheated and oppressed. The tone of the book is almost
entirely negative, its action determined by the author's pessimistic
vision. Mark, misnamed at the very font, is exploited by his family and
the evil Charlie Tulk; even the love of his young wife Nellie cannot
stand up to the brutality in man. Death, once more, is the rescuer,

personified in Mark's vision of the dogs who are pursuing him. At the end 'the dogs had him, the good dogs'.[13]

The wickedness of man is here seen as endemic in nature itself. In no other of Powys's novels is the country painted in such austere, drab colours, the action taking place against a predominantly winter landscape, with a great emphasis on dirt and smells. In places the book attains a Hardy-like grandeur, as in those moments when the figure of the ploughman is seen upon the skyline; but the narrative is overloaded with authorial comment and an almost mechanical insistence upon gloom. What gives it solidity and persuasiveness is the sensibility with which the character of Mark himself is presented, and the robustness and roundedness of the 'good' characters, who are treated here far more convincingly than are the innocents of Powys's later work: the friendly farmer Peter Andrews is alive in a way that few of Powys's puppet-like characters are alive. Moreover there begins to appear in this book that black humour which is one of Powys's most distinctive characteristics, a humour exemplified in the dialogue between Peter's two young grandsons about their grandmother's death (of rat poison).

> 'Did 'ee hear . . . what wold Potten did say when coffin went splash into water at bottom of grave? Parson were telling about dust when there were only mud on dirt heap, and Potten did whisper, 'Tis well wold 'oman be dead, or thik bloody puddle would have drownded she.' An' chalk stones did rattle down on thik box, same as hail an' rain on school window.'
> 'Will thik box go up to heaven?' asked Sam of the everwise Tom.
> ' 'Tis most like it will,' replied Tom, 'for God may take a fancy to they shined handles, and box when wold gran be tipped out will do fine to 'old 'Is winter onions.'[14]

II

There is still more humour in the novels of the middle period. *Mockery Gap* (1925), *Innocent Birds* (1926) and *Mr Weston's Good Wine* (1927) are mellower in tone than the earlier ones, partly because the author postulates some kind of alleviating activity within the general horror of existence. The figures of Tinker Jar, the Fisherman, and Mr Weston are attempts to define and illustrate what might be called this internal providence.

Powys's fictional world is full of presences and forces coming from outside man. In *Mark Only* there is a short but haunting passage concerning Mark's own personal fears.

> Once, as a child, he had been allowed to drive a blind horse to the station to bring back some coal. When he started to come home, he called to the horse from behind the cart to go on, without going to its head to lead it. The horse walked straight into the station wall. . . . As Mark drove home that day, he wondered why the horse, though she was blind, had not known that the wall was there. A curious thought crept then into the boy's mind – that there might be a station wall somewhere that he could not see.[15]

Such a sense of irrational disturbance is frequent in Powys's work; and it develops from novel to novel. In 'The Left Leg', the earliest of the tales to treat of providence, the disturbance takes the form of Tinker Jar's vengeance upon the cruel and greedy Farmer Mew; but Jar is little more than a figure of retribution. He is not integrated into the nature of the surrounding world like the Fisherman in *Mockery Gap* or the incomparable Mr Weston. Indeed Powys seems unsure as to whom Mr Jar represents. His name suggests identification with the God of the Old Testament, his come-and-go existence with the Son of Man wandering upon the face of the earth. But God is Himself invoked by name in a passage recalling Powys's earlier speculations in *Soliloquies of a Hermit* (1916).

This book, a collection of meditations in rural solitude, belongs to a genre frequently to be published at this time. *The Roadmender* has already been mentioned; another such book is *The Silences of the Moon* (1911) by Henry Law Webb, the husband of Mary Webb. It is a dignified and literate example of its kind; but one has only to set it alongside *Soliloquies of a Hermit* to see how Powys transcends the sensibility and attendant diction of his age. He creates the rural experience anew, and in doing so he sees the Deity revealed in the life of nature.

> It is the spring, and the apple-blossom is beautiful because He is there in it. To love Him is the only good thing in this world. It does not matter if He is true; He is beyond all truth. All things have breath in Him; I feel Him in the earth. When I hammer at the rocks and break away fossils that have been there for millions of years, I am only going a little way into His love.[16]

G

But the 'He' of this passage is not the creator of the world but the Son of man who suffers and endures in this world, as the preceding paragraph makes clear:

> With the terrible moods of God moving about me, as dark clouds, and then the lightning, and sometimes the ominous silence and calm, I turn to the stranger upon earth that once learned to bear the burden of God, calling Him Father, as Atlas held the world, upon His shoulders. I turn to the stranger upon earth, He who was not afraid to call the terrible moods 'Father', to take them into His life, to bear with them, to love them. And still more than that, He dared also to become the shepherd of men; to live Himself as a man and to fall before His Father's terrible mood of blind rage working in men. He alone dared to become one with the spoiler and the spoiled.[17]

There is a certain ambiguity here, a distinction suggested, rather than maintained, between God as first cause and God as absolute value – the contradiction between the two being at the root of all atonement theology, their resolution implicit in the doctrine of the Incarnation. Powys is more genuinely religious than his brothers in his continual awareness of the Son of Man, the redemptive aspect of God.[18] In his mature work the implications of the *Soliloquies* are followed through, and nature is seen as its own healer, love as a mitigation and death as a friend. The creative and redemptive activities of God are expressed in terms of natural processes. But in the earlier books God is seen rather uneasily as a being within his own world.

> Sometimes God makes His dwelling-place in the heart of a man. When He settles Himself there, there is generally trouble. The man usually ceases to prosper in a worldly way; his friends often desert him. God cuts all ropes that bind the man to his former ways, and the man often runs naked into the wilderness where strange voices sound. Those voices are the echo of God's voice speaking inside the man. . . . Sometimes they bid him destroy himself; this he does. God is a queer fellow.[19]

The wry irony of this is peculiarly the author's own. God represents the unpredictable and unknowable element in life that yet subserves man's opportunities for love and sacrifice.[20] Tinker Jar, in his work of rescue and vengeance, embodies the creative power for good which endures and works among the unpredictable vagaries of 'the moods of God'.

In *Mockery Gap* the interest is transferred from God to man. The book is a study of a village community, and of the nature of human desire and its fulfilment. In its quiet way it is a critique of romanticism. The villagers are stirred up to expect something exciting to happen, something symbolised by the elusive Nellie-bird, which is interpreted in various manners and according to their own natures by those who believe in its coming. But their real desires are met by the Fisherman, who for a while takes up his residence by the sea, which they are too unadventurous to visit.

The Fisherman is an interesting variant on Powys's figures of remedial providence. He is the youngest and sexually the most attractive of them, and while he influences the action he takes no part in it. Like Mr Weston after him he gives the two gifts of love and death; but he also brings life. In a beautiful passage the pregnant Mary Gulliver is saved from suicide by the sight of the Fisherman's naked body:

The sun . . . set a burning and a shining match to the fisherman's hair, that seemed at that moment to be on fire; while his limbs, white and still glistening with drops from the sea, appeared to belong, by reason of their perfect proportion, to some high spirit from above rather than to a plain, though unnamed, fisherman from those islands.

The man appeared by his gestures to be casting an invisible net over the girl.

It is possible to be awakened from the very saddest state of mind by a sudden burst of colour. A colour that burns can do more than make us merely happy: it can give us life.

The light that lightens the world can shine in a daisy; it can also shine in the human form when it is naked and fair.[21]

The Biblical overtones of this passage are frequently to be found in Powys's work;[22] but the particular Blake-like radiance and clarity are more uncommon. The Fisherman comes as the giver of the real desires of the heart, and his gift is not only one of death.

But *Mockery Gap* is remarkable less for its picture of the providence of God than for its portrayal of village life. The little community near the sea is more realistically treated than in the rest of Powys's work, the children especially, viewed as they are from the standpoint of an alarmed adult. The feud between the Prings and the Pottles has all the rancour and venom of something observed and experienced; and the particular quality of Powys's awareness is caught in his remark that 'In every village almost that we can think of . . . there is a blind lane that leads nowhere, or at least, if it does lead somewhere, 'tis but to a cottage and a pond, and there the lane ends.'[23] Close familiarity with his village world informs all Powys's writing; he conveys, for all the mannered quality of his prose, a keen sense of the slowness and monotony of rural life, and the feel, as much as the look, of stiles and paths and hedgerows. He himself married a Dorset girl, and it is possible that his novels and tales drew on anecdotes told by her and subsequently transformed. Out of the particular he realised the eternal: the very repetitiveness of his work adds to its force.

Innocent Birds, *Mockery Gap*'s companion, is an altogether grimmer affair, and is among the more reflective novels. Here too we are presented with a village community, but the inhabitants of Madder (*Innocent Birds* is a kind of sequel to 'The Left Leg') are more crudely contrasted in their good and evil. Once again a gift is awaited, prepared this time by a miniature theophany witnessed by the pleasant Miss Deborah Crocker upon Madder Hill. Her vision of the Burning Bush is commented upon with typical Powysian irony:

> Whether the words the vision had spoken came from the burning bush or no, Aunt Crocker was not sure. But anyhow, she had got them clear enough – that the Presence had promised a gift to Madder with its love, and that the gift would be given as a solace to someone. Aunt Crocker thought this a little vague, but she supposed that she hadn't listened as carefully as she should have done, and had thought more about the fate of a sparrow that had unluckily been perched upon the bush when it flared up.[24]

The Scriptual references will be readily apparent: such allusiveness and interlocking meanings within the allusion are frequent in Powys's work as it matures. The fate of the sparrow is related to the fate of the lovers Fred Pim and Polly Wimple, the 'innocent birds' to whom, after their trials and misfortunes, the good gift of death comes as a release. This novel has a continual undertow of resigned sadness, made explicit and ratified at the end of the book, as Mr Solly, whose appointed task it has been to wait for God's good gift, sits reading in the churchyard.

> In the silence Time came by. The seasons came too: spring with its chill snowflakes, hail and meek primroses; summer, with its hay-

making, and harvest, that follows so soon after the hay is gathered; and then autumn, with Chick and Pim throwing muddy mangels into farm carts, when the Madder leaves are yellow and the rain drips; and last of all winter came. The four seasons passed, coloured by all human pains, human passions and desires, and by good and evil.

Sorrow and joy passed too; while man born of a woman sat at the feet of life, each one waiting in his place until God's gift be given to him. . . .[25]

The slight transpositions of seasonal associations in this passage points to the fleetingness of time and the hardship of the human lot; but it also serves to present death as being integral to life and not simply as an escape from it. Not that Powys is unaware of death's terrors: in an earlier passage he wonders whether it be not 'the mere rounding of a point in the sea of time, where the memory of the old woes will beget again new torments, to be remembered again, and new-begotten again, through all eternity'.[26]

Threading the book is the theme of religion, which is played upon from a number of different angles. There is a repeated sardonic emphasis on human misunderstanding: Parson Tucker spends his days reading the Bible in the fields and the villagers suspect that it is pornography; Suzy the church cleaner is decried for neglecting her duties – because she spends all her time in prayer; the odious Miss Pettifer, who appears in several other tales as a symbol of hypocritical Christianity, ill-treats her servants in conformity with a theological position that only T. F. Powys could have imagined:

she very much approved of those words of Jesus – and applied them indeed more closely than He perhaps ever meant them to be, to herself – when He said that He was come amongst men as 'One who serves.'. . .

And so what could be better and more hopeful to her future well-being than those Christ-like promises and sayings? If the Son of God, of His own free will, came down to earth to be a servant, He must have done so, reasoned Miss Pettifer, 'because He liked the occupation.' And what, then, could be more natural and more proper a corollary than that He would like to be a servant in heaven too?[27]

Powys's treatment of Miss Pettifer in its combination of amusement and fury is typical of the way in which he handles characters of whom he disapproves.

The central weakness of *Innocent Birds*, as of *Mockery Gap*, is the feebleness of the forces for good; to be good in Powys's world seems to necessitate being a little stupid also. A naïvety of moral presentation is coupled with a theological uncertainty: this robs the books of an energy sufficient to keep them credible. Both *Mark Only* and *Mr Tasker's Gods* have more conviction. But these intermediate novels, the preludes to Powys's supreme achievements, are stronger than their predecessors in more important qualities than narrative power or certainty of aim – they are richer in compassion and more secure in their hold on the actualities of human life. There is a beautifully controlled pathos in the story, in *Mockery Gap*, of the lovelorn Miss Pink, while *Innocent Birds* is rich in moments of humorous melancholy, moments such as the following conversation between the postman Mr Moody and his wife:

> Mr. Moody placed one elbow upon the table, and his cheek into his hand, and stared still at his plate.
>
> 'Bread and butter bain't wrong side up?' said Mrs Moody.
>
> 'World be,' said Mr. Moody, finding his voice at last. 'World be sadly twisted.' Mr Moody sighed deeply.
>
> 'All my life long,' said Mr. Moody, looking up at his wife, 'leastways all my letter-carrying time, I've wanted to meet a maiden in they Madder fields who would say kindly, "There be they dark trees for we to go to, Mr. Moody." '
>
> 'Wouldn't the kindly maid 'ave called 'ee William?' Mrs Moody inquired.
>
> ' 'Twere always "Mr. Moody" in me fancy,' her husband replied. ' 'Twere "Mr. Moody" even on thik happy grass.'
>
> 'We bain't got no money to pay for they grassy doings!' said Mrs. Moody a little sulkily.
>
> The postman stared at his plate again. Suddenly he beat his fist upon the table.
>
> 'I won't hanker for none of they maids no more,' he cried out. 'I'll mind me letters and postcards.'
>
> 'Thee bain't been in no cold wind, 'ave 'ee?' asked Mrs. Moody feelingly, 'for thee's eyes be blinking.'
>
> 'Yes,' said Mr. Moody, wiping his eyes. 'Yes, they cold winds did drive into I cruel on they Madder hills.'[28]

Here plaintiveness, sardonic humour and mythological suggestion are nicely blended, in Powys's most thrifty manner. Puppet-like his people

may be, wooden representations of Jonsonian humours; but at his best
he treats them with a warmth and sure understanding that makes of
them characters who are richly human.

III

This humanity is abundantly present in *Mr Weston's Good Wine*,
which is Powys's undisputed masterpiece. It deserves that title by virtue
of its flawless construction and economy, its richness of texture and
delicate balance of values, its blend of humour and bleak tragedy.
Folly Down is the most completely realised of his villages, and its inhabitants represent an epitome of Powys's fictional world. To Folly
Down comes Mr Weston, together with his worldly-wise young assis-
tant Michael. They bring Mr Weston's gift of wine, wine which is
sold in two vintages, the stronger of which is death. Their advent in
Folly Down is a moment of judgement in which time stops still and
in which the desires of the inhabitants are fully met. In this story
Powys presents his most effective picture of the working of justice:
the wickedness of men is exposed, the meek are comforted and those
who yearn for love are given their desire. But the tone of the book is
nowhere simple. Mr Weston is not God omnipotent. At the very outset
of the tale, as his Ford van waits in Maidenbridge. we are presented
with a picture of nature in action:

> The winds with their wild gusts intended to do some mischief, and
> succeeded, for they blew against a wall two elderly ladies who
> wished to go by train to Weyminster to attend a sale where, it was
> said, a pair of nice new shoes might be bought for five shillings,
> and broke a leg of one of them.[29]

Mr Weston is neither held accountable nor does anything to remedy
the matter: what he might be said to represent is less the deity in any
strict theological sense than the essential truth in things, God within
creation rather than God outside it.

Such a viewpoint is in keeping with Powys's attitude to nature. He
is always conscious of its peace and innocence, and yet equally aware
of the cruelty built into the struggle to survive. The former quality is
abundantly present in this book:

> Every man who has imagination, and who lives in the country, is
> sure to find out some day or other that he is a lover. For all that

surrounds him and all that he sees informs him, in loving words, that beauty exists. He wakes in spring to see the rich meadows covered with yellow buttercups, while the most delicious scents fill the lanes. To live then oneself and to share such beauty with another is a proper desire. To be happy with another, in all the excitement and glamour of spring, is the proper thing to do.[30]

This free sharing with another is the lesser of the two gifts: in this case it is offered to Luke Bird (the young preacher in the earlier 'Abraham Men'), who has come to Folly Down and turned from ministering to uncaring men to ministering to animals.

Suddenly as he sat there and looked out of his door, he felt convinced that it was the beasts of the field and the fowls of the air that God's Son came down to save. It was they and they alone who possessed souls. The certainty of this new belief filled Luke with hope. God had sent His only son to be born in a stable, so that the most innocent and simple creatures, the oxen and asses, should have the first chance of salvation.

Luke pictured the scene in his heart: those quiet creatures whose sweet breath rose in holy adoration of the Divine Child – that was more likely a calf or foal than a human child – graciously accepted Him as their Lord. It was man, that unholy beast, that liar to the uttermost, who, with his gross conceit, must needs steal from the rightful heirs the birthright of heaven.[31]

For all its gentleness this passage is reminiscent of Swift. But Mr Weston does not ratify Luke's vision: indeed the character of Luke himself is a refutation of it.

Mr Weston's Good Wine would not be the masterpiece it is if it did not incorporate the darker side of Powys's imagination; but there is no morbidity. The crude brutalities of the early novels are exchanged for a more genuine realism.[32] The scene in which the Mumby brothers are taken to the graveyard to see the decomposing body of the girl whom they have raped and driven to suicide has a Webster-like gruesomeness; but it is also sombrely moral. Death is not simply oblivion – it is a physical process. The sexton, Mr Grunter, on whom the village wishes the paternity of all its misbegotten children, is described as a 'cold, clammy old man' who 'looked as though he had spent all his leisure hours, preferably in the winter-time, in standing in cold and damp lanes, looking at nothing and thinking of less'.[33] But Mr Grunter disowns his reputation at the end of the book: he, like the Mumby brothers, is brought to accept the truth. For others, like the procuress Mrs Vosper, the truth means extinction or, like the sorrowing widower, the Reverend Mr Grobe, deliverance from the knowledge of his loss. Indeed, he would seem to be promised more: when he asks whether, after drinking Mr Weston's good wine, he will see his Alice in heaven, he receives the reply, 'She is a little goose . . . and she will flap her wings at you.'[34] The delicacy of this, the quiet humour of it, are typical: in all his dealings with the men and women of the book, Mr Weston never behaves with false solemnity. And Powys's irony is nowhere more happily employed than when Mr Weston talks about his Book. 'I am a writer, Mr. Bird.'[35]

But the homeliness of Mr Weston's character does not obscure the essential solemnity of his visitation. Time stops while he is at Folly Down – that is to say, he is not involved in time as are the Fisherman or Tinker Jar, or John Death in the final novel, *Unclay*. This arrest of time also means that the effectiveness of Mr Weston as a symbol of the ultimate truth about life is the greater, for what happens during his sojourn is seen as being the true pattern of events underlying what has happened hitherto. This is the significance of the narrative flash-back in Chapters 11 to 19. Mr Weston brings the fears and dreams, the desires and lusts of the villagers to their logical conclusion. He reveals as much as he intervenes.

It is this timeless element in the book which gives it its artistic unity. The ingredients of the novel are those familiar to us from Powys's other work; but here they all subserve a central purpose, and centre upon a particular theme. It is the most optimistic of the books, suffused with a genial peacefulness that comprehends its darker insights. We are a long way from the bitterness of *Mr Tasker's Gods*. (It is also free from the archness and whimsicality that mar all the other novels, *Mark Only* excepted: the youthful and lamented Mrs Grobe is a great improvement upon all the tiresome merry maidens who frisk and skip their way through too many of Powys's pages.) The novel is the affirmation of an eternal world of values which underlies and supports the limited world of Folly Down, so that the oak-tree bed where the Mumby twins seduce the village girls can also be seen as the meeting place of earth and heaven. But there is nothing portentous about the treatment: all is seen as being natural, part of a single reality.

But perhaps because of this timeless element, *Mr Weston's Good Wine* is less vivid as a picture of country life than are the other novels. The bucolic element subserves the symbolic end; and, real as Landlord

Bunce, Mr Grunter and the rest are, we see them always in the light of Mr Weston's visit. It is this which most clearly demonstrates Powys's particular significance as a novelist of rural life. He used his knowledge of the country to create a representative world within which he could work out his speculations on the nature of God and man. Far from being a narrowly 'rustic' writer or the mere exploiter of a particular region, Powys is more in the nature of a seer – as his first champion, Louis Wilkinson, suggested.[36]

IV

It is in this capacity that Powys was to write the *Fables*, which are his other acknowledged masterpiece. This book was later published under the title *No Painted Plumage*; but the earlier title is the better. The *Fables* by their very nature underline Powys's particular quality as a novelist. The use of allegory and symbolism, which is intermittent in the earlier books, is here the predominating mode; and these short, cryptic, often dour and acrid tales illuminate his attitude to nature better than any other of his books except the *Soliloquies*. In all of them inanimate objects are imbued with wisdom, and are the instructors of erring man, or if not instructors then commentators, who behold with keen-sighted vision the vicissitudes of mortal life – a mortality in which they share. One exception to this is the tale of 'The Bucket and the Rope': the bucket, 'a large one, had been kicked over by a man who had hanged himself up by the neck, by means of an old piece of rope that he had tied to a strong beam'.[37] The bucket and the rope converse about their owner's suicide, quite unable to comprehend why he should have been distressed by the faithlessness of his wife.

> 'I believe the reason was,' replied the rope, 'that Mr. Dendy did not like to see others happy.'
> 'That is not easy to believe,' remarked the bucket, 'when one considers how happy he was himself.'
> 'His wife made him so,' said the rope, 'and feeling her success with him she naturally wished to make another happy too.'
> 'What could be more proper?' said the bucket.[38]

Powys uses his inanimates to voice a critique of established attitudes or to comment upon human life from abnormal angles. Thus in the story of 'The Corpse and the Flea' an inherently repellent situation is transformed by the power of the writer's imagination, and made the means of a complex and compelling vision of the nature of love and death. The poor man who has been neglected and cast off by his relations, but who has lived a life of unobtrusive goodness, is comforted after his death, in a temporary awakening, by the flea who at the end of the story takes on the nature of Christ Himself.

'You are my benefactor,' said a little soft voice. 'You are my dear friend upon whose blood I have reared grateful families. You, contrary to the custom of your race – unless you be gipsies or Indians – have ever permitted me to remain in comfort, hiding amongst your clothes. You have never tried to cast me from you with evil words, and, when I have bit you, you have only remarked, with a little shake of your body, that a small bite was a pleasure compared to the sneers and revilings of those old friends who had once pretended to love you.'[39]

What is especially remarkable about the *Fables* is their ability – and it is an ability characteristic of Powys's art as a whole – to combine a variety of viewpoints and experiences in a single complex pattern. In 'The Corpse and the Flea' the fact of death is nowhere softened, and yet it is seen as a healing, ultimately a beneficent, power; the 'little creatures', the beetle, the spider and the flea, discourse in judgement on human ways; but the first two embody disagreeable human characteristics themselves. The depredations of the old woman who lays Mr Johnson out are paralleled by the raid of a fox upon the stackyard; while the release that death affords is balanced by regret for everything that the dying man will have to leave behind. Especially poignant is the thought of the natural world.

Mr Johnson grew sadder. His thoughts now left the little room and wandered, for the last time, into the fields and lanes. He had come – and the more he was forsaken by man the further he went in this way – to dote upon these common fields and simple hedgerows, where a little mouse might rustle the dead leaves and a fern grow.
The day before he had been obliged to take to his bed Mr Johnson had crept out and knelt down upon the soft grass of the little hillside that was before his doors. He had wept for a while, but, feeling that whatever might happen to him, he would still belong to that sweet grass, he returned comforted.[40]

In the *Fables* we find Powys's definitive statement of the interrelated-
ness of all living things, and of the mingled cruelty and consolation
implicit in man's responsiveness to nature and in nature's ways with
man. The simplicity of style, the traditional and Biblical echoes and
cadences, the complexity of mood add up to a literary achievement of
a unique kind.

A preoccupation with death also marks *Kindness in a Corner* (1930),
the most humorous of Powys's novels. It originated in a short tale
called 'Tadnol'.[41] This novel is, like the numerous other stories about
the same village, of a genial and comic turn.[42] The book's tone is
established early on, in the account of Lottie Truggin, the most appeal-
ing of Powys's innocent maidens:

> A young girl is a deep mystery. When she enters a room something
> enters with her that belongs to the earth and to the sun, to the
> carnal and to the holy. A warm, earthly thing, a star of heaven.
> Pagan and yet merry with God, a presence that wishes to be kind,
> but opens a door to sorrow.[43]

The novel celebrates the holiness of carnality and the natural virtues
of kindliness and toleration. The title has a twofold meaning: the
ostensible one is that of the Reverend Mr Dottery's kindness in his
corner, that is Tadnol; the other emerges when 'thik corner where God
be kindness'[44] turns out to be a description of death. The chapter called
'The Dirt of God', in which Sexton Truggin persuades the terrified
Mr and Mrs Turtle that they have no need to fear the grave, is one of
Powys's supreme achievements. Truggin's speech attains the nobility
of poetry.

> 'Thik be a wide and vast place . . . though it do look so small. God,
> who do but lend 'Is love to the living, do give it to the dead for all
> time. There bain't no clod that do touch a bone that does not love
> with a greater love than the living do know of. And what be
> loneliness but to bide in our sorrows, for time bain't always kind?'[45]

In Powys's last books it is seen that death is bound up with life and
is good because life is good, though the equation is at times uncertainly
sustained. Indeed, this book is the most ostensibly Christian of the
novels; oblivion may be God's gift in death, but there is a God to give it.

> How pleasant to rest for ever in a corner of the kind earth, fearing
> nothing, loving nothing, while above and about us, never lessening,

never slackening for one moment its power of protection, is the peace
of God that passeth understanding.[46]

Death is itself a character in the last[47] and longest of the novels,
Unclay (1931). If the comparison be not too misleading, it may be said
to be Powys's equivalent of *The Last Chronicle of Barset*. In it most
of his fictional villages and characters are mentioned, and it includes
every facet of his work. But it is far from being his best book. John
Death's sojourn in Dodder is not worked out with anything approach-
ing the consistency of Mr Weston's visit to Folly Down, and the
narrative meanders and lacks an effective climax. Indeed, although the
novel reveals the author's increasing preoccupation with death, it does
not treat the subject with the same profundity as its predecessor.
Powys's inventive ingenuity leads him astray here: John Death's
relationship with the villagers, although narrated with a feeling for
what is appropriate in individual instances, is not portrayed with an
overall credibility. His mislaying of his instructions to 'unclay' (i.e.
kill) Joseph Bridle and Susie Daw is an amusing fancy; but it consorts
ill with Powys's understanding of death as being not only life's appointed term but also life's defining quality. There is a frivolity of a
limiting kind here. Moreover, the references to both Tinker Jar and
Mr Weston lead to a feeling that Powys has a pantheon of Gods: the
references do little for *Unclay* itself, and detract retrospectively from
the earlier work.

Nevertheless there is much to admire in the novel. Parson Hayhoe,
who prefers reading to his parishoners from Jane Austen to reading to
them from the Scriptures, is a figure of Powysian comedy at its best:
his continuous citation of Austenian texts neatly points up the habits
of other, more orthodox clergy. The sexual relationship between Susie
Daw and her slow, devoted lover is treated with a depth and seriousness that is far ahead of similar passages in earlier books; and there is
a notable increase in the use of scenery and of animal life to fill in
the pastoral background and illustrate the central truths of love and
death.

The evening gnats quivered and danced in the warm air, unmindful
of danger. The swallows caught them and they heeded not the act.
The tiny pig-louse that lived in the grass upon Madder Hill ate its
prey. Then it rolled up into a ball to sleep near an anthill, and was
eaten itself. A frog, seeking amusement, hopped out of Joe Bridle's
pond, only to find a grave in the cold body of a snake.[48]

Passages like this one are balanced by a more tranquil vision:

> The usual, the ordinary village sounds, were quieted. The new
> summer that was to come to Dodder brooded silently, thinking of
> her own loveliness. The fruitful sun had warmed the green earth.
> There was no hedge, no wayside place, that had not drunk a cup of
> the new life. The winds moved softly over the downs; the daytime
> flowers slept without dreams.[49]

The novel is continuously reflective, and almost every chapter begins
with a generalisation. At times its pessimism is expressed in language
that borders on self-parody:

> God is the great hunter. In order to fill his larder, He scatters mouldy
> cheese about – carnal desire. The sun is above, and all the fair flowers
> of the valley glisten with dew. The trap look pleasant.
>   Then there is the bait – woman. Her wiles are inconceivable, her
> arts manifold, her desires ever-lasting. My friend, you are caught. A
> laugh is heard in the sky, and for a while the child plays happily,
> all unconscious that he is trapped.[50]

A note of sententiousness is apparent here: Powys's hermit-like existence occasionally led him to play the sage. This is not always to his
advantage, though he had a gift for the gnomic aphorism:

> 'When God's finger first stirred the pudding. . . He let a tear fall in
> by mistake, and the tear became man's consciousness. Then to pre-
> serve man from everlasting sorrow, He put death in the pot.[51]

This kind of serio-comic jesting is indicative of Powys's ultimate scepti-
cism as to Christian dogma. What endures from a reading of his total
body of work is his awareness of the natural order, summed up for
him in Madder Hill, round which all his villages and hamlets appear
to cluster.

> But over all that happens a watcher stands and looks. This watcher
> is Madder Hill. Above life – that grand and woeful calamity –
> Madder Hill looks and yields a kind of consolation to those who
> bend to it. It may be but the sweet odour of white clover, or the
> winter's sun setting in the sea, that tells other tales than the fury of
> constant becoming and continuous ending. Madder Hill is the same
> yesterday, to-day, and for ever.[52]

And again :

> When the scene of our short vision ends, hardly a stone shall be
> moved, hardly a root gone. All the turmoil and trouble that love
> makes for a man, during the few years of his vanity, is of less con-
> sequence in the universe than the moving of one small worm from
> one burrow to another. Trouble Heaven as we will, make all the
> outcry we may, complain of our care to the wind and to the stars
> of the sky, nothing – no tittle – shall be left out of the law of our
> ways. We run our race blindfold, and when all is done, we have
> but moved one place, one step lower in degree, down Madder Hill.[53]

But this kind of pessimism depends to a degree on its lulling cadences,
and reveals a weariness of spirit peculiar to an author who has repeated
himself too often.

It is all the more remarkable, therefore, that Powys's final work
should show signs of fresh inventiveness and a development in style.
The three tales in *The Two Thieves* (1932) are altogether more purpose-
ful, fast-moving and authoritative than anything he had written to
date. Gone are the whimsical asides, the short, mannered sentences:
the prose, though still spare and simple, moves at a swift pace and is
flexible to changes of mood and narrative requirements. All three
tales are in effect fables, though 'In Good Earth' and 'God' are the most
formally 'realistic' that he ever wrote. The latter is especially ingenious
in its play upon the different aspects of religious belief (the hero thinks
that God is his father's top hat; in the end, though disenchanted with
this belief, he finds the lining stuffed with bank notes). The other two
are simpler in conception, 'The Two Thieves' being a clearly worked-
out moral allegory about a man who steals the properties of greed,
anger, pride and cruelty from the Devil, only to have them stolen from
him in his turn by Tinker Jar; 'In Good Earth' is a tragedy inspired
by the text 'To him that hath shall be given'[54] – applied here with
tragic irony. Nowhere more than in this tale does Powys approach a
Hardyesque vision of the tragic peasant :

> Although the hour was late, a figure stooped in the mangold patch –
> a bending creature, a man of many sorrows, who knew the earth
> only as a hard mother. . . . Anywhere else he would have been un-
> noticed, but, being the only thing to break the flat line of field, he
> attracted the eye. He had struggled with the earth so long that he
> had become gnarled and knotted, and it was easy to see which of

the two must at the last be defeated. That such a man who in his day had received, without being broken by them, more reverses than the unlucky prince, should have been utterly unnoticed is but the ordinary measure meted to the poor.[55]

The greater simplicity of this, the unselfconsciousness, are immediately apparent, as are the corresponding depth of sympathy. It seemed as if Powys were to progress into a new manner as a writer.

Instead of which he stopped. Other volumes of tales were to be collected, two of them posthumously; but his substantial work was done. Of his short stories, the finest is 'The Only Penitent', in which Tinker Jar confesses to Mr Hayhoe his responsibility for all the suffering inherent in human life, and is absolved because he also gives man death. But they all belong to the same coherent fictional world. From *Mr Tasker's Gods* to *The Two Thieves*, Powys's work is all of a piece.

It stands outside time or fashion. And although its bucolic world can feel monotonous and small, it *is* a world, a distillation of the rustic experience through which Powys's supremely original mind and sensibility could express their responses to the fundamental experiences of human life. He has nothing ostensibly to say to the twentieth century – in this respect he is the rural novelist *par excellence* – and he often utters the great platitudes in a voice that does little to disguise them; but for the most part it is the manner in which he works, his gifts as a literary artist, that put a new perspective on familiar matter, his style at its best being so clean-cut that simply to read it is to be mentally quickened and invigorated. Above all he celebrates the rural world, not by exploiting its historical aspect, not by any working up of regional scenery, but by relating it to the permanent realities of human existence. His originality provides a methodology; the quietness of his tone has a steady insistence comparable to the working of a mole. His own sophistication of mind prevents him from being an 'earthy' writer in the crude sense – though it is surprising how much one is aware, despite the absence of descriptive set-pieces, of the actual landscape and of primitive natural forces as one reads his work.

Powys succeeded in making out of the rural experience something entirely new in fiction. His success is a paradoxical one not least because it has in no way commended itself to a large audience. His account of village life does in some ways epitomise all that is wrong in the approach of the alienated townsman, and in this respect it deserves Stella Gibbons's burlesque. This is ironic in view of Powys's deliberate rusticity of life; but the oddity of his work, its mannered dialect and self-mockery, is a deliberate distortion of carefully observed realities. Powys plays on and exaggerates the remoteness of his pastoral world in order to make of it a symbol of human life in general. Even at his most prosaic he is a fabulist; meaning is organic in his work, not arbitrarily imposed or merely collocated. Compared with that of Lawrence, his achievement seems extremely limited, but this is less a matter of his skill as an artist than of the scale on which he chose to write. The geographical restrictions of the rural novel made it insufficient to meet the imaginative needs of an age of ever greater dispersion and mobility; instead it catered all too easily, as has been seen, to its emotions. T. F. Powys outraged those emotions, which accounts for his particular distinction; but, as was the case with Hardy and *Jude The Obscure*, it also accounts for his unpopularity with many admirers of the rural fictional tradition. Nonetheless his work, by its very power to disturb, represents that tradition at its most forceful and effective.

12 The Enduring Land: H. E. Bates

The symbolic narratives of Powys contrast revealingly with the far more popular tales of an equally fastidious craftsman, H. E. Bates (1905–74), to mention whom is to refer not only to a skilful novelist, but also to one whose career showed him to be something of a literary barometer. His work went on changing, if not developing, in response to the pressures and outlooks of the times, his war novels[1] and the opulent Larkins saga of the 1960s[2] being alike pointers to the moods and tastes of the periods in which they were written. But Bates's most popular work has probably been the group of rural stories which he published in the 1930s.[3] While written with all the grace and refinement of *The Two Sisters* (his first, intensely romantic novel, published in 1926, when he was twenty, with an introduction by Edward Garnett), these books are of their time in their concern with the hardships and practicalities of country life. Deborah Loveday, the farmer's wife in *The Fallow Land* (1932), and Luke Bishop in *The Poacher* (1935) are types of human endurance, of a basic simplicity that acts directly according to its nature and without the prevarication and complex motives of urban dwellers. They thus provide a kind of twentieth-century heroic ideal. Rosie Jefferys, the barmaid turned farmer's wife in *A House of Women* (1936) is another.[4] Bates's attitude to his people has none of the uncertainty of Booth or Trevena; they are treated with great naturalness, above all with a feeling for their inherent dignity. The background of the Nene valley, beautifully described though it is, remains a background; people are more important in these novels than landscape.

The books proceed on a straightforward narrative course; one thing happens, then another; there is no exaggeration, no implausibility, no rustic cliché. But also there are no obvious morals and no conflicting themes: the individual is presented as a world to himself. This is why, within its limits, *The Poacher* is such a satisfying novel. Luke Bishop, who panics at the thought of being suspected of murder, and who finally commits manslaughter as a result of an inevitable lapse back into a way of life he had in vain sought to repress, is a representative figure, one whose life is naturally parabolic and the centre of an austerely tragic picture of which the hardships and beauty of country life are inseparable components.

The strength of country life does indeed, in these novels, mean its capacity for tragedy. It provides a challenge not to be found in the life of towns. As Deborah, the embodiment of the spirit of work, passionately declares,

> 'What's wrong with the land, I should like to know? It's the same land – the same weather – the same seasons, everything the same except the people farming it. The people have changed, that's all. . . . If you're not master of the land the land will be master of you.'[5]

The enduring nature of the land is a feature of all these early novels. They are full of a sense of the timelessness of rural life. This can be conveyed through a delicate descriptive skill:

> In the pub, down in the town, with its narrow streets and the early mists coming up the river, she knew that it must already be winter. She could see and feel it all if she thought for only a moment; the fire in the bar, the gas bubbling and hissing, the glasses cold as ice to her hand first thing in the mornings, the smell of rain-wet horses waiting against the curb outside. There was a thickening in the flow of the pub's life in winter whereas on the farm . . . life seemed to thin and quieten and almost, at times, to come to a stillness entirely, turning in upon itself and coming to rest like a snake curling in for winter. In late summer the clack of the binder and a thousand sounds beside it had kept the air alive and the life in motion; now if there were sounds at all they were dying sounds, the somnolent fall of leaves, the mournful moan of cows housed-in, the dull rumble of muck-carts, sounds which sucked up and magnified the quietness as the hum of bees had stirred and magnified the silence of summer afternoons.[6]

The assonances and alliteration of this are evidence of the careful mind behind it. But the care can elicit a more prosiac timelessness.

He was almost an old man; his hands were twisted and skinny and the veins blue and prominent . . . he walked with a slight hobble and a heavy stoop of his shoulders, as though all his life he had been carrying loads too heavy for him. The skin of his arms and neck and face were deep and soft, and his eyes, coloured an old pale blue shade turning to grey, were mild with a profound tolerance. There was nothing aggressive about him. He had the same air of patience and servitude as an old horse, too old to canter but still strong enough to work until he dropped. He had worked for over sixty years and had never taken a holiday except on his wedding day.[7]

When one compares this with Trevena's account of old Barseba, or even Brett Young's of the ancient labourer in *The Black Diamond*, one sees the essentially detached nature of Bates's art: nothing is being 'made out of' the subject; the author has not a trace of the showman.

In *Spella Ho* (1938), the last and most conventional of this group of novels, Bates takes the well-worn theme of the self-made man. Bruno Shadbolt, the self-educated labourer who becomes a successful businessman, eventually buys the mansion in whose shadow he has grown up. It is a typical nineteenth-century story of endeavour; but Bates gives it a wry conclusion.

Standing between the house and the town he stood between much that had been created by twin forces in himself. Looking down, he could see the huge, more than tangible mass of his material endeavour for almost fifty years: the sprawling record of his undefeated ignorance, courage and strength. Looking up, he could see nothing but the house. . . . There was no record, except in his own mind, of things that had happened there. There was no record of the best in himself.[8]

Again, the representative nature of these novels is made clear; and the point is made still more insistently at the close. A young girl, sketching the house, attacks Bruno for the ugliness of the town, an ugliness for which his own prosperity is largely responsible.

'It just happened.'
'I know,' she said. 'A bit here, and a bit there. A street and then a hotel, and then something else. Anyhow. No plan. I know. Terrible . . . Didn't it ever occur to you to make it beautiful while you were at it?'
'I don't know. I don't think so.'

'Didn't you ever do anything beautiful?'

He did not answer. There was nothing he could say to that. If he had done anything beautiful there was no record of it. There was no record of beauty, he thought, and affection, love, happiness, things like that. . . . Everybody is shut up; part of everybody is shut away from everybody else.[9]

This fragmentation is what the rural writer condemns in the age of the city.

Such chaos, such slovenly lack of plan, is clearly antipathetic to Bates, the fastidious artist in words, whose own favourite literary form is the short story.

Its flexibility, almost unlimited range of subject and sympathy, and its very brevity, make it as perfectly suitable to the expression and mood of this age as the heroic couplet was to the age of Pope. To my mind it is in every way a finer means of expression of our age of unrest, disbelief and distrust, than either the novel or poetry.[10]

In view of this it is not surprising that Bates's own short stories should be among his most successful rural fiction. There is a total detachment in their artistry, an absolute objectivity, even in the frequent elements of violence; the reader is left free to draw his own deductions. The most satisfying stories are, however, the shortest, tales like 'The Plough', 'Harvest Moon', and 'Cut and Come Again'; for the objectivity, telling though it is, has an alienating effect when pursued at too-great length. 'The Mill', with its unremittingly sober account of a servant girl's seduction and dismissal, comes to mind here. The author's reticence works better in a story like 'Cut and Come Again', a brief vignette of a young newly-married labouring couple, or 'Cloudburst', in which an elderly pair see their barley crop destroyed in a storm; these are virtually prose poems, their whole theme being conveyed through carefully disposed detail. The overall picture of life is an austere one, despite Bates's preoccupation with ripeness, full-breasted women, well-stocked farm-houses and crusted characters like 'My Uncle Silas'. There is no softening of the realities of daily life, and a tale like 'Beauty's Daughters' skilfully conveys the tension within a single household in which the old rural and the new suburban values are in conflict. There is great immediacy of physical impact in the stories – more so than in the novels – and in this they suggest, rather than assert, the superior vitality of country life. And they do not gesture at their readers; they do not have the slightly self-conscious 'folk' quality of the tales of A. E. Coppard,[11] many of which also handle rural subjects with vividness, if with rather too obvious charm. 'Charm' indeed is a quality refreshingly absent from Bates's early stories; but nonetheless the author's refusal to comment or to colour his material other than by physical detail leads finally to a slight impression of futility. The detachment, the artistry diminish the sense of urgency, of personal engagement; and we do not find the sense of a living folklore, such as the best of Kipling's rural tales convey. Bates has nothing to compare with 'The Wish House' or 'Friendly Brook'. In his work the rural theme subserves the art presenting it.

However, art does make for clarity; and Bates, more than any other rural novelist, would seem to have understood the precise issues attendant on the writing of this kind of fiction. As a record of country life his work takes a high place; in it there is a perfect ease in the relation of author to reader, and it is entirely lacking in the self-indulgent exaggeration that can be detected in Trevena and Phillpotts, being written, one feels, as much for the country reader as for anyone else. In it the rural tradition becomes part of the general tradition of the novel. From being a genre, a specific literary product, it becomes a means of furthering genuine understanding of the countryman, his problems and attitudes; it thus fulfils a social as well as a purely literary function. Indeed, since the Second World War the most memorable rural writing has been documentary in character:[12] one thinks of books like Ronald Blythe's *Akenfield* (1969), a portrait of an East Anglian village, and of the work of George Ewart Evans, such as *The Pattern Under the Plough* (1966). The influence of George Sturt has grown, not lessened, with the years, and his lament for a bygone way of life was to prove prophetic in every sense.

This note of regret is absent from Bates's fiction, which is always firmly of the present. If in his very realism he can match the representative nature of T. F. Powys's work, he has an understanding of the term 'the land' more precise than that of Constance Holme, in whose novels it likewise frequently recurs. There it represents tradition, permanence. In Bates's work it stands for challenge, energy, life.

> The land was something more than the earth; the earth was something vague, primitive, poetic; the land was a composite force of actual, living, everyday things, fields and beasts, seed-time and harvest, ploughing and harrowing, wind and weather; bitterness and struggle; the land was an opponent, a master.[13]

Conclusion:
The Earth and the Land

I

H. E. Bates's distinction between 'the earth' and 'the land' highlights the changing attitudes to be found in the rural fiction of this period. The fact that the rural experience had come to be essentially alien from that of the majority of readers led inevitably, as has been seen, to a feeling for it as something 'vague, primitive, poetic'. The emasculating of the last-mentioned term is another symptom of the same estrangement; for 'poetic' has taken on the sense of 'fanciful' or 'decorative', much as the country comes to be thought of in conventional tourist terms as 'picturesque', 'refreshing', and so on. The paradox has been, however (and the very merits of the work of H. E. Bates illuminate it), that those novelists who have been most concerned with the land as a way of life have not been notably interesting novelists as such: praiseworthy as is, for example, the work of Street and Freeman, its value is historical rather than literary. The fidelity to observed truth serves only to indicate the limits of that truth's significance for art.

But those writers who concentrate on 'the earth' (in Bates's use of the term) are no less limited and limiting.[1] Walpole, Brett Young and Phillpotts all in their different ways treat landscape primarily as a means to feeling; but, being without the imaginative power or religious conviction necessary if this is to be done without solipsism, they induce a sense of superficiality. In their work (though Phillpotts is to some extent an exception to this) the feeling does not reach out exploratively beyond itself: it is an adornment of experience, not an illumination of it. In both these extremes, that of the 'earth' and that of the 'land', one is made aware of the contemporary schism between the scientific and religious interpretations of experience, what W. H. Auden has described as the divorce between the Historian and the Poet.

The primary world as perceived by the divorced Historian, is a desacralised, depersonalised world where all facts are equally profane. Human history becomes a matter of statistics, in which individual human beings are represented as faceless and anonymous puppets of impersonal forces. . . . The divorced Poet, on the other hand, can find materials for building his secondary worlds only in his private subjectivity. His characteristic virtue, a sense of the sacred, the personal, becomes concentrated upon himself.[2]

For the most part the rural writers are as much victims of the split in consciousness as are their urban contemporaries. That split is acutely felt in times of change. In the England of this period the increasing industrialisation of the landscape and its overrunning with motor traffic meant that it tended to be seen as the victim of change rather than as benefiting from it. To the conservative in outlook, to whom the idea of change was hurtful, the country seemed especially vulnerable, a case of the Historian victimising the Poet; while for the more radical and *avant-garde* it was, as the home of outworn social values, largely irrelevant, just as the Poet is an irrelevancy to the materialistic Historian. As a result the country was the literary preserve either of those writers who disliked and distrusted the social, political and economic developments of the twentieth century; or else of those whose concern with those developments was unaccompanied by any deep personal response to the rural experience as such.

The most interesting rural novelists are therefore those who have written against the grain of the times they lived in, and who resolved, or tried to resolve, the division in their thought and feeling. In the case of Henry Williamson and Mary Webb this was a deliberate undertaking: their work proffered an antidote to the social and personal malaise they found in existing urban attitudes. Mary Webb, however, was too cut off in her own imaginary world to speak effectively to the world outside it, so that, for her, artistic success involved the limiting of her ambition. In her work the Poet is in opposition to the Historian. Williamson is a writer of considerably greater stature, discussed here only in terms of his early work; but that work too draws its force more from the author's reaction against his times than from a participation in them. Compared with these two writers, novelists like Francis Brett Young and Sheila Kaye-Smith, for all their more even achievement, are relatively uninteresting; what they say is often unexceptionable, sometimes admirable, but there seems to be no particular reason why it should be said again. The insights of Poet and Historian seem to exist independently of each other in their work, as they do in that of Hugh Walpole and, to a lesser extent, that of Winifred Holtby. There is no effective relationship between them.

The opposite extreme is to be found in the novels of T. F. Powys, where the fact of change is ignored altogether in favour of a vision of life in which the Poet and Historian exchange roles, the facts of rural life providing a symbolism directed to expounding a meaning in terms of fable. In his finest work, in *Mr Weston's Good Wine*, *Fables* and *The Two Thieves*, there is a perfect coalescence of the two, just as there is in the very different work of Adrian Bell, where the Historian inspires the Poet.

In the novels of Constance Holme we find a reconciliation between the two through the portrayal of an ideal community: their inter-action is shown in terms of function within the social structure. An illuminating comparison may be made between them and those of Eden Phillpotts. In both cases we have a regional novelist who uses a particular landscape for dramatic ends, and who holds a par-picular philosophy of life. But Phillpotts's evolutionary humanism, interesting and often persuasive though it is, is imposed upon his material in order to give an added dimension to conventional and often artificial plots. The failure of his art reflects an insufficiently felt aware-ness of the nature of his subject matter: his work is more impressive in potential than in achievement. The novels of Constance Holme, how-ever, while apparently more slight, allow their philosophy to emerge from characters who determine the narrative, and, since it is these characters who give life to the landscape, inner and outer modes of ex-perience are fused. These novels, although not obviously related to their time, are in their limited but distinct success a comment on it.

II

The diversity of approach found in the numerous rural writers should of itself dissuade one from attempting any broad generalisations about a rural school: their best work proceeds from their own responses, not from an awareness of other people's books. Their existence is a re-minder that literature is not to be equated with the literary life; it is not, even, a conscious process of development, influences or move-ments, convenient though such concepts may be for the literary his-torian. Lawrence witnessed to this in his rejection of the contemporary world of journalists and academics; and it is notable that the most

significant rural writers have played little or no part in literary society
or politics but have, to use a metaphor appropriate for once, ploughed
their own furrows.

That this has involved them in a limitation of outlook and appeal
is obvious.[3] Inevitably they tended to be conservative and retrospective
in their views: the aspect of life on which they concentrated ensured
it, the times being what they were. And so some extent the significance
of any minor writer is bound to be expressed in terms of negatives. He
is the man of average height by whom the giant is measured, the
commonplace who provides the frame for the exceptional. With the
exception of T. F. Powys, all the novelists considered here reflect rather
than enlarge the consciousness of their time.

Nonetheless it is possible to make certain distinctions among them.
The writers whose novels can still be read with a sense of freshness and
continuing relevance are those who have tried to reconcile the manner
in which their contemporaries felt about the country with the economic
and social realities of the rural situation – those who, in Forster's words,
have tried to connect the prose and the passion.[4] They were concerned,
in however humble a way, with reordering a mythology, with providing moral and imaginative sanctions for a continuing emotional need.

III

One way of measuring their achievement, therefore, is to consider
the way in which they met the challenge to traditional human values
that arose with the contemporary changes in science, social structures
and the arts. Urban novelists, faced with that challenge, were prin-
cipally concerned with the question, What is human nature? Their
interests are essentially anthropological. The rural writers, however,
direct our attention to nature in a more general sense; and at their best
they succeed in giving a real imaginative content to what the term
'natural' may mean where men and women are concerned. It is their
most distinctive contribution to the literature of the time, and provides a perspective from which the achievement of more obviously
sophisticated writers can be assessed.

Man does not live by man alone, but by a vital struggle with his
environment: this is the repeated theme of the major rural novelists.
On occasion that struggle is seen as being potentially or actually de-
humanising (some of T. F. Powys's work makes this point); alternatively
it can be sentimentalised as a mock-heroic cliché. But its positive

affirmation is central to the tradition. As a result the rural novelists understand human nature in the sense of humankindness, of the community at work, rather than in the psychological, essentially solitary terms of so much modern fiction. They depict the 'natural' man as a role-fulfiller rather than as a role-player. Their insistence on the interdependence of human beings means that, for all the austerity of its finest proponents, the rural tradition is fundamentally optimistic with regard to the ability of men to live creatively together.

These novelists, however, do not ignore the need for solitude; they are aware of nature not only as an external force but also as a medium for spiritual intuition. This is an experience which lends itself less readily to treatment in fiction than in poetry – or music: one thinks of Elgar, Vaughan Williams, Butterworth and other composers of the time. It is certainly an experience which urban fiction finds it hard to come by; but the country, with its sense of an immemorial past, is more readily associated with the numinous and the transcendent than is the town. The tragedy is that, T. F. Powys apart, we do not find one rural novelist whose imagination fully answered to that sense of transcendence. But Powys is a genuine seer, and the development of his literary art is bound up with his quest for an appropriate symbolic portrayal of the workings of providence. In this he indicates what one achievement of the rural school might have been: the relating of history to myth through the depiction of what was happening in rural society as something that happens perennially in man. But Powys, for all his gifts, kept himself too far apart from contemporary awareness really to accomplish this; and the other rural novelists are too often content with responding emotionally to natural scenery.

Not that the latter experience need be decried; and there is a wealth of loving, careful writing to enjoy in these novels, writing which plays its part in sensitising one's responses. A love of landscape is one thing these novelists all have in common, together with an awareness of the potential in human experience arising from it. And together with this there is to be found in most of them a narrative compulsion that helps to create a sense of the significance of human beings as a vital and vitalising part of their surroundings. Such a sense can be inflated (as it tends to be in the work of Eden Phillpotts), but it provides a corrective to the rather quivering presentation of life in terms of passive consciousness, which can infect even so fine a novelist as Virginia Woolf. The rural tradition indeed provides a bridge between the introspective, subjective novelists and naturalistic writers like Maugham and Arnold Bennett.

For complementing the response to natural beauty we find an awareness of economic necessity such as the urban novel of personality can
too easily avoid. The very structure of village life, still more of farming life, makes the economic factor easy to portray. This is not a world,
the great houses apart,[5] where money can be taken for granted and
thus ignored. The novels of Phillpotts, Sheila Kaye-Smith, Bates and
even T. F. Powys are full of questions of rents, mortgages and wills:
the economy of the land is always prominent, and the novels' plots are
as often as not dictated by it. This is one constant factor throughout
the heyday of the tradition. The kind of people with which it was
concerned were those who had to earn their own living; and it is in the
rural novels, coming between the work of the Edwardian realist school
and such novelists of the 1950s and 1960s as Stan Barstow and Alan
Sillitoe, that one must look for the most thorough fictional study of
working-class life.

IV

The more serious rural novelists raised, in fact, many of the same
issues in their work as are dealt with in less obviously parochial fiction.
Their books are not just a sincere celebration of natural beauty and
traditional value: they reflect a tension, a clash of experience, an ex-
tending of that conflict between the individual and corporate experiences of life which is at the root of the major novelist's concerns.
In the case of the minor writer this conflict expresses itself in the very
way in which his novels are written: it is reflected as much in his
method as in his subject matter. An uncertain tone of voice, a hyper-
consciousness of his readers proclaim the artist who lacks conviction
of his own authority. In the case of writers handling the rural theme,
this uncertainty was built into the very social situation of which they
wrote, so that the challenge to their creativity was the more exacting.
In this respect it is fruitful to compare the work of the rural novelists
with that of Lawrence, as a brief examination of one novel will show.
The White Peacock, precisely because it is an early work, is the more
striking as evidence of the timeliness of its author's genius.

In this first novel, published in 1910 when only Eden Phillpotts, of
all the novelists considered above, was fully launched on his career,
Lawrence comes straight to the heart of the rural tragedy, the tragedy
of necessary change. He was of course fortunate in being born in a
landscape which in its very configuration showed that change at work;

the farms and collieries are in dramatic juxtaposition. In *The White Peacock* the passing of the valley of Nethermere is aligned with the moral breakdown of George Saxton; and underlying both is the deeper tragedy of the divorce between the rational and instinctual aspects of human nature. The rich, in the person of the misguided Lettie, become bored and sterile, the poor like George are brutalised. The novel is of its time in its lushness, the overwriting and too obvious schematisation; but, while giving the idyllic pastoral mode its head, it points to the situation that encompassed the life it celebrates. It has a far wider intellectual grasp than other contemporary novels of its kind.

> 'To the Vita Nuova !' said Lettie, and we drank, smiling.
> 'Hark !' said George, 'the hooters.'
> We stood and listened. There was a faint booing noise far away outside. It was midnight. Lettie caught up a wrap and we went to the door. The wood, the ice, the grey dim hills lay frozen in the light of the moon. But outside the valley, far away in Derbyshire, away towards Nottingham, on every hand the distant hooters and buzzers of mines and ironworks crowded small on the borders of the night, like so many strange, low voices of cockerels bursting forth at different pitch, with different tone, warning us of the dawn of the New Year.[6]

This kind of appropriateness is the sign of the major artist : he uses such symbolism with perfect naturalness. It is the blending of subjective with objective. But Lawrence goes beyond this, seeing an acceptance of the situation that can transcend it. Cyril's experience in South London presages a sequel different from that adumbrated despairingly by Jefferies in *After London* : it is a victory won through the transfiguring power of the artist's imagination.

> The spring came bravely, even in South London, and the town was filled with magic. I never knew the sumptuous purple of evening till I saw the round arc-lamps fill with light, and roll like golden bubbles along the purple dusk of the high road. Everywhere at night the city is filled with the magic of lamps : over the river they pour in golden patches their floating luminous oil on the restless darkness; the bright lamps float in and out of the cavern of London Bridge Station like round shining bees in and out of a black hive; in the suburbs the street lamps glimmer with the brightness of lemons among the trees. I began to love the town.[7]

From his country boyhood Cyril draws strength to encounter the forces that apparently were threatening it. In *Sons and Lovers* (1913) and still more notably in *The Rainbow* (1915) and *Women in Love* (1920) Lawrence moves out from the rural world to encompass the changing society of the England that was growing away from it likewise.

We may find a concluding illustration in the work of Joyce Cary, a wide-ranging novelist who on occasion wrote memorably of English rural life, seeing in it, as Lawrence had before him, the living heart of the life of the nation as a whole. Both novelists came to this view in a convincing manner because they did not centre their entire interest upon the country. Both are aware of change and of the world outside and are interested in them. Cary gives memorable expression to this robust and balanced viewpoint in *To Be A Pilgrim* (1942), where the old lawyer, Thomas Wilcher, comes at the end to accept his farmer nephew's desecration of the saloon of the old manor house, Tolbrook – itself an emblem of England in the same way that Ford's Groby or Forster's Howard's End are emblems. The room is now used to house farm machinery.

> . . . the very ruin of this beautiful room is become a part of my happiness. I say no longer 'Change must come, and this change, so bitter to me, is a necessary ransom for what I keep.' I have surrendered because I cannot fight and now it seems to me that not change but life has lifted me and carried me forward on the stream. It is but a new life which flows through the old house; and like all life, part of that sustaining power which is the oldest thing in the world. . . . Robert does not destroy Tolbrook, he takes it back into history, which changed it once before from priory into farm, from farm into manor from manor, the workshop and court of a feudal dictator, into a country house where young ladies danced and hunting men played billiards; where at last, a new rich gentleman spent his weekends from his office. And after that, I suppose it was to have been a country hotel, where typists on holiday gaze at the trees, the crops, and the farmer's men, with mutual astonishment and dislike. Robert has brought it back into the English stream . . . a wisdom and a faith so close to death and life that we could not tell what part of it was God's and what was man's sense. . . .[8]

Here the union of Poet and Historian is achieved; but the passage none the less epitomises the social dilemma with which the rural novelists were concerned. That dilemma remains a contemporary and tragic one. Change, even for the better, always has to be paid for; and the price paid for the social benefits of twentieth-century technology has been exacting. But there is no way back, and the predicament would seem to be an enduring part of the consciousness of the modern English world.

> How with this rage shall beauty hold a plea,
> Whose action is no stronger than a flower?[9]

That question, however, is its own reply. 'The absence of noise is not in all cases the same thing as the presence of peace.'[10]

Notes

Chapter 1

1 *The Return of the Native* (1878), Book V, Chapter 1.
2 Ibid., Book V, Chapter 7.
3 Ibid., Book V, Chapter 8.
4 Jane Austen, *Sense and Sensibility*, Vol. I, Chapter 16.
5 Preface to the second edition (1800) of *Lyrical Ballads*.
6 A Vision of the Last Judgement, *Poetry and Prose of William Blake*, ed. Geoffrey Keynes (1948), p. 652.
7 Charles Williams, *The Place of the Lion*, 1952 edition, p. 96.
8 See especially Williams's last novel, *All Hallows Eve* (1945), and his portrayal of the ideal Britain as 'Logres' in his two volumes of Arthurian poems, *Taliesin Through Logres* (1938) and *The Region of the Summer Stars* (1944).
9 Postscript to Preface to *Jude the Obscure* (1912).
10 Quoted in Florence Emily Hardy, *The Life of Thomas Hardy*, 1962 edition, p. 274.
11 For example, the description of the country town of Marney in Book II, Chapter 3 of *Sybil*. Compare that of the squatter settlement of Wodgate in Book III, Chapter 4. The squalor of Wodgate is partly attributed to its being built on common land.
12 *Hard Times* (1852), Book I, Chapter 5.
13 'George Bourne' (George Sturt), *Lucy Bettesworth* (1913), p. 262.
14 See especially Chapter 37, 'Looking South', and Chapter 46, 'Once and Now'.
15 *Howards End*, Pocket edition (1947), p. 47.
16 One has only to compare *The Lilac Sunbonnet* and the early work of J. M. Barrie, such as *The Little Minister* (1891), with the *Scots Quair* trilogy of 'Lewis Grassic Gibbon' (Leslie Mitchell, 1901–35) – *Sunset Song* (1932), *Cloud Howe* (1933) and *Grey Granite* (1934) – to see in Scottish terms the strengthening of fiction by the firmer grasp of external realities in the 1930s.
17 Details of Sturt's life and work can be found in E. D. Mackerness's introduction to the 1967 edition of the *Journals*. See also Arnold Bennett's introduction to Sturt's *A Small Boy in the Sixties* (1927) and Geoffrey Grigson's introduction to the *Journals* of 1890–1902, published in 1941. For a more limiting assessment of Sturt's achievement, see Raymond Williams, *Culture and Society* (1958), Part III, Chapter 4.

18   *Change in the Village* (1912), p. 226.
19   Ibid., p. 118.
20   Ibid., p. 144.
21   William Ashworth, *An Economic History of England* (1960), p. 49.
22   For an example of this in practice, see Richard Jefferies, 'Landlords' Difficulties', in *Hodge and His Masters* (1880),
23   The author was the journalist J. W. Robertson Scott (1886–1963). *Who's Who* listed his recreations as 'Most outdoor recreations, except hunting, racing and fishing'.
24   See *Culture and Environment* (1933). The influence of this theme on the academic imagination has been an important one, thanks to Leavis's own high reputation and persuasiveness as a critic.
25   For a valuable account of Massingham's life and work, see W. J. Keith, *The Rural Tradition* (Brighton: Harvester Press, 1975).
26   *Change in the Village*, p. 308.
27   For an important corrective to the myth of a lost rural golden age, the reader is referred to Raymond Williams, *The Country and the City* (1973).
28   For Carpenter's influence on Forster, see *Two Cheers for Democracy* (1951) and the terminal note to *Maurice* (1971). For Lawrence the evidence is discussed at length in Emile Delavenay, *D. H. Lawrence and Edward Carpenter: A Study in Edwardian Transition* (1971).
29   Edward Carpenter, *Civilization, Its Cause and Cure* (1889), pp. 44–5, quoted in Delavaney, *D. H. Lawrence and Edward Carpenter*. For a sharply critical view of the followers of nature cults, see Helen Thomas's memoir of her husband Edward Thomas, *World Without End* (1931), especially Chapter 7.
30   This has been powerfully argued by F. R. Leavis, most notably in his *D. H. Lawrence: Novelist* (1955) and *Thoughts, Words and Creativity: Art and Thought in Lawrence* (1976).
31   Adrian Bell, 'English Tradition and Idiom', in *Scrutiny*, II (1933).
32   Ibid.

Chapter 2

1   Christopher's novels have disturbing implications with regard to contemporary conservative attitudes, and his *Prince in Waiting* trilogy (1970–72) in particular is an interesting rehabilitation of the machine age.
2   *Hodge and His Masters* (1966 edition), Vol. II, p. 95.
3   *Change in the Village*, pp. 163–4.
4   For details of Booth's life see J. B. Priestley's introduction to Vol. I (*The Cliff End*) of the Holderness Edition of the novels (Putnam, 1956).
5   *The Tree of the Garden* (1922), pp. 40–1.
6   *Fondie* (1916), p. 317.
7   *The Tree of the Garden*, p. 75.
8   Ibid., p. 31.
9   Ibid., p. 78.
10   Ibid., pp. 81–2.
11   Ibid., p. 196.

12 See the essay 'John Galsworthy', in *Phoenix* (1936), pp. 539–50.
13 *The Tree of the Garden*, p. 452.
14 'Surgery for the Novel – or a Bomb', in *Phoenix* (1936), p. 517.
15 *The Tree of the Garden*, pp. 9–10.

Chapter 3

1 Katherine Mansfield, *Novels and Novelists* (1930), p. 152, reviewing (favourably) Eric Leadbitter's *Shepherd's Warning* (1920).
2 See Margaret Lane, 'Flora Thompson', in *Purely for Pleasure* (1967).
3 *The Heart of the Moor* (1914), p. 52.
4 *A Stepson of the Soil* (1910), p. 246.
5 Published by J. M. Dent and Sons (1933).
6 *English Country Life* (1910), p. 191.
7 Ibid., pp. 393–4.
8 *Tess of the D'Urbervilles*, Chapter 24.
9 For the autobiographical promptings of this theme see 'The Challenge of Our Time' in *Two Cheers for Democracy* (1951).
10 *The Broken Halo* (1913), p. 109.
11 *Harmony* (1916), p. 1.
12 *Kenneth Grahame* (1959), p. 252. Grahame was a senior official in the Bank of England.
13 *The Wind in the Willows* (1908), Chapter 7.
14 Ibid., Chapter 1.
15 Ibid., Chapter 4.
16 See W. S. Palmer and D. M. Haggard: *Michael Fairless. Her Life and Writings* (1913).
17 See, for example, *Hills and the Sea* (1906).
18 *Farewell Victoria* (1933), p. 68.
19 Ibid., p. 61.
20 *Earth Stopped* (1934). p. 186.
21 For example, in *Mistress Masham's Repose* (1946). A more considered self-portrait is that of 'Mr White' in *The Elephant and the Kangaroo* (1948).
22 *Gone to Ground* (1935), p. 172.
23 *Earth Stopped*, p. 177.
24 *The Letters of D. H. Lawrence*, ed. Aldous Huxley (1934), p. 578.
25 *Bachelor's Knap* (1935), pp. 119–20.
26 *Lolly Willowes* (1926), pp. 238–9.
27 Ibid., p. 230.
28 A similar dual notation attaches to the village of Kings Barton in John Cowper Powys's *Wolf Solent* (1929), a novel which emcompasses this kind of rural fiction and uses its motifs for purposes of psychological exploration. In *Lolly Willowes* the psychic ambience of Great Mop is left unexamined.
29 *Lolly Willowes*, p. 29.
30 Ibid., p. 29.
31 For an account of T. F. Powys by Sylvia Townsend Warner, see Kenneth Hopkins, *The Powys Brothers* (1967), p. 129.

32   *The Happy-Go-Lucky Morgans* (1913), pp. 102–3.
33   Ibid., pp. 98–9.

Chapter 4
1   See W. G. Hoskins: *The Making of the English Landscape* (1955), pp. 216–24.
2   From 'A Study of Thomas Hardy', in *Phoenix* (1936), p. 419.
3   Widecombe Edition, Vol. I (*Widecombe Fair*), p. viii.
4   But for an apt comment on this see Edward Thomas, *A Literary Pilgrim in England* (1917), p. 143.
5   *Eden Phillpotts: An Assessment and a Tribute*, ed. Waveney Girvan (1953), p. 19.
6   *The Thief of Virtue*, Widecombe edition, (1927) p. 269.
7   *The River*, Widecombe edition, (1927) p. 222.
8   Ibid., pp. 27–8.
9   *The Mother*, Widecombe edition (1927) pp. 134–5.
10   *Children of the Mist*, Widecombe edition, (1927) p. 277.
11   *The Secret Woman*, Widecombe edition, (1927) p. 264.
12   *The Portreeve*, Widecombe edition, (1928) pp. 134–5.
13   *The Whirlwind*, Widecombe edition, (1928) pp. 150–1.
14   *Widecombe Fair*, Widecombe edition, (1927) pp. 143–5.
15   *Children of Men*, Widecombe edition, (1928) pp. 57–8.
16   Preface to *Widecombe Fair* (1913), p. ix.
17   A. M. Allen, *Baxters o' the Moor* (1923), p. 84.
18   *Times Literary Supplement*, 30 Jan 1908.
19   *Heather* (1908), p. 29.
20   Ibid., p. 322.
21   Ibid., p. 292–3.
22   *Sleeping Waters* (1913), pp. 43–4.
23   *Granite* (1909), p. 11.
24   *Furze the Cruel*, p. 99.
25   *Granite*, p. 146.
26   Ibid., p. 67.
27   *Furze the Cruel*, p. 98.
28   Ibid., p. 233.
29   Ibid., pp. 64–5.
30   *Off the Beaten Track* (1925), p. 22.
31   *Heather*, p. 297.
32   *Furze the Cruel*, p. 330.

Chapter 5
1   But not exclusively. Blackmore tried equally romantic settings for other novels – South Wales for *The Maid of Sker* (1872), Dartmoor for *Christowell* (1882), the New Forest for *Cradock Nowell* (1864) – without success. It was *Lorna Doone's* merits as a romantic tale which maintained its popularity for so long; and it is worth noting that the centre of the book is the Ridd family, farmers and not 'romantic' aristocrats, even though Lorna herself turns out to be of noble birth.
2   Rupert Hart-Davis, *Hugh Walpole* (1952), p. 334.

3 The four novels were published in a single volume under this title in 1939.

4 Hart-Davis, *Hugh Walpole*, p. 224.

5 A further quotation from *The Happy-Go-Lucky Morgans* seems apposite here. Commenting on Borrow's 'There's the wind on the heath, brother; if I could only feel that, I would gladly live for ever', Jack comments, 'Jolly good . . . but what puzzles me is how the man who knew that could bother to write a book. There must have been something the matter with him. Perhaps he didn't really believe what he wrote' (p. 155).

6 *The Herries Chronicle*, pp. 727–8.

7 Ibid., p. 1459.

8 *A Prayer for My Son* (1935), p. 202.

9 Hart-Davis, *Hugh Walpole*, pp. 166, 180. See also the Preface to *The Herries Chronicle*.

10 See Walpole's letter to Arnold Bennett, quoted in Hart-Davis, *Hugh Walpole*, pp. 216–17.

11 'In all his seventeen years at Brackenburn he was never there for longer than five weeks at a stretch, and very seldom for more than two or three' (Hart-Davis, *Hugh Walpole*, p. 249).

12 Published in 1928 in 'The English Men of Letters' series.

13 Clive Holland, *Wessex* (1907), pp. v–vi.

14 Compton Mackenzie, *Literature in My Time* (1933), p. 215.

15 *Talking of Jane Austen* (1943), *More Talk of Jane Austen* (1950).

16 *All the Books of My Life: A Bibliography* (1956), pp. 95–6.

17 *The Ploughman's Progress* (1933), p. 293.

18 *Tamarisk Town* (1919), p. 112. This study of a seaside town may be compared with *A Pier and a Band* (1918) by Mary MacCarthy (the wife of Desmond MacCarthy) as a variant on the usual treatment of the town–country theme with regard to the coastal resorts.

19 *Three Ways Home* (1937), p. 86.

20 *Sussex Gorse* (1916), p. 460.

21 Ibid., pp. 413–14.

22 *Joanna Godden* (1921), pp. 222–3.

23 Cf. also *Susan Spray, The Female Preacher* (1931).

24 *Iron and Smoke* (1928), p. 306.

25 D. H. Lawrence, *Sons and Lovers* (1913), Chapter 5.

26. *Joanna Godden*, p. 43.

27 *Little England* (1918), p. 255.

28 From a review of *The George and the Crown* in *The Nation and Athenaeum*, 18 Apr 1925.

29 *Little England*, p. 264.

30 Katherine Mansfield, *Novels and Novelists* (1930), p. 252.

Chapter 6

1 Brett Young contributed seven poems to *Georgian Poetry*, 1918–19, ed. Edward Marsh. They are graceful, profuse and over-dulcet.

2 *The Young Physician* (1919), pp. 235–6.

3 *The Crescent Moon* (1918), *Pilgrim's Rest* (1922), *Woodsmoke* (1924),

They Seek a Country (1937) and *The City of Gold* (1939) – the last two part of a projected trilogy.

4   *The Tragic Bride* (1920).
5   *The Key of Life* (1927).
6   *Black Roses* (1929).
7   Eric Brett Young (b. 1893), later secretary to Compton Mackenzie. (See *My Life and Times*, Octave V (1966). The two brothers also collaborated in a study of the poems of Robert Bridges: *Robert Bridges* by 'F. E. Brett Young' (1914).
8   *The Crescent Moon*, p. 26.
9   *The Iron Age* (1915), pp. 299–300.
10 *The Black Diamond* (1921), pp. 183–4.
11 Ibid., p. 321.
12 Jessica Brett Young, *Francis Brett Young, A Biography*. *With a preface by C. P. Snow* (1962), pp. 157, 171.
13 *My Brother Jonathan* (1928), p. 176.
14 *White Ladies* (1935), pp. 22–3.
15 Ibid., pp. 474–5.
16 There is an instructive indication, in the Author's Foreword, of his attitude to novel writing: 'In those distressful days, when the very existence of Britain was imperilled, the writing of anything so flimsy as fiction seemed out of tune with the time' (*The Island* (1944), p. vi).
17 *Portrait of Clare* (1927), pp. 814–15.
18 Jessica Brett Young, *Francis Brett Young*, p. 166.
19 Ibid., p. 114.
20 Ibid., pp. 164–5.
21 Ibid., p. 99.
22 *Far Forest* (1936), p. 232.
23 'E. M. Delafield' was the pseudonym of Elizabeth Monica Dashwood (1890–1943), daughter of the Edwardian novelist Mrs Henry de la Pasture, and a fellow director (with Winifred Holtby) of *Time and Tide*. Her *Diary of a Provincial Lady* (1930) and its successors give an amusing account of life in the country (as distinct from country life) in a middle-class home between the wars.
24 *The Land of Green Ginger* (1927), pp. 58–60.
25 Quoted in Vera Brittain, *Testament of Friendship* (1940), p. 138.
26 Ibid., pp. 433–4.
27 *South Riding* (1936), p. 18.
28 Ibid., pp. 433–4.
29 See Vera Brittain, *Testament of Friendship*, pp. 103, 138, 160.
30 *South Riding*, p. 339.
31 Ibid., p. 486.
32 Ibid., pp. 346–7.
33 Ibid., p. 97.
34 Ibid., p. 226.
35 Ibid., p. 499.
36 Ibid., p. 3.
37 Ibid., p. 82.

38   Ibid., p. 507.
39   Ibid., p. 476.

Chapter 7
  1   Moult was also the author of studies of Barrie (1928) and W. H. Davies
       (1934) and a contributor to Georgian Poetry, 1918–19.
  2   Snow Over Eldon (1920), p. 202.
  3   Down in the Valley (1930), p. 188.
  4   Joseph and His Brethren (1928), p. 257.
  5   Pond Hall's Progress (1933), pp. 172–3.
  6   Joseph and His Brethren, p. 177.
  7   Ibid., p. 8.
  8   R. H. Mottram (1883–1971), author of The Spanish Farm (1924), one of
       the first serious treatments in fiction of the First World War, later
       wrote a number of novels about East Anglian life, of which the best
       known are probably Our Mr Dormer (1927) and The Boroughmonger
       (1929).
  9.   Joseph and His Brethren, p. vii. To do Mottram justice, however, one
       can quote his remark that 'We must have books of this sort written
       and read if our literature is to have its basis in reality and not in mere
       realism.'
 10   Hester and Her Family (1935), p. 187.
 11   Wessex Wins (1941), pp. 31–6.
 12   Strawberry Roan (1932), p. 326.
 13   The Gentleman of the Party (1936), p. 311.
 14   Ibid., pp. 356–7.
 15   Ibid., p. 12.
 16   Ibid., p. 14.
 17   Ibid., p. 54.
 18   Ibid., p. 40.
 19   Ibid., p. 48.
 20.   The Endless Furrow (1934), p. 153.
 21   The Gentleman of the Party, p. 270.
 22   Ibid., p. 224.
 23   Ibid., p. 70.
 24   Strawberry Roan, p. 165.
 25   The Endless Furrow, p. 368.
 26   This judgement is confirmed by Bell's actual autobiography, My Own
       Master (1961).
 27   Corduroy (1930), p. 5.
 28   The Cherry Tree (1932), p. 11.
 29   Silver Ley (1931), p. 49.
 30   For example, 'The Manor Farm', 'Swedes', 'Sowing', 'October', 'Digging'
       in Collected Poems.
 31   Folly Field (1933), pp. 193–4.
 32   Corduroy, p. 177.
 33   Ibid., p. 46.
 34   Ibid., p. 59.
 35   Silver Ley, p. 97.

36 *The Balcony* (1934), p. 131.
37 *The Cherry Tree*, p. 41. But compare the account of the rival pulls of farm work and contemplation in the character of Tony Fortune in *The Shepherd's Farm* (1939).
38 *Corduroy*, p. 43.
39 *The Balcony*, p. 67.
40 *Folly Field*, p. 103.
41 Ibid., pp. 202–3.
42 Ibid., p. 266.
43 *By-Road* (1937), pp. 118–19.
44 *The Cherry Tree*, p. 125.
45 That this involvement is no matter of mere familiarity can be seen from the beautiful account of Westmorland farming life in *Sunrise to Sunset* (1944).

Chapter 8

1 Later expanded as *An Autobiography* (1954). At the end of the latter, Muir has some words which might serve as an epigraph for many writers of the rural school : 'I think that if any of us examines his life, he will find that most good has come to him from a few loyalties, and a few discoveries made many generations before he was born, which must always be made anew' (p. 281).
2 For a detailed exposition of the theme see Peter Coveney, *Poor Monkey* (1957), reprinted 1967 as *The Image of Childhood*, with an introduction by F. R. Leavis.
3 The two collections, *The Peregrine's Saga* (1923) and *The Old Stag* (1926), with the longer stories, *Tarka the Otter* (1927) and *Salar the Salmon* (1935).
4 *The Peregrine's Saga* (1923), p. 5.
5 *The Lone Swallows* (1922), pp. vi–vii.
6 *The Dream of Fair Women* (revised ed. 1931), p. 65.
7 Ibid., p. 16.
8 *The Beautiful Years* (revised ed. 1929), p. 135.
9 See especially *The Longest Journey*, Part II, Chapter 7, for Mr Pembroke's opening address. 'And it seemed that only a short ladder lay between the preparation-room and the Anglo-Saxon hegemony of the globe. Then he paused, and in the silence came "sob, sob, sob," from a little boy, who was regretting a villa in Guildford and his mother's half-acre of garden.'
10 *Dandelion Days* (revised ed. 1930), p. 214.
11 Ibid., p. 184.
12 *The Beautiful Years*, pp. 234–5.
13 *The Dream of Fair Women*, p. 359.
14 Ibid., p. 375.
15 *The Flax of Dream* (1936), p. 1415.
16 *The Pathway* (1928), p. 81.
17 *The Dream of Fair Women* pp. 139–40.
18 Ibid., p. 60.
19 Ibid., p. 107.

20 *Richard Jefferies. Selections of his Work, with Details of his Life and Circumstance, His Death and Immortality* (1937), pp. 24–5.
21 *The Labouring Life* (1932), p. 64.
22 *The Pathway*, p. 191.
23 *The Flax of Dream*, pp. 1029–30.
24 Besides Llewelyn Powys's two writer brothers, John Cowper and T. F. Powys, other members of the family achieved distinction, notably Gertrude Powys (1877–1952) as a painter, and A. R. Powys (1881–1936) as an architect. For a good general account of the family, see Kenneth Hopkins, *The Powys Brothers* (1967).
25 *Skin for Skin*, 1948 edition, p. 69.
26 *The Blackthorn Winter* (1930), pp. 61–2.
27 'I like it as a banner or battle cry, but . . . it has many faults. I wrote it too quickly and too carelessly' (*Letters of Llewelyn Powys* (1943), p. 185).
28 See Malcolm Elwin, *The Life of Llewelyn Powys* (1946), pp. 53–7.
29 *Apples Be Ripe* (1930), p. 274.
30 Ibid., p. 256.
31 A curious sleight of hand is taking place here: the character of Dittany is in fact modelled on that of Gamel Woolsey, the American poet (later married to Gerald Brenan) with whom Powys had a tragic love affair. See Alyse Gregory, *The Cry of a Gull*, and Llewelyn Powys, *So Wild a Thing* (both Dulverton: Ark Press, 1973).
32 *Love and Death* (1939), p. 166.
33 Ibid., p. 282.

Chapter 9
1 The fullest account of Mary Webb's life is to be found in Dorothy P. H. Wrenn, *Goodbye to Morning* (Shrewsbury, 1964).
2 *Religio Medici*, Part I, section 34.
3 See especially Jefferies's *The Story of my Heart* (1883) and Powys's *Impassioned Clay* (1931).
4 *The Spring of Joy*, Collected edition (1928) p. 128.
5 *Gone to Earth*, Collected edition (1928) p. 183.
6 *The House in Dormer Forest*, Collected edition (1928) pp. 16–17.
7 *The Golden Arrow*, Collected edition (1928) p. 48.
8 Ibid., p. 174.
9 See especially his novels *A Glastonbury Romance* (1933) and *Weymouth Sands* (1934).
10 *The Golden Arrow*, p. 79.
11 Ibid., p.82.
12 Ibid., p. 71.
13 Ibid., p. 24.
14 Ibid., p. 51.
15 *Gone to Earth*, p. 65.
16 Ibid., p. 118.
17 Ibid., p. 185.
18 Ibid., p. 69.
19 Ibid., p. 206.

20 Ibid., p. 184.
21 *The House in Dormer Forest*, p. 23.
22 Ibid., p. 191.
23 Ibid., p. 191.
24 *Seven for a Secret*, Collected edition (1928) p. 466.
25 'Pity, to her, had but one task – to console; and at the bottom it was built upon rebellion against pain, whether her own or another's' (Dorothy P. H. Wrenn, *Goodbye to Morning*, p. 110).
26 *Precious Bane*, Collected edition (1928) p. 96.
27 Ibid., p. 97.
28 Ibid., p. 141.
29 *Poems; and the Spring of Joy*, Collected edition (1928) p. 109.
30 *Precious Bane*, p. 269.
31 *Yonder*, Collected edition (1928) p. 272.
32 Ibid., p. 152.
33 *The Vicar's Daughter*, Collected edition (1928) p. 93.
34 *Chatterton Square* (1947), p. 300.
35 *A Corn of Wheat* (1911), p. 5.
36 Ibid., p. 384.
37 Ibid., p. 358.
38 Ibid., p. 4.
39 Ibid., p. 62.
40 That E. H. Young had something of Jane Austen's skill can be seen from her delineation of Margaret Stack in *The Vicar's Daughter*. Her marriage to a clergyman, whose beliefs she does not share, results in an occasional callousness based ultimately on a species of contempt. Her teasing of her stuffy but sensitive cousin Maurice (a good study of the erosion of personality by professional posturing) is matched by an equal insensitivity towards the husband whom she loves. When Edward's manuscript article is returned to him she comments, 'Oh dear, what a nuisance! I do wish editors would show a little consideration for authors' wives. And you must cost them quite a lot in those printed slips! But really and truly, darling, I'm very sorry. Very sorry. But we all know what stupid people they are, and you see, if they took your articles, it would be almost like saying you were stupid, too. So of course it's a compliment. Every writer knows that' (p. 246). The author's touch here is very sure: implicit in the speech are all the complexities of the situation: Margaret's boredom, her high spirits turned by that boredom to mockery, her desire to please vitiated by her desire to be thought pleasing, her too-easy charm, her sense of guilt. Underlying it all is the problem of how to create a satisfying life out of circumstances that are dangerously restricting. It is a measure of E. H. Young's quality that she is as aware of the perils of the remedy as she is of the perils of the disease.
41 *Moor Fires*, Collected edition (1928) p. 198.
42 Ibid., p. 10.
43 *The Misses Mallett*, Collected edition (1928) p. 68.
44 Ibid., p. 308.
45 Ibid., p. 70.

46 Ibid., p. 94.
47 Ibid., p. 37.
48 *Jenny Wren* (1932), p. 139.
49 *The Curate's Wife*, Collected edition (1928) pp. 78–9.
50 *Jenny Wren*, p. 140.
51 *Miss Mole*, Collected edition (1928) p. 61.
52 *Caravan Island* (1940), p. 50.
53 *The Spectator*, 7 Sept 1934.

Chapter 10

1 Most of the places described in the novels are composite pictures, but one or two can be confidently identified. Crump is Dalham Tower, outside Milnthorpe, and the almshouses in *The Trumpet in the Dust* are on the main road from Milnthorpe to Heversham.
2 An early work, *Hugh of Hughsdale*, was serialised in the *Kendal Mercury and Times* in 1909. It was not reprinted. Another novel, *The Jasper Sea*, was left unfinished at her death. (I am indebted to Mr Donald Hopewell for these and other particulars concerning Constance Holme.)
3 26 Jan 1939.
4 Preface to *Crump Folk Going Home*, World's Classics edition (1934) p. viii.
5 Another early novel by Constance Holme, written in 1912 but unpublished, is 'about a Florentine tour, in a lively (though at one point tragic) vein. Early aviation is mixed up with it too.' (From a letter by Constance Holme, quoted in *Letters and Manuscripts*, Bertram Rota catalogue 185, Summer 1973).
6 *Crump Folk Going Home*, p. 97.
7 Ibid., p. 44.
8 *The Lonely Plough*, World's Classics edition (1931) p. viii.
9 Ibid., p. 159.
10 Ibid., pp. 326–7.
11 9 July 1936.
12 *The Old Road from Spain*, World's Classics edition (1932) p. 208.
13 Ibid., p. 208.
14 *The Splendid Fairing*, World's Classics edition (1933) pp. 151–2.
15 'The Crooked Branch', for instance, is a story that has strong affinities with *The Splendid Fairing*.
16 *The Things Which Belong* – World's Classics edition (1934) p. 188.
17 *Beautiful End*, World's Classics edition (1935) pp. 202–3.
18 Ibid., p. 120.
19 Ibid., p. 219.
20 *The Things Which Belong* –, p. 114.
21 *Beautiful End*, pp. 70–1.
22 Ibid., p. 219.
23 'Dots are believed by many writers of our day to be a good substitute for effective writing. They are certainly an easy one. Let us have a few more. . . . . . .' (M. R. James: *Collected Ghost Stories* (1931), pp. 646–7).
24 *The Splendid Fairing*, pp. 80–1.

25 Ibid., p. 210.
26 *He-Who-Came?*, World's Classics edition (1936) p. 133.
27 Ibid., pp. 98–9.
28 *The Splendid Fairing*, pp. 98–9.
29 *The Old Road from Spain*, p. 54.

Chapter 11

1 It is to be hoped that the story is untrue, for the house is very ugly.
2 For further details, see the Bibliography in H. Coombes, *T. F. Powys* (1960).
3 *Mr Tasker's Gods* (1925), p. 1.
4 Ibid., p. 51.
5 Ibid., pp. 223–4.
6 Ibid., p. 42.
7 See 'The Only Penitent', in *Bottle's Path* (1947).
8 *Mr Tasker's Gods*, p. 34.
9 Ibid., p. 45.
10 Ibid., p. 47.
11 *The Left Leg* (1923), p. 99.
12 Ibid., pp. 196–7.
13 *Mark Only* (1924), p. 267.
14 Ibid., pp. 202–3.
15 Ibid., p. 118.
16 *Soliloquies of a Hermit* (1916), pp. 65–6.
17 Ibid., pp. 64–5.
18 John Cowper Powys, however, introduces the figure of the suffering Christ into A *Glastonbury Romance* with telling effect, in his account of the mystical experiences of Sam Dekker.
19 *The Left Leg*, p. 46.
20 Although there is no direct evidence of this, Powys was probably influenced by the story of Jacob and the Angel (*Genesis* xxxii, 23–31) in which Jacob receives his name of Israel, 'He Who Strives With God' or 'God Strives'.
21 *Mockery Gap* (1925), p. 234.
22 His first book, *An Interpretation of Genesis* (1908) is clearly influenced by the style of the Authorised Version.
23 *Mockery Gap*, p. 5.
24 *Innocent Birds* (1926), pp. 5–6.
25 Ibid., p. 276.
26 Ibid., p. 152.
27 Ibid., p. 95.
28 Ibid., p. 193.
29 *Mr Weston's Good Wine*, New Phoenix Library edition (1950), p. 13.
30 Ibid., p. 182.
31 Ibid., p. 178.
32 In view of the fact that Powys has frequently been accused of exaggeration and morbidity – an example of this can be found in Norman Nicholson's account of him in *Man and Literature* (1943) – it is worth quoting once more from George Sturt. 'I myself heard and wondered at

the happy prattle of two little girls . . . as they told of the fun they had
enjoyed along with their father and mother, in watching a dog worry
a hedgehog' (*Change in the Village*, pp. 263–4).

33 *Mr Weston's Good Wine*, pp. 134–5.
34 Ibid., p. 307.
35 Ibid., p. 273.
36 Louis Marlow, *Seven Friends* (1953), p. 98.
37 *Fables* (1929), p. 137.
38 Ibid., p. 145.
39 Ibid., p. 183.
40 Ibid., p. 187.
41 This tale was submitted to Chatto and Windus in 1923, but was not
   published until 1967. (T. F. Powys, *Two Stories*, ed. Peter Riley
   (Hastings: R. A. Brimell).)
42 The various tales about Tadnol are distributed as follows: 'Lady Louise
   and the Wallflower', 'The Lost Proofs', 'Adder's Brood' and 'No Room'
   in *The House with the Echo* (1928); 'Archdeacon Truggin', 'Mr
   Dottery's Trousers' and 'Feed My Swine' in *The White Paternoster*
   (1930); 'Only the Devil' and 'Godfather Dottery' in *Captain Patch*
   (1935); and 'Circe Truggin' in *Bottle's Path* (1946).
43 *Kindness in a Corner* (1930), p. 11.
44 Ibid., p. 246.
45 Ibid., p. 234.
46 Ibid., p. 201.
47 At least one other mature novel by Powys exists in manuscript. It is
   called 'The Market Bell', and from internal evidence would seem to
   have been written at the same time as *Mockery Gap* and *Innocent Birds*.
   See J. A. Boulton, 'A Note on T. F. Powys', in *Delta, a Literary Review*,
   no. 52 (1974).
48 *Unclay* (1931), p. 117.
49 Ibid., p. 116.
50 Ibid., p. 173.
51 Ibid., p. 306.
52 Ibid., pp. 180–1.
53 Ibid., pp. 311–12.
54 *Matthew* xxv, 29.
55 *The Two Thieves* (1932), p. 7.

Chapter 12
1 For example, *Fair Stood the Wind for France* (1945), *The Purple Plain*
  (1947).
2 *The Darling Buds Of May* (1958) and its successors.
3 The short stories, originally issued in several volumes, were collected
  by the author in *Country Tales* (1938).
4 A similar type of woman is more fully and memorably portrayed as
  Sara Munday in Joyce Cary's *Herself Surprised* (1941). It is interesting
  to compare her character with that of the old landowner Wilcher, her
  employer, in *To Be a Pilgrim* (1942), with regard to their different roles
  in society. Sara has vitality, Wilcher sanity.

5   *The Fallow Land* (1932), pp. 165–6.
6   *A House of Women* (1936), pp. 101–2.
7   *The Fallow Land*, p. 13.
8   *Spella Ho* (1938), p. 400.
9   Ibid., pp. 410–11.
10 *Country Tales* (1939), p. 10.
11 A. E. Coppard (1878–1957), like W. H. Davies, was an outsider in the literary world of his day; his stories enjoyed a vogue in the 1920s and 1930s. *Adam and Eve and Pinch Me* (1921) was the first publication of the Golden Cockerell Press. Coppard's autobiography *It's Me, O Lord* appeared posthumously in 1957. He was an attractive and unusual writer of considerable self-taught skill; but his work is only peripheral to the themes considered here.
12 It might be argued that the most determined attempt to find contemporary relevance through rural fiction is to be found in the radio serial *The Archers*.
13 *The Fallow Land*, p. 71.

Conclusion

1   John Cowper Powys (1872–1963) is the exception to this. He was the eldest and most prolific of the three writing brothers. His fourteen novels fall into two distinct periods, the later group, written after he returned from America to live in Wales, being concerned with Welsh history and mythology – as in *Owen Glendower* (1942) and *Porius* (1951) – and with fantasy. But the first seven – all of them set in his boyhood homes in Somerset (*Wood and Stone* (1915) and *A Glastonbury Romance* (1933), Dorset (*Ducdame* (1925), *Wolf Solent* (1929), *Jobber Skald* (*Weymouth Sands*) (1935) and *Maiden Castle* (1936)) and Norfolk (*Rodmoor* (New York 1916)) constitute intricate and exploratory studies of inner states of feeling and sexual desire, in relation to climate, landscape and the whole spiritual aura of particular places – in the latter being alien to the spirit of their time. In them the purely rural novel is subsumed to a more comprehensive picture of human life. Powys's work complements that of Lawrence, in its emphasis on the rural experience as emblematic of spiritual rather than of material health, and is remarkable for its simultaneous realisation of complex psychological and mystical experience with a humorous and realistic acceptance of the ordinary and day-to-day. For an assessment of his work, in relation to the rural theme see H. P. Collins, *John Cowper Powys: Old Earth Man* (1966).
2   W. H. Auden, *Secondary Worlds* (1968), p. 83.
3   Not as limited as all that, however. Phillpotts, Walpole, Brett Young, Mary Webb, Street and Williamson continue to have a considerable following, as a glance at public library shelves will confirm.
4   See *Howards End*, Chapter 22.
5   It is notable that very few of the rural novelists concerned themselves with the great house: it is viewed as being by and large remote from the essential rural experience, except, as in the novels of Constance Holme, where local loyalties and responsibilities are in question.

6   *The White Peacock* Part III, Chapter 2.
7   Ibid., Part III, Chapter 3.
8   *To Be a Pilgrim,* Carfax edition (1951) p. 328.
9   William Shakespeare, Sonnet 65.
10 Charles Williams, *The Place of the Lion* 1952 edition, p. 96.

Bibliography

Part One contains a representative list of novels dealing with rural life, published for the most part between 1900 and 1939.

In Part Two are listed other works of general or particular interest in connection with the novelists discussed above.

Unless otherwise stated, the place of publication is London.

Part One

Allen, A. M.	*Baxters O' The Moor* (1923)
Bates, H. E.	*The Fallow Land* (1932)
	The Poacher (1935)
	A House of Women (1936)
	Spella Ho (1938)
	Country Tales (1938) (stories)
	My Uncle Silas (1939) (stories)
Bell, Adrian	*Corduroy* (1930)
	Silver Ley (1931)
	The Cherry Tree (1932)
	Folly Field (1933)
	The Balcony (1934)
	By-Road (1937)
	The Shepherd's Farm (1939)
Benfield, Eric	*Bachelor's Knap* (1935)
	Saul's Sons (1938)
Booth, E. C.	*Fondie* (1916)
	The Tree of the Garden (1922)
	Kith and Kin (1929)
Carmichael, Frances	*The Witch of Brent* (1934)
Cary, Joyce	*Charley Is My Darling* (1940)
	To Be a Pilgrim (1942)
'Elizabeth' (Countess Russell)	*The Princess Priscilla's Fortnight* (1905)
	The Caravaners (1909)
Forster, E. M.	*The Longest Journey* (1907)
	Howards End (1910)
'Francis, M. E.' (Mrs M. E. Blundell)	*The Manor Farm* (1902)

	Lychgate Hall (1904)
	Wild Wheat (1905)
Freeman, H. W.	*Joseph and His Brethren* (1928)
	Down in the Valley (1930)
	Fathers of Their People (1932)
	Pond Hall's Progress (1933)
	Hester and Her Family (1935)
	Andrew to the Lions (1938)
Garnett, David	*Lady into Fox* (1922)
	The Sailor's Return (1925)
	Go She Must (1927)
Gibbons, Stella	*Cold Comfort Farm* (1932)
Grahame, Kenneth	*The Wind in the Willows* (1908)
Hall, Radclyffe	*The Forge* (1924)
	The Sixth Beatitude (1936)
Holme, Constance	*Crump Folk Going Home* (1913)
	The Lonely Plough (1914)
	The Old Road from Spain (1915)
	Beautiful End (1918)
	The Splendid Fairing (1919)
	The Trumpet in the Dust (1921)
	The Things Which Belong – (1925)
	He-Who-Came? (1930)
	The Wisdom of the Simple (1937) (stories)
Holtby, Winifred	*Anderby Wold* (1923)
	The Land of Green Ginger (1927)
	South Riding (1936)
Kaye-Smith, Sheila	*Spell Land* (1910)
	Isle of Thorns (1913)
	Three against the World (1914)
	Sussex Gorse (1916)
	Little England (1918)
	Green Apple Harvest (1919)
	Tamarisk Town (1919)
	Joanna Godden (1921)
	The End of the House of Alard (1923)
	Iron and Smoke (1928)
	Shepherds in Sackcloth (1930)
	Susan Spray (1931)
	The Children's Summer (1932)
	The Ploughman's Progress (1933)
	Rose Deeprose (1936)
Kent, Nora	*Barren Lands* (1926)
	Endless Furrows (1928)
Klickmann, Flora	*The Flower Patch among the Hills* (1916)
	Between the Larch Woods and the Weir (1918)
	The Trail of the Ragged Robin (1921)
Lawrence, D. H.	*The White Peacock* (1910)
	Sons and Lovers (1913)

	The Rainbow (1915)
	Lady Chatterley's Lover (1928)
	The Virgin and the Gipsy (1929)
	Love among the Haystacks (1934) (stories)
Leadbitter, Eric	*Shepherd's Warning* (1920)
MacCarthy, Mary	*A Pier and a Band* (1918)
Manning-Sanders, Ruth	*Hucca's Moor* (1929)
	The Crochet Woman (1934)
Moult, Thomas	*Snow Over Eldon* (1920)
Owen, John	*The Shepherd and the Child* (1929)
	The Road and the Wood (1936)
Peake, C. M. A.	*Eli of the Downs* (1920)
	Pagan Corner (1923)
Phillpotts, Eden	*Children of the Mist* (1898)
	Sons of the Morning (1900)
	The River (1902)
	The Secret Woman (1905)
	The Portreeve (1906)
	The Whirlwind (1907)
	The Mother (1908)
	The Virgin in Judgement (1908)
	The Fun of the Fair (1909) (stories)
	The Three Brothers (1909)
	The Thief of Virtue (1910)
	Demeter's Daughter (1911)
	The Beacon (1911)
	The Forest on the Hill (1912)
	Widecombe Fair (1913)
	Brunel's Tower (1915)
	Miser's Money (1920)
	Orphan Dinah (1920)
	Children of Men (1923)
	Brother Man (1926) (stories)
Powys, John Cowper	*Wood and Stone* (1915)
	Rodmoor (New York, 1916; London, 1973)
	Ducdame (1925)
	Wolf Solent (1929)
	A Glastonbury Romance (1933)
Powys, Llewelyn	*Apples Be Ripe* (1930)
	Love and Death (1939)
Powys, Philippa	*The Blackthorn Winter* (1930)
Powys, T. F.	*The Left Leg* (1923) (stories)
	Black Bryony (1923)
	Mark Only (1924)
	Mr Tasker's Gods (1924)
	Mockery Gap (1925)
	Innocent Birds (1926)
	Mr Weston's Good Wine (1927)
	The House with the Echo (1928) (stories)

	Fables (1929) (stories)
	Kindness in a Corner (1930)
	The White Paternoster (1930) (stories)
	Unclay (1931)
	The Two Thieves (1932) (stories)
	Captain Patch (1935) (stories)
	Bottle's Path (1947) (stories)
Prior, James	*A Walking Gentleman* (1907)
Raymond, Walter	*Gentleman Upcott's Daughter* (1893)
	Tryphena in Love (1895)
	Two Men O' Mendip (1898)
	Verity Thurston (1926)
Skrine, M. J. H.	*A Stepson of the Soil* (1910)
	A Romance of the Simple (1911)
	Shepherd Easton's Daughter (1925)
Street, A. G.	*Strawberry Roan* (1932)
	The Endless Furrow (1934)
	The Gentleman of the Party (1936)
	Already Walks Tomorrow (1938)
Sutcliffe, Halliwell	*A Man of the Moors* (1897)
	Ricroft of Withens (1898)
	Through Sorrow's Gates (1904)
	The Winds of March (1927)
Thomas, Edward	*The Happy-Go-Lucky Morgans* (1913)
Tilden, Philip	*Noah* (1932)
'Trevena John' (Ernest G. Henham)	*A Pixy in Petticoats* (1905)
	Arminel of the West (1906)
	Furze the Cruel (1907)
	Heather (1908)
	Granite (1909)
	Bracken (1910)
	Wintering Hay (1912)
	Sleeping Waters (1913)
	No Place Like Home (1913)
	The Vanished Moor (1923)
	Off the Beaten Track (1925)
Uttley, Alison	*The Country Child* (1931)
Walpole, Hugh	*Rogue Herries* (1930)
	Judith Paris (1931)
	The Fortress (1932)
	Vanessa (1933)
	A Prayer for My Son (1935)
Ward, E. M.	*Far Easdale* (1931)
	Deborah in Langdale (1933)
Warner, Sylvia Townsend	*Lolly Willowes* (1926)
	The True Heart (1929)
	The Salutation (1932) (stories)
Webb, Mary	*The Golden Arrow* (1915)
	Gone to Earth (1917)

	The House in Dormer Forest (1920)
	Seven for a Secret (1922)
	Precious Bane (1925)
	Armour Wherein He Trusted (1929) (stories)
White, T. H.	Farewell Victoria (1933)
	Earth Stopped (1934)
	Gone to Ground (1935)
	The Sword in the Stone (1939)
Williamson, Henry	The Beautiful Years (1921)
	Dandelion Days (1922)
	The Peregrine's Saga (1923) (stories)
	The Dream of Fair Women (1924)
	The Old Stag (1926) (stories)
	Tarka the Otter (1927)
	The Pathway (1928)
	Salar the Salmon (1935)
Young, E. H.	A Corn of Wheat (1911)
	Yonder (1912)
	Moor Fires (1916)
	The Misses Mallett (1922)
	William (1925)
	The Vicar's Daughter (1927)
	Miss Mole (1930)
	Jenny Wren (1932)
	The Curate's Wife (1934)
	Celia (1937)
	Chatterton Square (1947)
Young, Francis Brett	Undergrowth (1913) (with E. Brett Young)
	The Dark Tower (1914)
	The Iron Age (1915)
	The Black Diamond (1921)
	Cold Harbour (1924)
	Portrait of Clare (1927)
	My Brother Jonathan (1928)
	The House under the Water (1932)
	This Little World (1934)
	White Ladies (1935)
	Far Forest (1936)
	Portrait of a Village (1937)
	Mr Lucton's Freedom (1940)
'Zack' (Gwendolen Keats)	Tales of Dunstable Weir (1901) (stories)
	The White Cottage (1901)
	The Roman Road (1903)

Part Two

| Addison, Hilda L. | Mary Webb: A Short Study of Her Life and Work (1931) |
| Anonymous | The Life of Florence L. Barclay, by One Of Her Daughters (1921) |

Baker, Ernest A.	*The History of the English Novel*, 10 vols (1924–1939)
Baker, Ernest A., and Pachman, James	*A Guide to the Best Fiction* (1967)
Bell, Adrian	*My Own Master* (1961)
Bentley, Phyllis	*The English Regional Novel* (1941)
Brittain, Vera	*Testament of Friendship* (1940)
	Selected Letters of Winifred Holtby and Vera Brittain (1960)
Brook, Donald	*Writer's Gallery* (1944)
Chappell, W. Reid	*The Shropshire of Mary Webb* (1930)
Coombes, H.	*T. F. Powys* (1960)
Cooper, Frederick Taber	*Some English Story Tellers* (1912)
Coveney, Peter	*The Image of Childhood* (ed. 1967)
Elwin, Malcolm	*The Life of Llewelyn Powys* (1946)
Ford, Basil (ed.)	*The Pelican Guide to English Literature*, Vol. VII ('The Modern Age') (1961)
Forster, E. M.	*Two Cheers For Democracy* (1951)
Garnett, David (ed.)	*The White–Garnett Letters* (1968)
Girvan, Waveney (ed.)	*Eden Phillpotts: An Assessment and a Tribute* (1953)
Green, Peter	*Kenneth Grahame* (1959)
Hart-Davis, Rupert	*Hugh Walpole* (1952)
Hopkins, Kenneth	*The Powys Brothers* (1967)
Hopkins, E. Thurston	*Sheila Kaye-Smith and the Weald Country* (1925)
Joad, C. E. M.	*The Horrors of the Countryside* (1931)
	A Charter for Ramblers (1934)
Kaye-Smith, Sheila	*Three Ways Home* (1937)
	All the Books of my Life (1956)
Keith, W. J.	*The Rural Tradition* (Brighton: Harvester Press, 1975)
Lawrence, D. H.	*Phoenix* (1936)
Leavis, F. R. and Thompson, Denys	*Culture and Environment* (1933)
Leavis, Q. D.	*Fiction and the Reading Public* (1932)
Leclaire, Lucien	*Le Roman Régionaliste dans les Îles Brittaniques 1800–1950* (Paris, 1954)
Lovell, Robert M. and Hughes, Helen S.	*A History of the Novel in England* (1933)
Mackenzie, Compton	*Literature in My Time* (1933)
Mansfield, Katherine	*Novels and Novelists* (1930)
Marlow, Louis	*Welsh Ambassadors* (1936)
	Seven Friends (1953)
Massingham, H. J.	*In Praise of England* (1924)
	Remembrance (1942)
	Men of Earth (1943)
	The Tree of Life (1943)
	Where Man Belongs (1946)

Nicholson, Norman	*Man and Literature* (1943)
Powys, Llewelyn	*Skin for Skin* (1926)
	The Letters of Llewelyn Powys (1943)
Raymond, Walter	*English Country Life* (1910)
Robertson-Scott, J. W.	*England's Green and Pleasant Land* (1925)
Sewell, Brocard (ed.)	*Theodore: Essays on T. F. Powys* (Aylesford: St Albert's Press 1964)
Stevenson, Lionel	*The English Novel* (1960)
Street, A. G.	*Thinking Aloud* (1933)
	Wessex Wins (1941)
Sturt, George	*The Bettesworth Book* (1901)
('George Bourne')	*Change in the Village* (1912)
	Lucy Bettesworth (1913)
	The Wheelwright's Shop (1923)
	A Small Boy in the Sixties (1927)
	The Journals of George Sturt 1890–1927, ed. E. D. Mackerness (1967)
Swinnerton, Frank	*The Georgian Literary Scene* (1935)
	Background with Chorus (1956)
	Figures in the Foreground (1963)
Thomas, Edward	*A Literary Pilgrim in England* (1917)
Twitchett, E. G.	*Francis Brett Young* (1935)
Ward, Richard Heron	*The Powys Brothers* (1935)
Warner, Sylvia Townsend	*T. H. White* (1967)
West, H. F.	*The Dreamer of Devon: An Essay on Henry Williamson* (1932)
Weygandt, Cornelius	*A Century of the English Novel* (1927)
White, Evelyne	*Winifred Holtby As I Knew Her* (1938)
Williams, Harold	*Modern English Writers* (1918)
Williams, Raymond	*Culture and Society* (1958)
	The Long Revolution (1961)
	The English Novel From Dickens To Lawrence (1970)
	The Country and the City (1973)
Williams-Ellis, Clough	*England and the Octopus* (1928)
Williamson, Henry	*The Village Book* (1930)
	The Labouring Life (1932)
	The Linhay on the Downs (1934)
Wrenn, Dorothy P. H.	*Goodbye to Morning: A Biographical Study of Mary Webb* (Shrewsbury, 1964)
Young, Jessica Brett	*Francis Brett Young* (1962)

Index